Imperial Encyclopedia

Volume III
M – Z

by members of the
National Imperial Glass Collectors' Society

Edited by James Measell

Front Cover:
A. Murrhina vase.
B. Peachblow 4037 10½" vase (satin finish).
C. Milk Glass 1950/461 footed (Eagle) covered box.
D. Ruby Slag No. 459 cocktail pick, cigarette holder or egg cup.
E. Forget-Me-Not Blue No. 80 Vinelf candleholder.
F. Stiegel Green 71757 Bellflower pitcher (made for the Metropolitan Museum of Art).

Back Cover:
G. Purple Slag No. 192 tricorn vase.
H. Stamm House Dewdrop Opalescent 1886/201 footed lamp.
I. Milk Glass 1950/60 Honey Jar with gold decoration on bees, ribbon and base.
J. Verde C165 box and cover (Cambridge mould).
K. Antique Blue No. 341 Old Williamsburg goblet.
L. Murrhina vase.

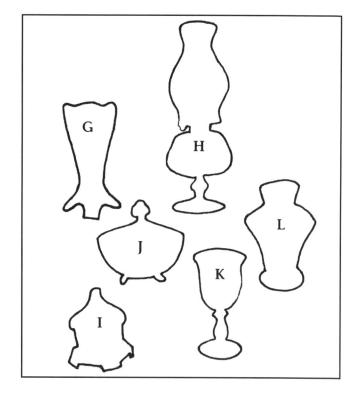

© October 1999

The Glass Press, Inc.
dba Antique Publications
P. O. Box 553 • Marietta, Ohio 45750

ALL RIGHTS RESERVED

PB ISBN #1-57080-065-0   HB ISBN #1-57080-066-9

No part of this book may be reproduced, stored in a retrieval system or transmitted in any form or by any means, electronic, mechanical, photocopying, recording, or otherwise, without the prior permission of the publisher.

Table of Contents

Introduction and Acknowledgments iv

M section 495

N section 511

O section 523

P section 533

R section 551

S section 562

T section 595

U section 607

V section 608

W section 618

Y section 631

Z section 635

Color Plate Descriptions 639

Color Plates 651

Milk Glass 731

Index 747

Value Guide 757

INTRODUCTION AND ACKNOWLEDGMENTS

The book you are holding is part of an encyclopedic series which discusses Imperial glass from A to Z. This is the third and final segment, "M-Z." (the first, covering "A-Cane," and the second, covering "Cape Cod-L," were published by The Glass Press/Antique Publications in 1995 and 1997, respectively). Like its predecessors, this volume contains eighty pages of color photography and numerous black-and-white photos, many of which are from original Imperial catalogs or advertisements.

Eye-catching headings appear throughout the book in the upper left or upper right corner of each page. For example, after the end of the "M" section, on page 507, the heading "M/miscellaneous" can be found. The respective "miscellaneous" sections contain information about those Imperial products for which a full page could not be constructed. Captions to the eighty color pages can be found on pages 639-650.

Readers seeking specific articles can consult the comprehensive index (starting on p. 747), which embraces both this book and the previous two volumes. The index lists colors, item designations, pattern names and other terminology important for a thorough understanding of Imperial glass.

These three books on Imperial glass would not have been possible without the determined efforts of the National Imperial Glass Collectors' Society Book Committee: Douglas Archer; Joan Cimini; Kathy Doub; Marion George; Lucile Kennedy; and Willard Kolb. They secured information, located glassware to be photographed, and checked (and re-checked!) facts about Imperial glass.

Photography for this book was done at the homes of Bob and Myrna Garrison in Texas and Paul and Judy Douglas in Illinois. Several days of photo work at the Bellaire Glass and Artifact Museum were made easy through the help and cooperation of Helen M. Clark, Jean Mountain and the late Clara Dankworth. Glassware was also photographed during the NIGCS conventions in 1997 and 1999.

Many people loaned glass or provided information about Imperial and its products. Special thanks go to Doug and Margaret Archer; Roy Ash; Bob Burns; Joan Cimini; Helen M. Clark; Bill Crowl; Ron and Connie Doll; Kathy Doub; Paul and Judy Douglas; Bob and Linda Frost; Bob and Myrna Garrison; Marion George; Kirk and Jackie Glauser; Charles Hartman; Paul and Carole Hrics; Don Jennings; Lucile Kennedy; Mrs. Donald Kent (daughter of Ray Weekley); Willard Kolb; Dave and Mary Kuster; Richard Lancione; Gene and Flora Ross; Wilma and Richard Ross; E. Ward Russell; John Sampson; Nathan Taves; Ronnie Vickers; Paul and Suzanne Weimer; Monte Schroer; and Berry Wiggins. The Gutman Advertising Agency made its files available, and some of the original black-and-white photos in this book came from those records.

James Measell, Editor
David E. Richardson, Publisher

September 24, 1999

Manhattan Cut Glass Assortment

The No. 2502 Manhattan Cut Glass Assortment from the early 1930s consisted of eight articles decorated with a cut floral motif imparted by a copper wheel (this sort of decoration was known as "grey cutting" or "light cutting" in the glass tableware industry to distinguish it from other wares which were both cut and polished, such as "rock crystal"). Imperial's No. 2502 Manhattan Cut Glass Assortment included the following: No. 169 mayonnaise; No. 716 candy box; bowl and plate from the No. 725 line; and four items from the No. 728 Octagon line. The No. 2502 Manhattan assortment was available in Topaz, Rose Pink, Green or crystal.

MAYONNAISE SETS

629B. 3 Piece Mayonnaise Set
6 dozen sets in barrel

682. 3 Piece Mayonnaise Set, Square
4 dozen sets in barrel

602. 3 Piece Mayonnaise Set
7 dozen sets in barrel

602/5. 3 Piece Mayonnaise Set
7 dozen sets in barrel

By adding a small glass ladle (such as Imperial's No. 169 ladle) to a footed bowl suitable in size for a few dollops of mayonnaise, the glassware manufacturer created a basic mayonnaise service set. Some sets were a bit more elaborate, as a flat-bottomed bowl rested upon a matching underplate. These four sets were shown in Imperial's Catalog No. 201.

MILK GLASS

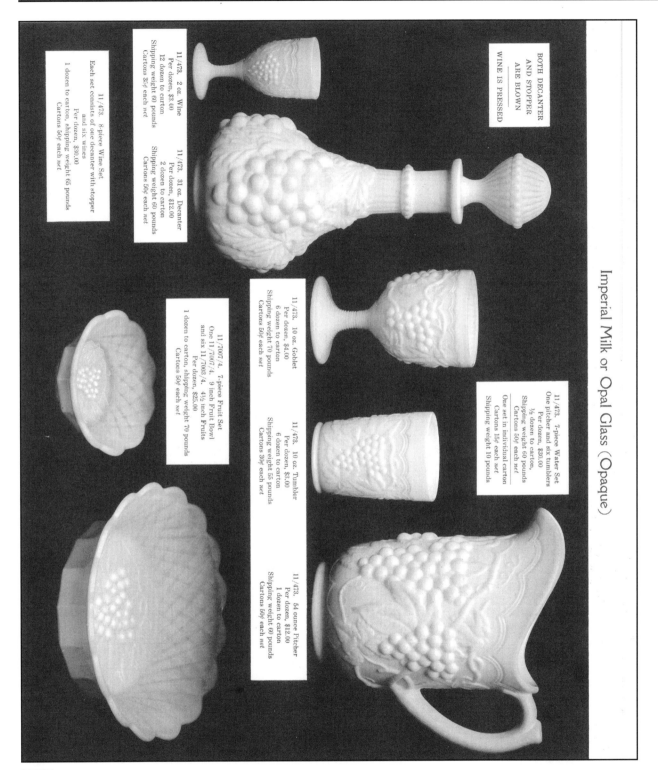

Imperial Milk or Opal Glass (Opaque)

BOTH DECANTER AND STOPPER ARE BLOWN
WINE IS PRESSED

11/473. 8-piece Wine Set
Each set consists of one decanter with stopper and six wines
Per dozen, $30.00
1 dozen to carton, shipping weight 65 pounds
Cartons 50¢ each net

11/473. 2 oz. Wine
Per dozen, $3.00
12 dozen to carton
Shipping weight 60 pounds
Cartons 35¢ each net

11/473. 31 oz. Decanter
Per dozen, $12.00
2 dozen to carton
Shipping weight 60 pounds
Cartons 50¢ each net

11/473. 7-piece Water Set
One pitcher and six tumblers
Per dozen, $30.00
½ dozen to carton,
Shipping weight 60 pounds
Cartons 50¢ each net
One set in individual carton
Cartons 15¢ each net
Shipping weight 10 pounds

11/473. 10 oz. Goblet
Per dozen, $4.00
6 dozen to carton
Shipping weight 70 pounds
Cartons 50¢ each net

11/7007/4. 7-piece Fruit Set
One 11/7007/4. 9 inch Fruit Bowl
and six 11/7003/4. 4½ inch Fruits
Per dozen, $25.00
1 dozen to carton, shipping weight 70 pounds
Cartons 50¢ each net

11/473. 10 oz. Tumbler
Per dozen, $3.00
6 dozen to carton
Shipping weight 55 pounds
Cartons 30¢ each net

11/473. 54 ounce Pitcher
Per dozen, $12.00
1 dozen to carton
Shipping weight 60 pounds
Cartons 50¢ each net

This was Imperial's most popular color in the 1950s and 1960s, so it is not surprising that there are many collectors interested in Imperial's milk glass today. Although most Imperial milk glass items date from the 1950s and thereafter, the company did produce a good deal of opal (pronounced "o-pal") ware in its earlier years. Smoke bells were made before 1910, and the company developed an opal glass called Pura which was used for lighting goods after about 1910.

The first major opal lines came in the 1930s, and these are well-documented with the catalogue sheets found on the next few pages. Opal glass was Imperial's color 11 in the 1930s and 40s. When Imperial's full milk glass line was in production during the 1950s, each item was designated with the prefix 1950/ fol-

Milk Glass

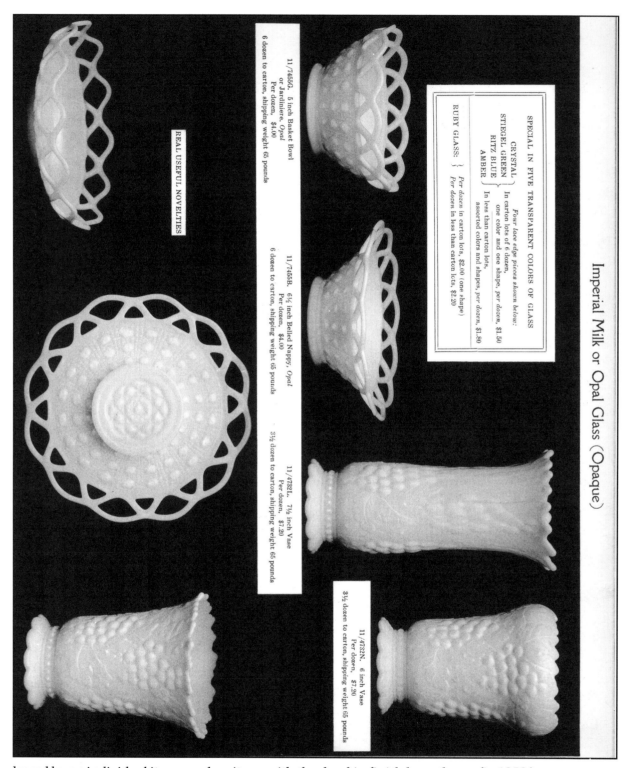

lowed by an individual item number; items with the doeskin finish have the prefix 1952/.

Some of the moulds used in the 1930s had their roots in iridescent ware made two decades earlier. Many more were used in the 1950s, of course, but the company added its distinctive "IG" mark to them during this period in response to the growing concerns of collectors who were leery of unmarked reproductions. The company also recognized its responsibility when it launched the Belknap Collection in the mid-1950s. E. McCamly Belknap had authored a book, *Milk Glass* (1949), which did much to spur the enthusiasm of collectors for this distinctive American glass. Imperial's marketing captured this enthusiasm, and success was theirs!

MILK GLASS

11/550. Wing Footed Bowl
Diameter 12 inches, height 6 inches

The descriptions below and at the right of this interesting Milk Glass footed bowl are from the original Imperial catalog.

11/550F. 12 inch Footed Bowl, *All Opal*
Per dozen. $48.00

ALSO MADE IN THE FOLLOWING COMBINATION OF COLORS:

116/550f. 12 inch Footed Bowl, $48.00 per dozen
Opal Bowl with Ritz Blue Foot

611/550F. 12 inch Footed Bowl, $48.00 per dozen
Ritz Blue Bowl with Opal Foot

311/550F. 12 inch Footed Bowl, $48.00 per dozen
Stiegel Green Bowl with Opal Foot

113/550F. 12 inch Footed Bowl, $48.00 per dozen
Opal Bowl with Stiegel Green Foot

1/2 dozen in carton, shipping weight 35 pounds
Cartons .50c each net

ILLUSTRATION SHOWS OPAL BOWL WITH RITZ BLUE FOOT

1950/377 5" Pie Wagon and cover. Note: Arthur L. Reber was a longtime Imperial glass salesman.

499

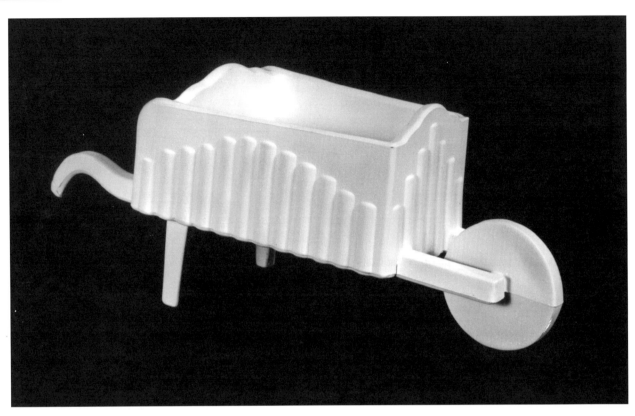

1950/376 Wheelbarrow (11¾" long).

1950/347 Sleigh (11" long).

Milk Glass

1950/134 Hobby Horse cigarette box.

1950/346 little sleigh.

1950/809 Colonial Belle.

Pair of No. 75 candelabrum.

1950/567 Pineapple marmalade jar, cover, and ladle.

1950/154 Bird box and cover.

1950/906 six-piece miniature Lamb set.

MONTICELLO, NO. 698

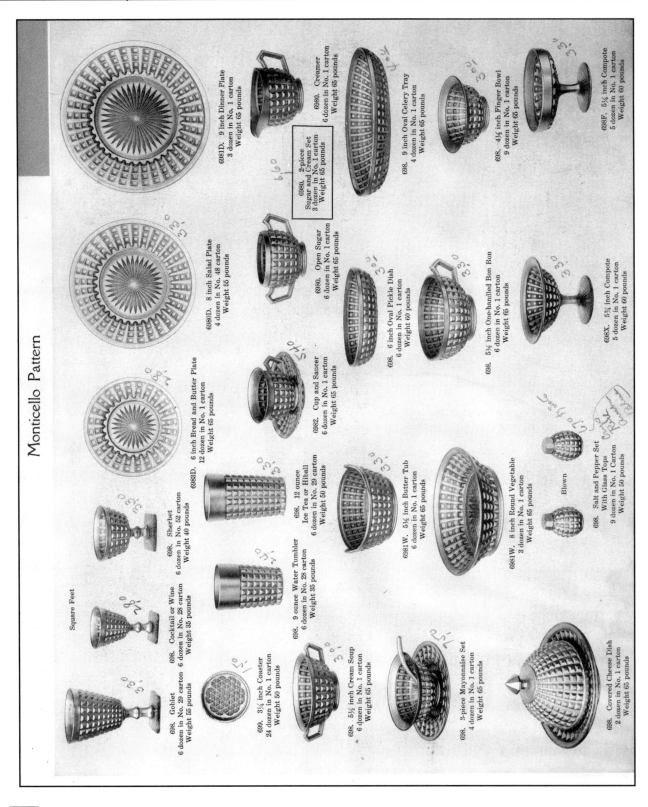

This was an extensive pattern line, and it appears in Imperial's Catalog No. 300 as well as in subsequent loose-leaf catalogs. Items were made in crystal and Rubigold as well as other Imperial colors of the 1920s-1940s, including milk glass (see Figs. 2091-2113). This pattern should not be confused with Heisey's No. 1425 (Victorian), which, after Imperial purchased the Heisey moulds in 1958, was called Early Americana Waffle and then Americana Waffle (see p. 156 in the first volume of this series).

MONTICELLO, NO. 698

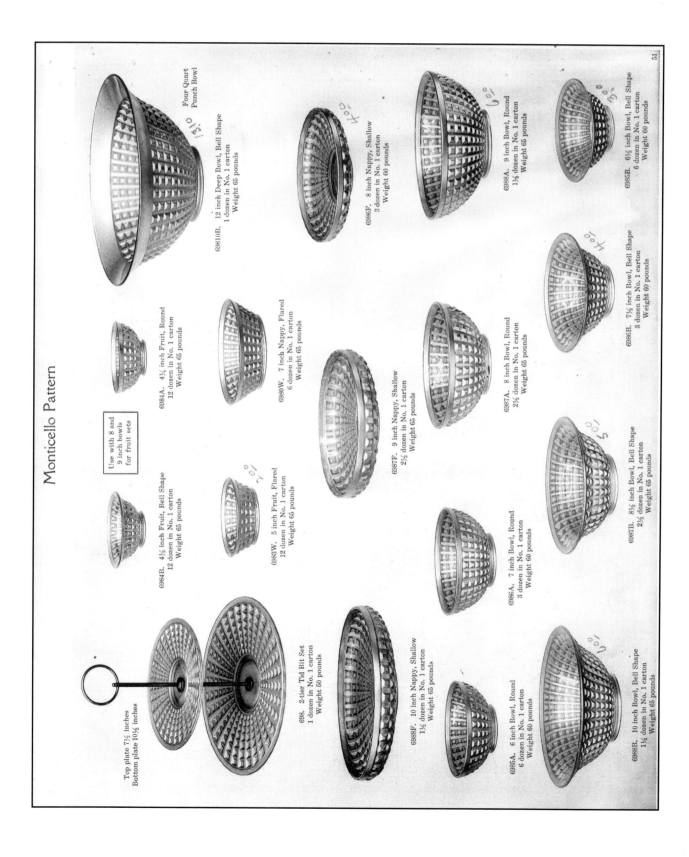

Monticello Pattern

Monticello, No. 698

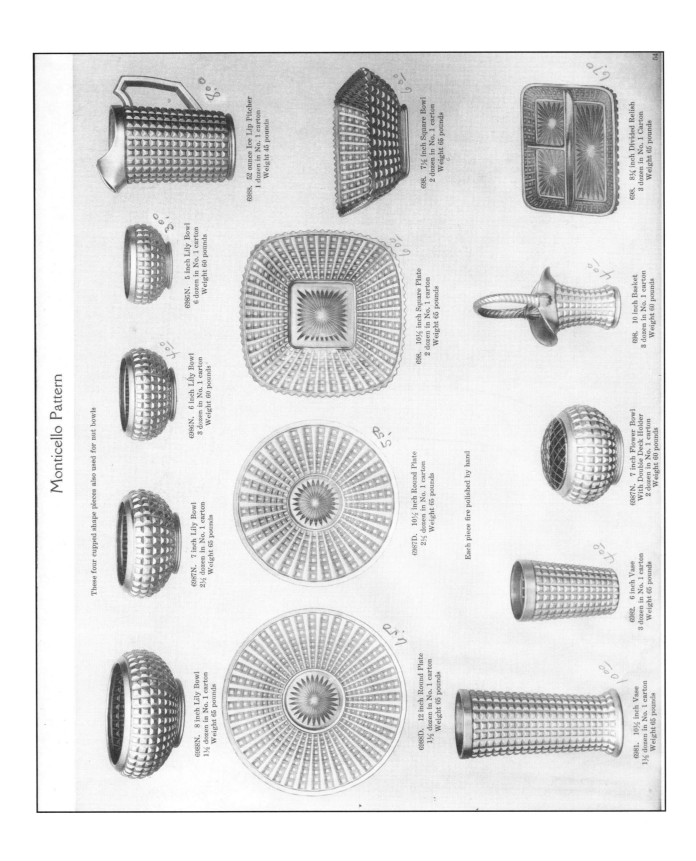

Monticello Pattern

Monticello, No. 698

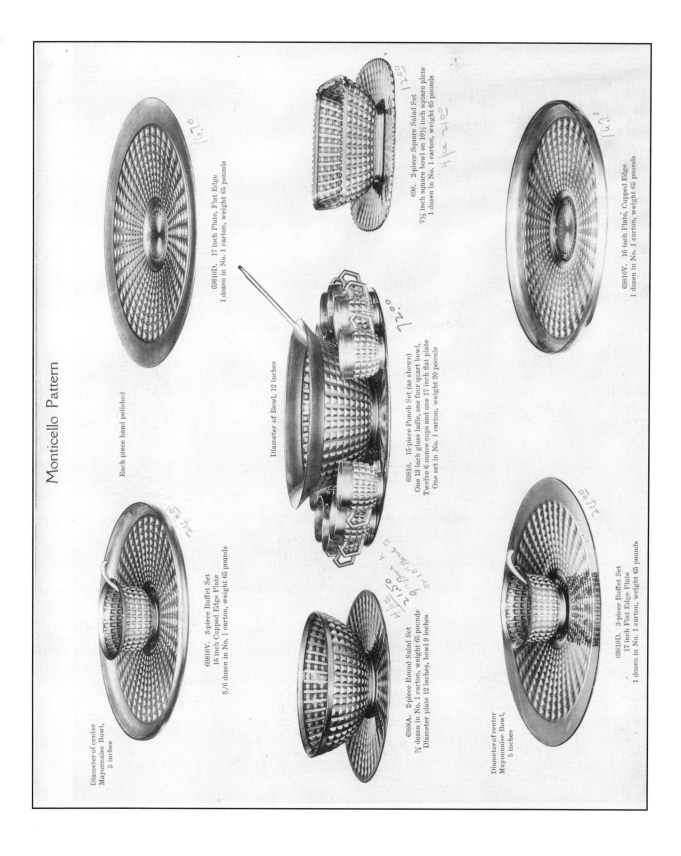

MOUNT VERNON ASSORTMENT

This assortment of Imperial glassware, which dates from the early 1930s, was decorated with a cut motif combining a central flower with a plethora of leaves. The phrase "rock crystal" on the original catalog sheet suggests that these pieces might be cut and polished. To obtain this effect, the cutting ("light cutting" in the glass industry) operation was followed by polishing to eliminate some of the grey appearance in the cut areas. Imperial's Mount Vernon Assortment consisted of the following: No. 724 covered dish (three partitions inside the bottom); No. 725 bon bon tray with heart-shaped handle; three pieces from the No. 727 line; two pieces from the No. 728 line; and the No. 760 sugar/creamer set. The Mount Vernon Assortment was available in crystal only.

M/MISCELLANEOUS

Magic Swirl, No. 115

MADEIRA GLASS COLOR

Imperial's color 51, Madeira was described this way in the July, 1949, issue of *Crockery and Glass Journal*: "Like a piece of real amber. It is both light and dark in tone, catching and reflecting sun or candlelight." Along with Burgundy, Evergreen and the unusual Indigo, Madeira was used in conjunction with the No. 123 Chroma line in the early 1950s (see Figs. 2549-2551). The No. 50 All-Glass Bird Feeder was also made in Madeira (see p. 57 in the first volume of this series).

MAGIC SWIRL, No. 115

These tumblers, intended for iced drinks, were introduced by Imperial in April, 1955. Four colors were offered (Pink, Blue, Flask Brown, Mustard and Crystal), but the most interesting feature of these tumblers is the swirl optic. Because of its low relief on the inside of the tumbler, the optic dissapears when the tumbler is filled with liquid, and it reappears when the glass is emptied! Imperial president Carl Gustkey had this advice: "Demonstrate before buyers! Play with! Seeing is believing! Suggest a jar of water on retail sales display for use of salespeople."

MANDARIN GOLD GLASS COLOR

Shown in Imperial's 1962 catalog, this color was used for a just a few items, including a plate and four pieces of stemware in the No. 1401 Jefferson pattern, which was made with moulds purchased from the Cambridge Glass Company in the 1950s (see **Jefferson, No. 1401** in the second volume of this series).

MARDI GRAS, No. 176

This line of stemware and drinking glasses was featured in a 1943 Imperial folder along with other stemware lines such as La France (No. 4600), Swedish Pinched Crystal (No. 220), and Twisted Crystal (No. 110). Although Mardi Gras was primarily a line made in "standard quality lead crystal," the 10 oz. tumblers were also available in special assortments which included two each in Aquamarine (color 75), Green (85), Cranberry (65), and Topaz (2). An Imperial price list (dated June 19, 1940) indicates that these colors were then in production: Sage Haze (30), Clover Honey (41), Chestnut Cola (42), Slight Blush (64), Green Oriolo (70), Quiet Stratosphere (80), and Wood Ash (82); a note in one of salesman Ed Kleiner's notebooks says that the colors were named by Imperial president Carl Gustkey, and a brownish color called Ripe Olive may also have been made. A trade-mark for Mardi Gras was registered on November 3, 1940.

MARINE LAMP

Also called Lantern or Marine Lights, these tumblers were fixtures in the Imperial line from the mid-1950s until well into the 1970s. Made in both ruby and dark green, they resemble the running lights on the side of a boat (see p. 712).

MARTHA WASHINGTON

Despite the name, the Martha Washington motif was a simple decalcomania decoration consisting of "sprays of flowers and leaves done in natural colors." The No. 15 Duplex Bedroom Set was done in crystal glass, but the decoration was also available on Rose Pink or Green glass. The Martha Washington decoration was apparently also available on items from Imperial's No. 727 and No. 728 lines. Martha Washington is mentioned in an Imperial price list (dated September 17, 1931).

MATCH STANDS

A few of these appear in Imperial's first catalog, which was published in 1904. Like the No. 9 match stand, some were part of extensive pattern lines, while others, such as the unique No. 245 shown here, were individual items.

MAYTIME DECORATION
(see **black glass**)

MEADOW GREEN CARNIVAL GLASS

In 1962, Imperial revived its production of the iridescent ware collectors had come to call "Carnival glass." New colors were introduced throughout the 1970s and the early 1980s before Imperial's closure. Meadow Green Carnival glass (see Figs. 1957-1981), which debuted in the firm's 1980 catalog, was among the colors made in the latter years of Imperial's existence. The catalog described the color as "the fresh spring hues of a Vermont meadow ... merged with the shimmering iridescence of a rainbow." Many of the moulds used for production of Meadow Green Carnival glass were old moulds, but all pieces should have the "LIG" (Lenox/Imperial Glass) mark. See **Carnival glass** in the second volume of this series.

MENAGERIE SET
(see **Animal decorated tumblers**)

METROPOLITAN MUSEUM OF ART

Imperial's relationship with this prestigious American museum began in 1968 when the glass company began to make special orders for articles to be sold exclusively through the MMA's gift shop and mail order catalog. During the summer of 1977, Imperial announced that it had been granted an "exclusive license to market these pieces nationally" (Wheeling *Intelligencer*, July 29, 1977). Ten different items were being made in 1977, and the number grew to 15 when they appeared in Imperial's 1980 catalog. Some pieces (71155, 71661 and 71762) were available in colors (Amber, Canary Yellow, Emerald Green, Sapphire, and Sky Blue). Each of these pieces should bear the MMA hallmark on its underside (see Figs. 1982-1998).

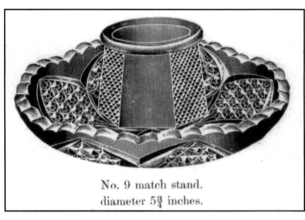

No. 9 match stand. diameter 5¾ inches.

245 match stand. 2⅝ inches high.

MEXICANA TUMBLERS, NO. 60

Shown in Imperial's Supplement One to Our Catalog 62, these three plain tumblers (13 oz., 10½ oz. and 7 oz) were available in Beer Bottle Brown. Interestingly, these tumblers were made by cutting beer bottles which Imperial had purchased from an outside source.

MIDAS

These items were produced in early 1957 by applying an all-over gold decoration to crystal articles from the No. 701 Reeded line (see p. 689 in this book and p. 463 in the previous volume of this series). The effect is quite vivid, for the gold has a remarkably brilliant quality.

MIDNIGHT DECORATION
(see **black glass**)

Midwest Custard

Along with Forget-Me-Not Blue and the short-lived Lichen Green, Imperial introduced Midwest Custard in January, 1955 (see Figs. 2219 and 2232). This opaque color was reasonably popular for several years, but it should not be confused with Ivory Satin, which was made 1978-1980.

Milk Jars

A few of these are shown in Imperial's first catalog, which was published in 1904. The unusual lid on the milk jar from the No. 1 line, which does not have a knob, would be quite difficult to grasp.

Miniatures

A short line of "new miniatures" appears in one of salesman Ed Kleiner's notebooks and is dated January 1, 1941. Six items were listed: No. 101 jug, No. 102 urn, No. 103 pitcher, No. 390-N rose bowl, No. 386-K bouquet and No. 100 boot. These were available in four colors: Green (color 21), Burgundy (30), Golden Amber (41), and Viennese Blue (80). Two years later, the list of miniatures had changed somewhat, and they were available only in crystal and satin-finished crystal; these pieces were listed: No. 101 jug, No. 103 pitcher, No. 100 boot, No. 428 handled basket (which held a pair of salt/pepper shakers), No. 104 cornucopia, No. 162 rabbit on nest, No. 145 chicken on nest and No. 147 swan on nest. Many of these moulds were used in conjunction with Imperial's slag colors in the 1960s and thereafter.

Mint Green Satin

This color debuted in Imperial's 1981 Supplement (see Figs. 2073-2090), where it was described as "a cool refreshing new Imperial tone" and one that was both "fashionable and feminine."

Moderna Decoration
(see black glass)

Molasses Cans
(see illustrations on next page)

A staple of imperial's early production years, several of these are shown in the company's first catalog, which was published in 1904. Some molasses cans were produced as blown ware, but others were pressed and finished using a method called "cut shut" (many collectors mistakenly think that the bottom of a cut shut molasses can, salt/pepper shaker or cruet has a "pontil mark").

Milk Jars

No. 1 milk jar and cover.
4¾ inches high including cover.
6 dozen in barrel.

Molly

This is Weatherman's name for Imperial's No. 725 line, but some confusion is created because she also calls it "Munsell" elsewhere.

Moonstone Blue

Designated Imperial's color 7 in the early 1930s, Moonstone Blue is a light opalescent blue. Imperial sometimes referred to its opalescent colors as Sea Foam. Moonstone Blue was used for some articles in Imperial's No. 749 Lace Edge line. Items from the No. 710 line (Beaded Block/Frosted Block) can also be found in Moonstone Blue, but it is not a common color.

Mosaic Tile tumbler
(see Tile Tumblers)

Mount Vernon
(see Washington, No. 699 later in this volume)

Mulberry color

Mentioned only in the supplement (c. mid-1920s) to Imperial's Bargain Books, this was Imperial's color 30. Described as a plain color (i. e., "without iridescence"), it was simply "a plain amethyst glass."

No. 67 blown molasses can.
shown with patented tin top.
6¼ inches high including top.
6 dozen in barrel.

No. 69 blown molasses can.
shown with common tin top.
6½ inches high including top.
6 dozen in barrel.

No. 7 pressed molasses can.
shown with nickel top.
6⅜ inches high including top.
6 dozen in barrel.

MUNSELL

Weatherman used this name for some of Imperial's No. 725 and No. 727 pieces, but she also called some No. 725 articles "Molly." Using Imperial's original number designations might be preferable.

MURRHINA

Imperial's Murrhina glass was on the market in early 1959. This glassware is made by an interesting process. First, a gob of molten crystal glass on a blowpipe is rolled in finely crushed glass fragments (called "frit" in the glass industry) which has been spread out on a steel plate called a marver. The fragments are picked up by the hot glass, and then additional crystal glass is gathered so that the frit becomes trapped between the layers of crystal. As the glass is rolled and then expanded when blown into a final shape mould, the frit becomes elongated and creates dramatic swirls of color. The technique for making Imperial's Vigna Vetro is essentially the same, but milk glass is used for the initial gathering. Imperial's 1959 price lists record some 25 different pieces of Murrhina. Some of the Murrhina shapes were made in other color treatments (see **Bittersweet**, **Spangled** and **Burnt Orange** in the first volume of this series). The dominant colors of frit in Imperial's Murrhina seem to be cobalt blue and green (see Figs. 2114-2130), but one can find ruby, orange or brown frit from time to time.

MUSTARD COLOR

This vivid, transparent yellow hue is first mentioned in Imperial's Supplement One to Our Catalog 62, and just a few items are scattered throughout the supplement. Mustard was not made for a lengthy period (see Fig. 1908 in the second volume of this series).

NAPPY PROMOTION

In 1960, Imperial created a special wholesale offer to sell these 5 to 5¼" round bowls. These were offered in crystal only,

NIAGRA

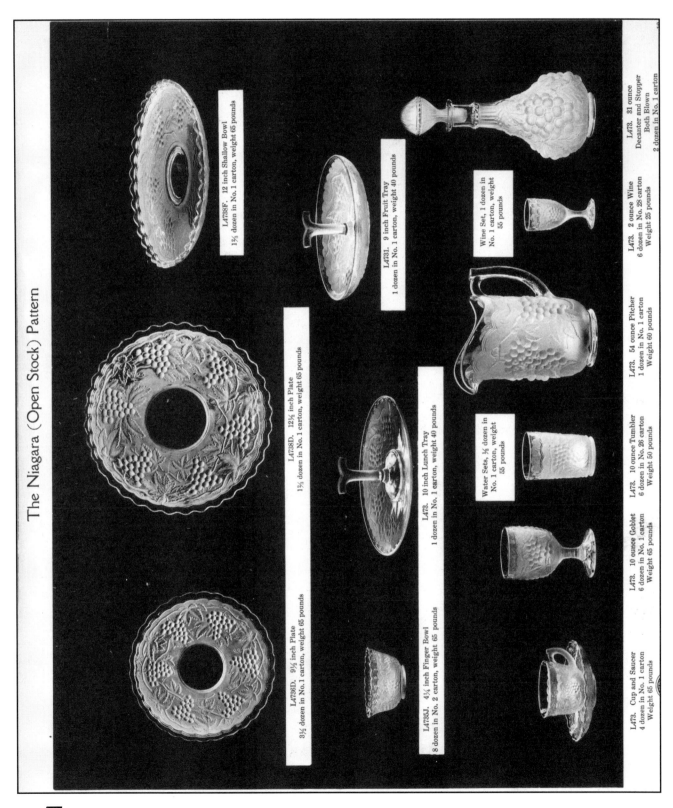

In Imperial's catalog 400, this was a revival of Imperial's No. 473 Grape design from the 1909 era. Items were made in crystal and then satin-finished with acid (the rims/edges were left clear).

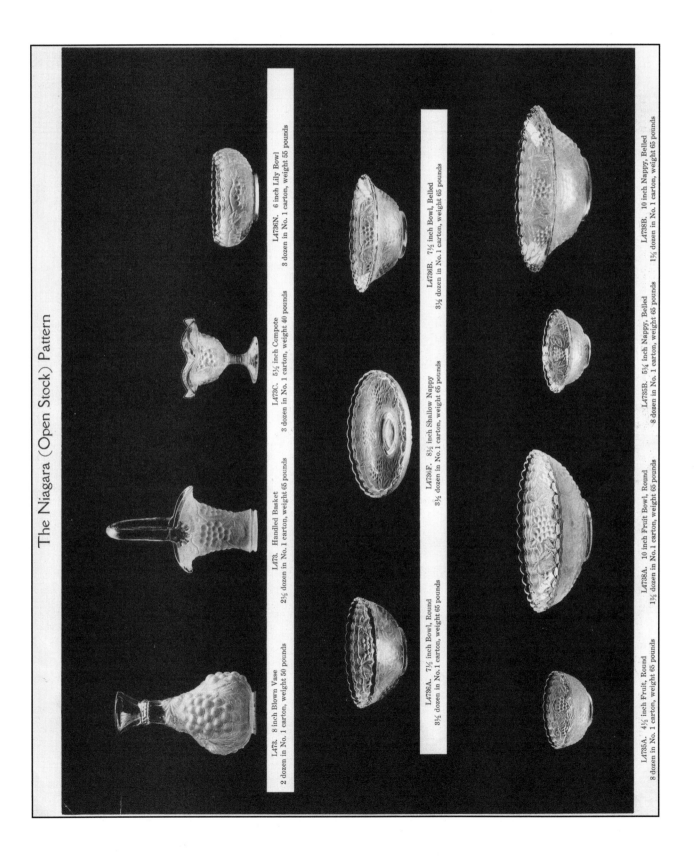

The Niagara (Open Stock) Pattern

L473. 8 inch Blown Vase
2 dozen in No. 1 carton, weight 50 pounds

L473. Handled Basket
2½ dozen in No. 1 carton, weight 65 pounds

L478C. 5½ inch Compote
3 dozen in No. 1 carton, weight 40 pounds

L4736N. 6 inch Lily Bowl
3 dozen in No. 1 carton, weight 55 pounds

L4736A. 7½ inch Bowl, Round
3½ dozen in No. 1 carton, weight 65 pounds

L4736F. 8½ inch Shallow Nappy
3½ dozen in No. 1 carton, weight 65 pounds

L4736B. 7½ inch Bowl, Belled
3½ dozen in No. 1 carton, weight 65 pounds

L4738B. 10 inch Nappy, Belled
1⅓ dozen in No. 1 carton, weight 65 pounds

L4735A. 4½ inch Fruit, Round
8 dozen in No. 1 carton, weight 65 pounds

L4738A. 10 inch Fruit Bowl, Round
1⅓ dozen in No. 1 carton, weight 65 pounds

L4735B. 5¼ inch Nappy, Belled
8 dozen in No. 1 carton, weight 65 pounds

Noel Cut Glass Assortment

Despite the name, Imperial's Noel Cut Glass Assortment No. 2503 does not seem to have anything to do with the Christmas holiday. Dating from the early 1930s, the cut decoration is similar to the **Mount Vernon Assortment** (see p. 506). The Noel Cut Glass Assortment No. 2503 consisted of the following: five items from the No. 725 line; a cheese and cracker set from the No. 727 line; two candleholders from the No. 727 line combined with a comport from the No. 728 line; and the No. 760 sugar and cream set. The Noel Cut Glass Assortment No. 2503 was available in crystal as well as Topaz, Rose Pink, and Green.

NUCUT

From about 1910-11 through the 1930s, the Imperial Glass Company was a major force among those American glass factories which produced imitation cut glass. Imperial's products were top-quality pressed ware made from pot glass, and the moulds imparted intricate geometric patterns. Furthermore, many articles were finished into shapes which closely resembled the brilliant lines made by Libbey and other cut glass manufacturers. Indeed, Imperial's wares sparkled in the light with almost as much dazzle as did Libbey's, but (and more importantly), Imperial's NUCUT imitation cut glass was just a fraction of the price of the real thing.

A design patent for the distinctive NUCUT trademark was granted on September 15, 1915, but the application papers (filed March 17, 1913) claimed that the trade mark had been in use since September, 1911. Indeed, ads for Imperial's NUCUT began to appear in the glass tableware trade publications in September, 1911, and appeared regularly during the fall of 1911. An extensive NUCUT line surely appeared in the firm's January, 1912, general catalog, for the 1913 supplement carried some fourteen pages of "numerous new pieces in NUCUT glass."

A large NUCUT offering was shown in the firm's Catalog No. 100C, which described the ware as "a line of fancy glass pieces in cut glass effects." "The illustrations cannot show you however the wonderful brilliancy of the glass," the catalog continued modestly, "nor the exquisite workmanship of the moulds which distinguish NUCUT from all similar products. There is absolutely no exaggeration in this statement: NUCUT is simply as nearly perfect as glass cast in moulds can be, for please bear in mind that NUCUT is not cut glass, though it looks like cut glass and answers the purposes of cut glass."

The NUCUT pieces in Catalog 100C are showy indeed—footed punch sets, footed bowls and comports, water sets and all manner of bowls, plates and vases. Catalog 101C offered even more items in NUCUT, and the firm claimed that NUCUT was "being handled by many stores that do not carry a general line of glassware" and by "hundreds and hundreds of the most successful glass stores in this country as well as other parts of the world." Merchants were urged to "keep the ware clean" when on display in the store, for it "appeals to the very best class of people."

When Catalog 104A was issued (c. 1920-22), the NUCUT line had been slightly scaled back. It occupied just four pages in the two editions of the Bargain Book (it's offered in Special Lots rather than as individual pieces, and the "$^1/_2$" designation appears after some articles, so it was probably being made from tank glass, which is typically somewhat inferior in quality to the earlier "mirror" pot glass). In Bargain Book 2, a line of "Heavy Part Cut Glass" was introduced; some 14 different articles were designated as No. 678.

In Catalog 200, NUCUT appeared in the index, but the assortments were intermixed with other crystal lines. In Catalog 201, many NUCUT pieces were offered for the first time in the new Rose Marie color. The catalog proclaimed this "a wonderful combination of the most exquisite moulds with the most exquisite glass" and asserted that "a table full of NUCUT Rose Marie will be in your department like a bed of roses in a garden."

NUCUT

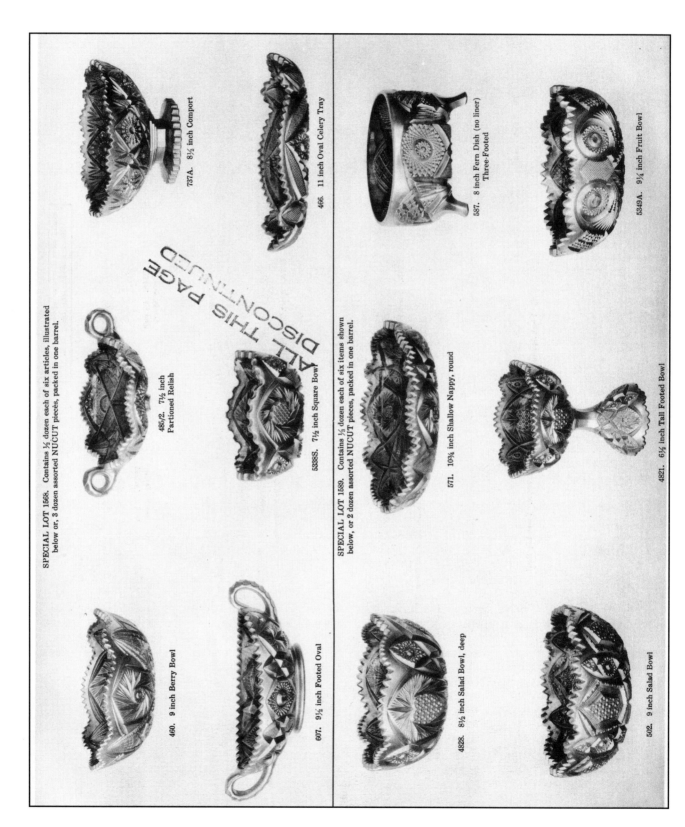

No. 313

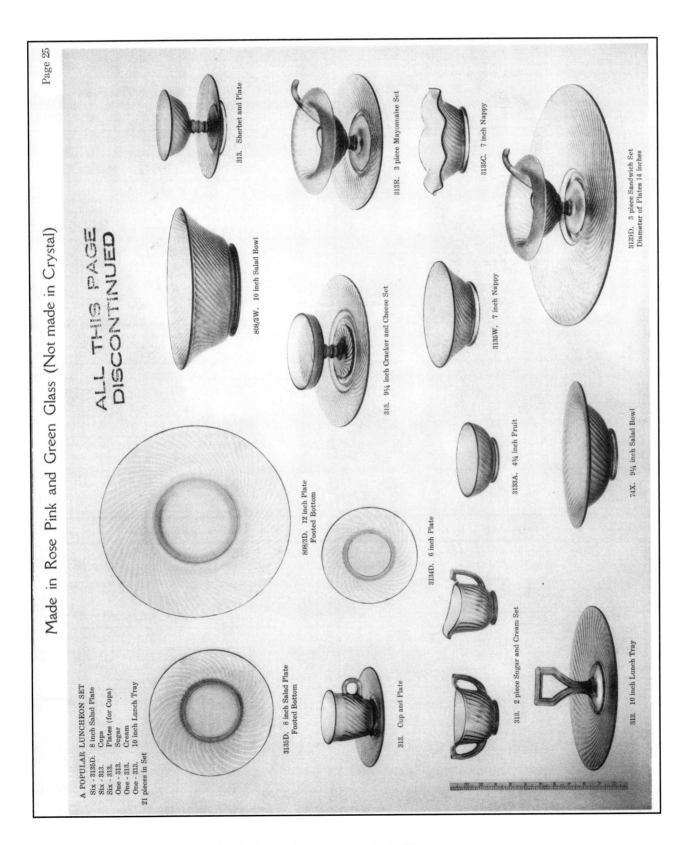

Imperial's No. 313 was made in the late 1920s and early 1930s.

No. 414

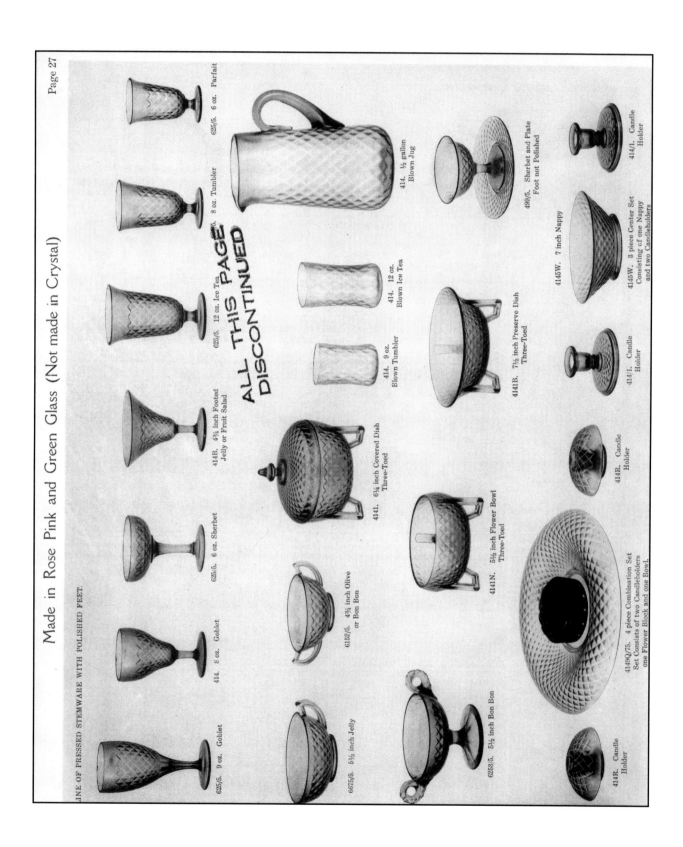

No. 414 (called "Diamond Quilted" by Weatherman) was made in the late 1920s and early 1930s.

No. 414

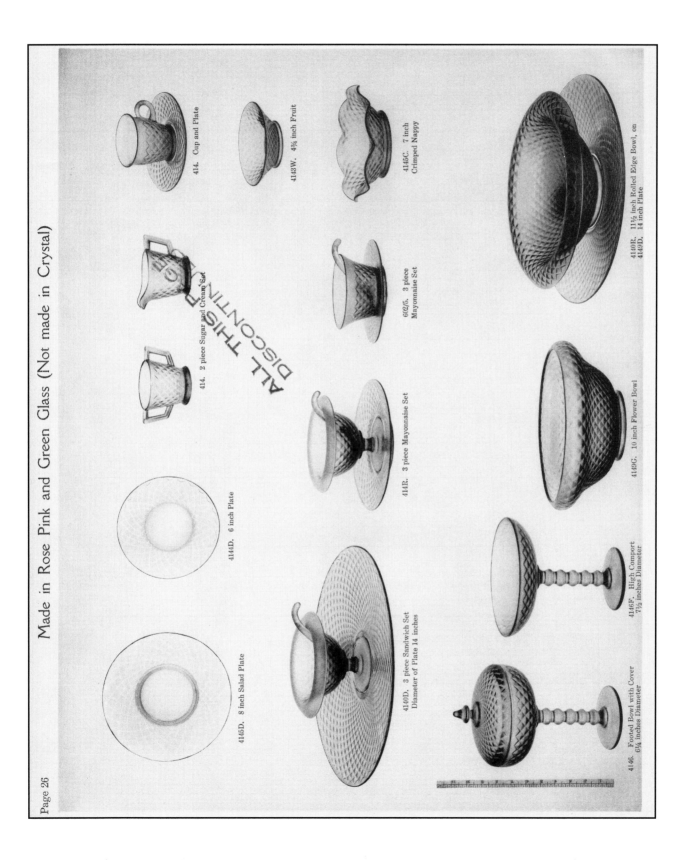

No. 719

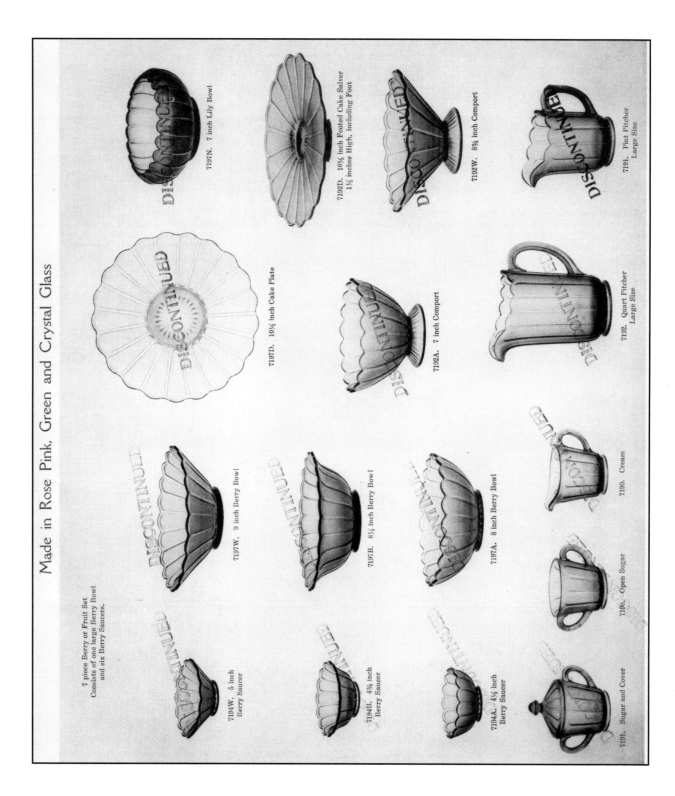

No. 719 (called "Lindberg" by Weatherman) was made in the late 1920s and early 1930s.

No. 721

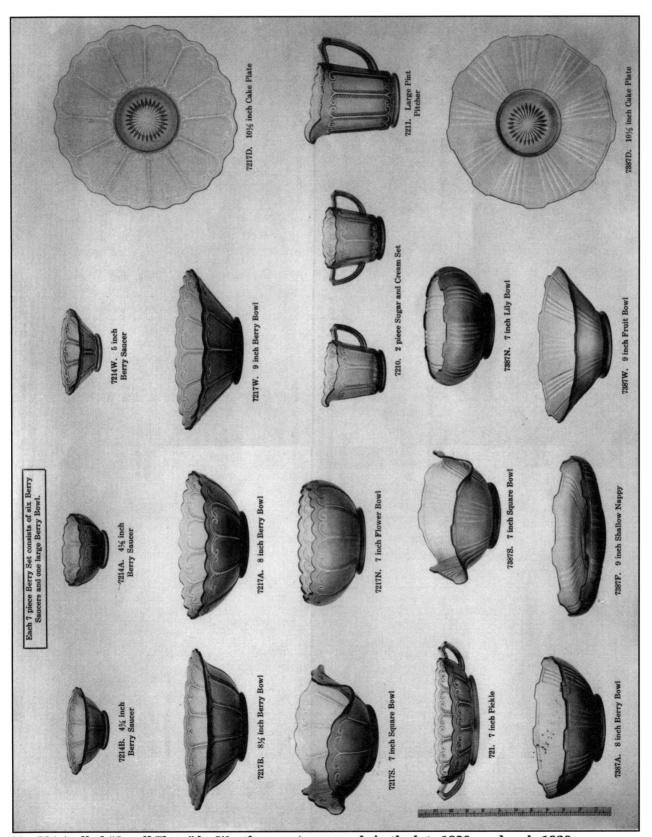

No. 721 (called "Scroll Flute" by Weatherman) was made in the late 1920s and early 1930s.

N/MISCELLANEOUS

NARCISSUS DECORATION

This handpainted decoration was shown in the May 27, 1948, issue of *Retailing* and in the June, 1948, issue of *China, Glass and Decorative Accessories*. Other decorations being shown at this time include Brown-Eyed Susan, Hawthorne, Western Apple and Western Rose. See Fig. 797 in the first volume of this series for a tumbler with the Narcissus decoration.

NEWBOUND

This is Weatherman's name for Imperial's No. 153 console set (see Figs. 1450-1467 in the second volume of this series).

NORMANDIE DECORATION

(see **black glass**)

NUART SHADES AND VASES

Imperial used the term NUART in conjunction with both vases and shades designed for gas or electric fixtures (see Figs. 2131-2139). The shades, which come in a variety of iridescent colors, may be marked with NUART in the fitter. The vases, which are typically found in iridescent green glass, may be marked NUART in small letters near the base of the vase.

NUGREEN

Along with amber and Mulberry, Nugreen was listed as a new color in an Imperial flyer which dates from the mid-1920s. It was described as "a bluish green plain glass" (see Figs. 970-972, 1578, 1580, 1584, 1588, 1592-1593, and 1596 in the second volume of this series). Many items from Imperial's No. 582 Fancy Colonial line were made in Nugreen.

NURUBY GLASS COLOR

This was one of three "bright iridescent colors" (Nuruby, Sapphire and Peacock) described in the Supplement to Imperial's Bargain Book.

NUT BROWN

This transparent glass color was introduced in Imperial's 1969 catalog, and some articles remained in the Imperial line through 1982-83 (see Figs. 636-650 in the first volume of this series).

OLD STURBRIDGE VILLAGE

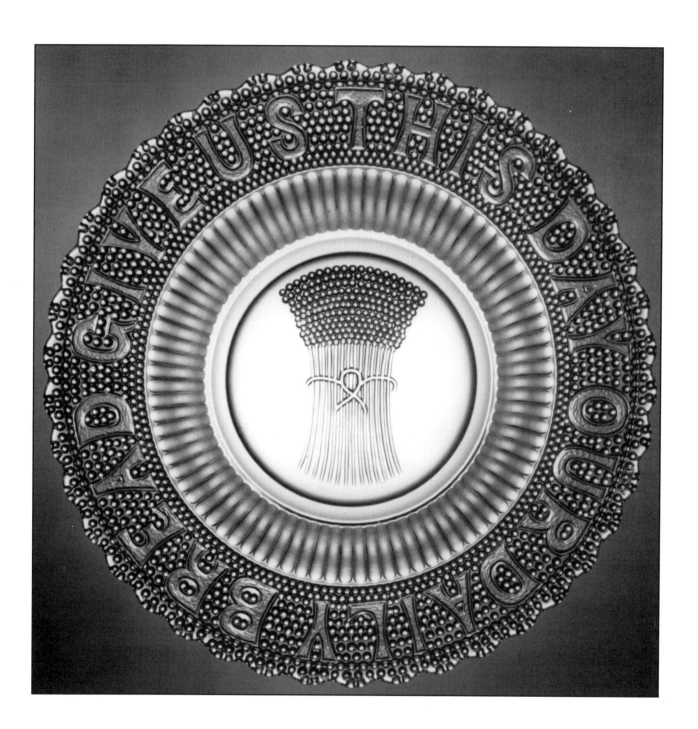

First produced as private mould orders for the Old Sturbridge Village in Massachusetts, these crystal items made their way into Imperial's general catalog in 1977. The 61206 Ribbed Palm goblet was a new item at that time, but the round bread plate depicting a shock of wheat and bearing the legend "GIVE US THIS DAY OUR DAILY BREAD" had been made for quite some time (a local newspaper, the *Times-Leader*, carried a story about this plate in its December 15, 1976, edition).

OLD WILLIAMSBURG, NO. 341

One of Imperial's successful lines, No. 341 Old Williamsburg was produced from moulds acquired from A. H. Heisey and Co. in 1958 (see figs. 2165-2216). Orders were strong for Old Williamsburg when Heisey was making it, and Imperial was confident that this interest would continue. Within a year, Imperial had more than 40 different pieces of Old Williamsburg on the market in crystal. Imperial's 66A Catalog showed the Old Williamsburg 341/5D 8" plate and four pieces of stemware in Amber, Antique Blue, Azalea, and Verde. These colors proved popular, so Imperial decided to make Old Williamsburg (especially stemware) in other colors and to keep all of the shapes in the line. Blue Haze and Nut Brown followed. Sunshine Yellow was available beginning in 1974-75, and Ultra Blue came the next year. Rose Pink (beginning in 1978) and Ruby (beginning in 1982-83) were also produced.

OLDE JAMESTOWNE

More than a dozen specialty items are shown in Imperial's catalog 53. These were available in Bead Green, Flask Brown, Heather, Hickory and crystal, which was called "Olde Flint." Some Olde Jamestowne items were marketed as flower holders in 1951. As shown above, these feature a rough looking, multi-holed flower frog inside. See **Olde Jamestown ashtrays** and **Jamestown Festival** items in the other volumes of this series.

Olde Jamestowne

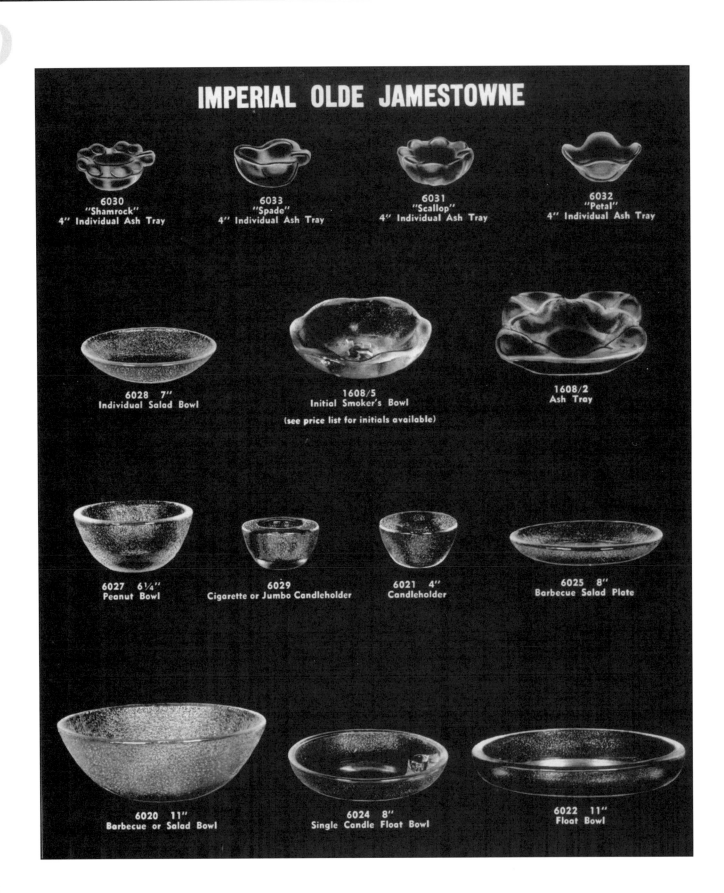

ON-THE-ROCKS TUMBLERS

These 11 oz. tumblers were decorated with cut motifs and intended for particular drinks, as follows: Scotch (#1 Thistle cut), Bourbon (#2 Corn cut), Rye (#3 Rye cut) and other alcoholic or non-alcoholic beverages (#4 Fancy cut). Each motif was sold in an eight-piece set for $6.50 retail in the early 1960s. The tumbler shape, called "roly-poly" in the glass tableware industry, was marketed by Imperial as No. 289 (which was made at Imperial) or as No. 785, which was purchased as blanks by Imperial from the Federal Glass Company.

Opaque, Colored

In January, 1955, Imperial released three new opaque colors—Forget-Me-Not Blue, Lichen Green and Midwest Custard. They were also called "Olden Opaque," but Lichen Green (color 87) was soon withdrawn from the market and not made again (see figs. 3035-3036 in this book). Both Forget-Me-Not Blue (color 86) and Midwest Custard (color 88) enjoyed continued popularity. The items shown here were included in the initial assortment in 1955, as pictured in the June issue of *House and Garden* magazine. Top row (l. to r.): No. 356 10" Loganberry vase, No. 132 Urn and No. 80 Vinelf candleholder; (middle row) No. 778 Dolphin comporte, No. 103 footed fruit bowl, No. 5002 Shang candy jar and cover and No. 67 Vinelf comporte; (bottom row) No. 180 Grape vase, No. 422 Atlantis cigarette box, No. 5026 Phoenix bowl, No. 181 Rose vase and No. 125 Scroll footed bowl with cover.

Optic Flute

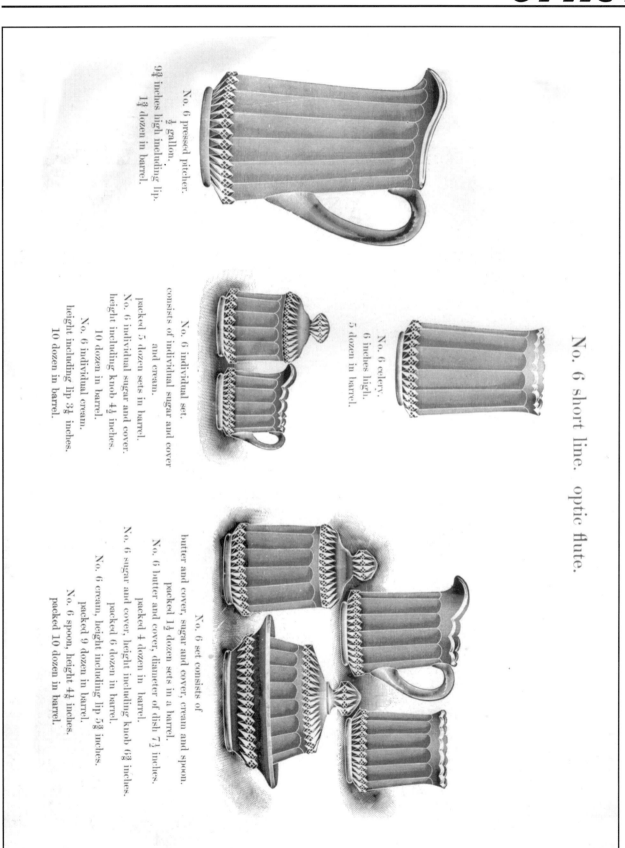

No. 6 short line, optic flute.

No. 6 pressed pitcher, ½ gallon, 9¾ inches high including lip. 1¾ dozen in barrel.

No. 6 celery, 6 inches high, 5 dozen in barrel.

No. 6 individual set, consists of individual sugar and cover and cream, packed 5 dozen sets in barrel.
No. 6 individual sugar and cover, height including knob 4½ inches, 10 dozen in barrel.
No. 6 individual cream, height including lip 3⅜ inches, 10 dozen in barrel.

No. 6 set consists of butter and cover, sugar and cover, cream and spoon, packed 1½ dozen sets in a barrel.
No. 6 butter and cover, diameter of dish 7¼ inches, packed 4 dozen in barrel.
No. 6 sugar and cover, height including knob 6⅜ inches, packed 6 dozen in barrel.
No. 6 cream, height including lip 5⅝ inches, packed 9 dozen in barrel.
No. 6 spoon, height 4⅜ inches, packed 10 dozen in barrel.

This small group of distinctively-patterned items was shown in Imperial's first catalog, which was published in 1904. These were probably made in crystal glass only.

O/MISCELLANEOUS

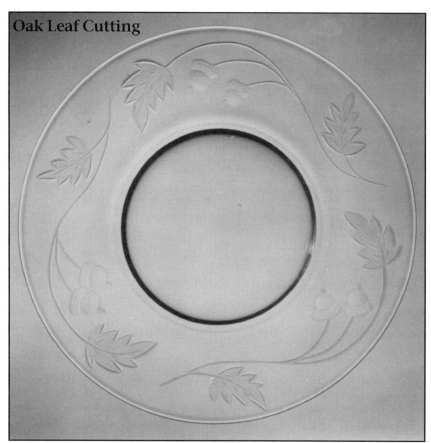

Oak Leaf Cutting

OAK LEAF CUTTING

This cut motif (C902), which depicts both oak leaves and acorns, was shown in Imperial's Catalog 53.

OCTAGON, NO. 725

According to an Imperial price list (dated September 17, 1931), the No. 725 Octagon line was available in crystal, Black, Topaz, Ritz Blue, and Ruby, but the most popular and long-lived colors were probably Rose Pink and Green (see p. 692). One Moonstone (opalescent) color was also mentioned, Sea Green. Sometimes, saucers in Black or Ruby were sold in combination with crystal cups.

OLD ENGLISH, NO. 166

This line was launched during the late 1930s, and at least one Imperial catalog shows articles on the same page with No. 165 Tradition and No. 134 Olive, both of which it resembles. Old English has elongated thumbprints, however, while No. 165 Tradition has crosshatching and oval areas which are not elongated. No. 134 Olive also lacks the elongated thumbprints, and it has rings on the base or underside (see the various items illustrated on p. 668 of this book).

OLD GOLD IRIDESCENT

This treatment appears in a color illustration in Imperial's 100B catalog, and it is described as "a real amber glass, with a deep, rich gold iridescent covering, which sometimes has beautiful warm tintings of red" (see fig. 1104 in the second volume of this series). The same description is found in Imperial's 101B catalog, but a copy of Imperial's 103B catalog in the files of the National Imperial Glass Collectors' Society has the word "Dropped" handwritten over the illustration and description of Old Gold. Carnival glass collectors readily acknowledge that Imperial was one of the few producers of amber iridescent ware, but they seem to prefer less precise terminology than the original appellation, Old Gold.

OLIVE, NO. 134

This little-known pattern is often confused with Imperial's No. 165 Tradition and No. 166 Old English lines. The No. 134 Olive line was launched during the 1930s, and at least one Imperial catalog

O/MISCELLANEOUS

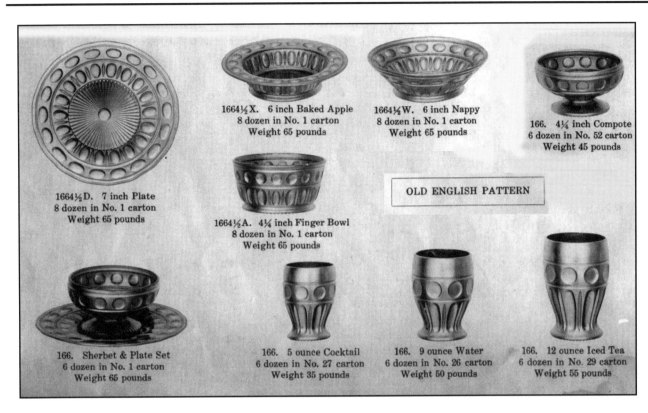

OLD ENGLISH PATTERN

1664½D. 7 inch Plate
8 dozen in No. 1 carton
Weight 65 pounds

1664½X. 6 inch Baked Apple
8 dozen in No. 1 carton
Weight 65 pounds

1664½W. 6 inch Nappy
8 dozen in No. 1 carton
Weight 65 pounds

166. 4¼ inch Compote
6 dozen in No. 52 carton
Weight 45 pounds

1664½A. 4¼ inch Finger Bowl
8 dozen in No. 1 carton
Weight 65 pounds

166. Sherbet & Plate Set
6 dozen in No. 1 carton
Weight 65 pounds

166. 5 ounce Cocktail
6 dozen in No. 27 carton
Weight 35 pounds

166. 9 ounce Water
6 dozen in No. 26 carton
Weight 50 pounds

166. 12 ounce Iced Tea
6 dozen in No. 29 carton
Weight 55 pounds

Olive

1346N. 7 inch Flower Bowl
2¾ dozen in No. 1 carton
Weight 65 pounds

134. 10 ounce Mug
6 dozen in No. 26 carton
Weight 60 pounds

1346A. 9 inch Comport or Pretzel Bowl
2⅓ dozen in No. 1 carton
Weight 65 pounds

O/MISCELLANEOUS

shows articles on the same page with No. 165 Tradition and No. 166 Old English. No. 134 Olive has rings on the base or underside. Original Imperial price sheets from 1938 and 1939 list the following No. 134 items: 1346A 3-pc. console set; 134 2½" candlestick; 1346A 9" comport; 1348A 10¼" salad bowl; 1346N 7" rose bowl; 1344-1/2B 6" comport; 1344-1/2F 6½" comport; 134 3-pc. mayonnaise set; 134 candy jar and cover; 1344D 6" plate; 1345D 8" plate; 1348D 12" plate; 134 cup and saucer; 134 sugar and cream set; and 1348A 4-pc. salad set.

OPALESCENT GLASS

Sometimes called Moonstone or Sea Foam, Imperial's earliest opalescent colors (blue and green) were produced in the late 1920s and early 1930s. The two pattern lines which seem to be found most often in opalescent glass is No. 710 (Beaded Block/Frosted Block) or Lace Edge. In the 1960s, Imperial produced Stamm House Dewdrop Opalescent (see figs. 2665-2672).

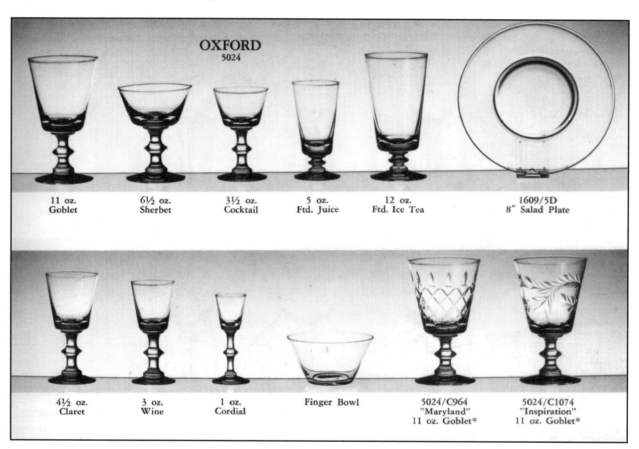

OXFORD, NO. 5024

Made from moulds acquired by Imperial from A. H. Heisey and Company in 1958, the plain No. 5024 Oxford line consists mainly of stemmed beverage items which have a distinctive shape to the stem. Imperial's 1962 catalog indicates that several cut decorations (C964 Maryland and C1074 Inspiration) were available on Oxford items in crystal.

Pacesetter Tumblers, No. 855

These were introduced in the early 1950s, and the name was changed from "Pacesetter" to "Terrace" in Imperial's 1953 Catalog, although the number designation (No. 855) remained the same. This is an original Imperial publicity photo, taken about 1953 by photographer Robert McDonald (top row, left to right): 6 oz. juice tumbler and 8 oz. Old Fashion; (bottom row, left to right): 18 oz. tumbler, 14 oz. tumbler, 10 oz. tumbler, and 14 oz. Double Old Fashion. These were made in crystal, Heather, Hemlock and Madeira.

PARLOUR PUPPIES

Also called Parlour Pups, this doggie quartet is well-known to collectors of Imperial's milk glass and slag colors (see **Animal figurines** in the first volume of this series). The four were described as Terrier (tail up), Terrier (tongue out), Scottie (standing), and Bulldog.

PASTIME TUMBLERS

Designated Imperial's No. 176/P/8 "Pastime tumbler set," these crystal, hand-decorated tumblers depict a variety of sports—tennis, football, archery, fishing, etc.—as well as a couple relaxing after a round of golf. These were being sold about 1943.

PEACHBLOW

These remarkable items were introduced in early 1964, as Imperial sought to recapture the much of the color and design style of Hobbs-Brockunier's famous glass from the 1880s. These cased glass pieces have an interior lining of milk glass, and the outer layer is a heat-sensitive ruby glass containing gold (see p. 676 and Figs. 2260-2280). When the pieces were exposed to heat during production, the outer layer would become a rich ruby red, shading smoothly to a warm yellow. This process, called "striking" the color, was quite difficult for the glassworkers to master, and Imperial president Carl Gustkey was far from satisfied with his company's Peachblow. Satin-finishing, called velvet, helped to achieve the effect (or to cover up the poor striking on many pieces). A number of Peachblow pieces were shown in Imperial's 66A catalogue.

PIE CRUST BOWLS

Designated Imperial's No. 1592, these three items were first made in 1960. Produced from the same mould, the pie crust bowls were shaped by a skilled finisher. The bowls were available in these styles: 1592 CC (double crimped); 1592 F (shallow crimped); and 1592 B (flared and crimped). Each could be ordered in any of four colors—Heather, Mandarin Gold, Pink or Verde. These pieces were also offered with a sueded finish (see **Velvet Pie Crust** later in this volume).

Pie Crust Crystal, No. 588

First shown in the supplement to Imperial's Bargain Book in the mid-1920s, this rather plain line was made until late in 1945. There may have been some subtle changes in the moulds for the creamer and sugar. Some illustrations indicate that selected panels were given a satin finish. This undated black and white photograph (perhaps from the mid-1940s) taken at Cress Studios in Wheeling shows four No. 588 items with a handpainted floral decoration.

Pie Crust Crystal, No. 588

Hand Cut Patterns on Hand Made Blanks

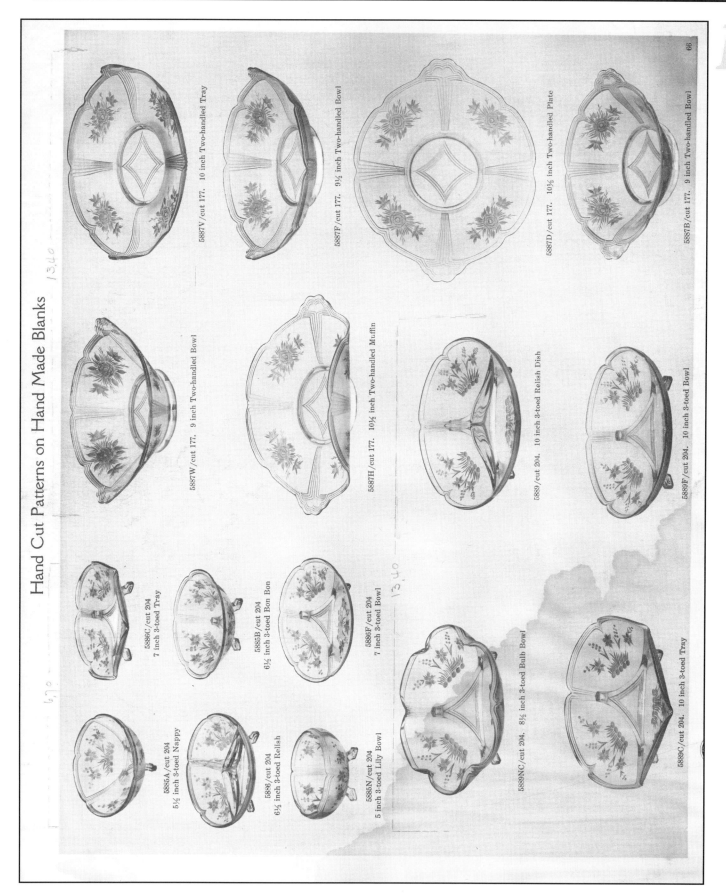

Pillar Flute, No. 682

This pattern dates from the late 1920s. A wide range of items was offered in crystal and Imperial's transparent colors—Nugreen, Red Glow, Blue Glow, etc. Items are also known in Rubigold and Peacock iridescent.

PROVINCIAL, NO. 56

These four pieces of blown stemware with pressed stems (l. to r.: 12 oz. goblet, 8 oz. sherbet, 7 oz. juice or wine and 16 oz. ice tea) were made in the following colors during the 1950s or 1960s: Amber, Azalea (formerly Cranberry), Forest Green, Golden Smoke, Larkspur Blue, Milk Glass, Topaz, Turquoise Opaque and Verde. Imperial's Catalog 66A shows the colored goblets with a cut decoration (C555). Crystal examples may be found with the Western Apple or Western Rose handpainted decorations.

Provincial, No. 1506

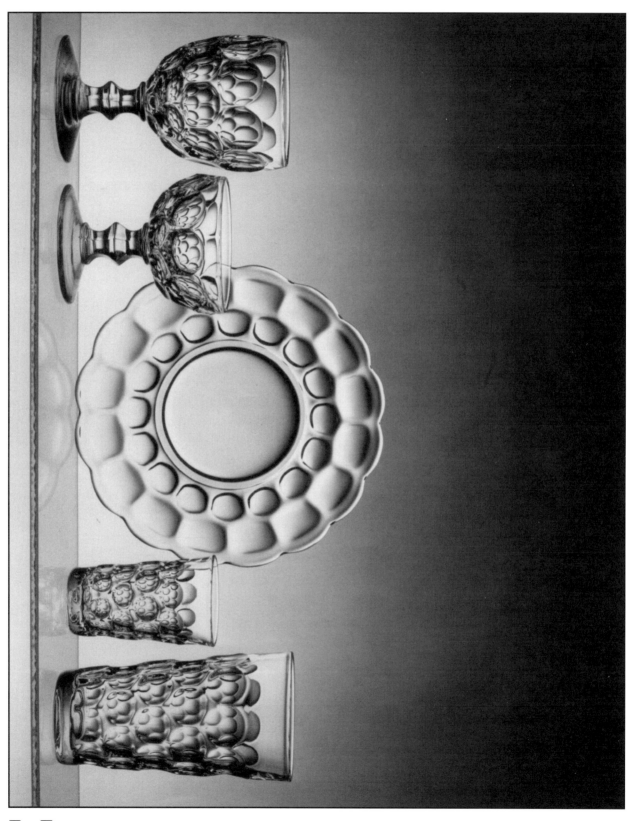

Made with moulds purchased from A. H. Heisey and Company, this was one of Imperial's most successful lines from about 1962 until its closure. In addition to crystal, No. 1506 Provincial items were made in these colors: amber, Antique Blue, Azalea, Blue Haze, Nut Brown, Rose Pink, Ruby, Sunshine Yellow, Ultra Blue and Verde (see Figs. 2334-2384).

PROVINCIAL, NO. 1506

Provincial
STEMWARE

In 4 lovely Colors

Heisy by Imperial

Fits every drinking usage, with handsome plates to match! All in your choice of four flashing colors... Amber, Verde, Heather and Crystal. Here is a proven, wanted pattern—traditional yet utterly charming in its multi-thumbprint design. Priced for profit and fast turnover. Better send that order in... NOW!

		List
1506	8" Salad Plate	$2.00
1506	5 oz. Sherbet	1.50
1506	10 oz. Goblet	1.50
1506	3½ oz. Wine	1.50
1506	5 oz. Regular Tumbler	1.00
1506	13 oz. Regular Ice Tea	1.30

New Accounts:
We'll gladly tell you how to become an Imperial Dealer. Please, write us!

IMPERIAL GLASS CORPORATION, Bellaire, Ohio

Punch Sets

The earliest of these dates from Imperial's initial offering of pattern glass in 1904. Those shown here are from the 1953 catalog.

Purple Slag

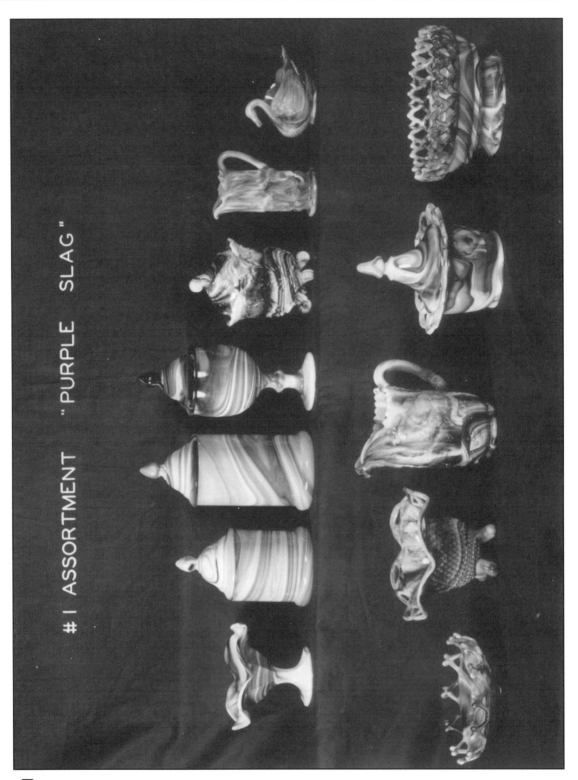

Among the "New Items" listed in Imperial's January 1, 1959, Price List were nine pieces of Purple Slag. More than 20 articles were pictured in Imperial's 1962 catalog, and the line continued to grow over the next few years. Caramel Slag took hold in 1964, followed by Jade Slag and Ruby Slag. This is the "#1 Assortment" of Imperial's Purple Slag, which was offered in 1962. Top row (l. to r.) No. 5930 6" compote, No. 702 7½" apothecary jar and cover, No. 704 9½" apothecary jar and cover, No. 464 Pokal, No. 176 4-toed jar and cover, No. 981 Olden pitcher/vase, and No. 147 Swan mint whimsy; bottom row (l. to r.): No. 363F 6" bowl, No. 274C 7" 4-toed compote, No. 240 one-pint pitcher, No. 780 6" covered bowl, and No. 159/1 7¼" bowl.

P/MISCELLANEOUS

Pansy, No. 478

Individual sugar, pansy design
packed 10 dozen in barrel.

Individual cream, pansy design
packed 12 dozen in barrel.

10 inch oval plate, pansy pattern

10 inch oval plate, pansy pattern
made in the following colors:

packed 9 dozen in barrel, per dozen	barrel lots	smaller lots
M358D Rubigold oval plate	$0.70	$0.80
L58D Azur oval plate	0.75	0.85
K123D Helios oval plate	0.75	0.85
R102D Old Gold oval plate	0.80	0.90

PACKARD

This is Weatherman's name for Imperial's No. 320 console set (see Figs. 1468-1478 in the second volume of this series).

PANSY, NO. 478

This was the original name for several articles made in iridescent ware from about 1910 through most of the 1920s. When Imperial revived Carnival glass in the 1960s and 1970s, some of the original Pansy pattern moulds were used for production.

P/MISCELLANEOUS

678—pitcher
1¾ dozen in barrel
per dozen $38.40

71/Dec.
"Patio" 12 oz. Tumbler
(see price list for sizes available)

PARISIAN PROVINCIAL, NO. 563

First shown in Imperial's Supplement One to Our Catalog Number 62 (issued January 1, 1964), these articles combine milk glass with colored glass (see Figs. 2236-2259). Pairing up a colored nappy with a milk glass plate (both from the No. 46 Hoffman House line) was simply a matter for the packing department, but the stemware pieces were created by fusing pressed milk glass stems to bowls made of Imperial's Amber, Heather, Ruby or Verde glass. In similar fashion, one of these milk glass stems was fused to a colored bowl (Amber, Antique Blue, Heather or Mustard) and given a milk glass cover to create Imperial's "No. 615 Hobnail bowl & cover."

PART-CUT GLASS, NO. 678

Weatherman calls this line "D'Angelo." At first glance, the glassware bears some resemblance to NUCUT, but these pressed articles were made so that particular areas (flower petals and the centers of the hobnails) could be cut later. These pieces were made in crystal, Imperial Green and Rose Marie/Rose Pink.

PATIO TUMBLERS

Shown in Imperial's General Catalog 53, these decorated tumblers were made from blanks (No. 71) purchased by Imperial from the Federal Glass Company.

PATRIOT

This decanter/tumbler set is described as "etched" in a 1943 catalog sheet. The tumblers were from the No. 176 line (14 oz. capacity), and the decanter was No. 627. Both the tumblers and the decanter have cut and polished fluting (designated C17½). Each of the eight tumblers is decorated with a different military or national motif. A similar set was available with etched, gold filled crests (see **America Always** in the first volume of this series).

PEACOCK IRIDESCENT

The first Bargain Book issued by Imperial called Peacock "our new, but already famous ... glass." The color (which was designated by the number 22) was described as "a very brilliant iridescence, but the effect is not loud. Every color of the rainbow is represented; a golden yellow predominates. Many color variations." Three pages of assortments in Peacock were offered, including several sizes and shapes of the No. 693 vases and articles from the plain optic crystal lines such as No. 615.

Pickle dishes

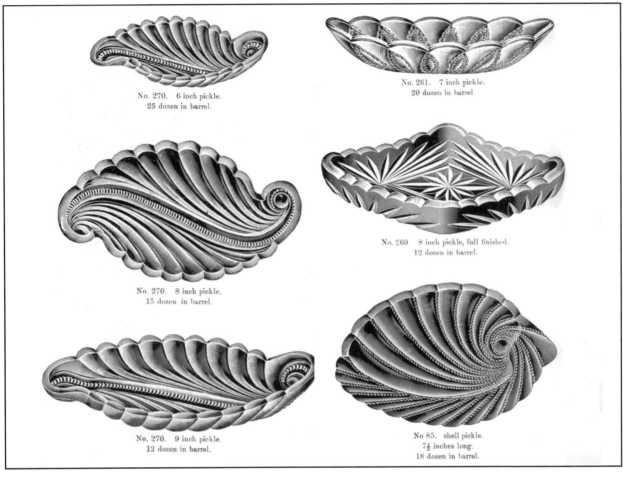

PEARL VENITIAN

During 1916-1918, Imperial produced five art glass colors—Pearl Amethyst, Pearl Green, Pearl Ruby, Pearl Silver and Pearl White (see **Art Glass** in the first volume of this series). Pearl Venitian is listed in just a single Imperial catalogue, which was issued in 1921 or 1922. The catalogue page clearly indicates that Pearl Venitian was an "art glass" color, but the shapes shown are all rather conventional pressed ware colonial-style pieces (see p. 678). Indeed, most of them were made "pressed to shape" and would not require the warming-in and subsequent shaping by a skilled glassworker that distinguishes must of Imperial's Art Glass, which is called "stretch glass" by many collectors.

PERSIAN TUMBLERS, No. 8401

Made in three sizes (5½ oz., 10½ oz., and 13 oz.), these blown, opalescent tumblers are intriguing Imperial products (see Figs. 2803-2813). In each case, the subtle drapery optic combines with an interesting color. these colors were offered: Dusk, Mulberry, Pecan, and "Vert" (not a spelling error, this color should not be confused with Verde).

PERUVIAN

The same tumbler motif, Imperial's No. 996 Toltec, had four different names, depending upon the color of the glass and the decoration. "Peruvian" was decorated with satin white on crystal, while "Aztec" consisted of matte black on crystal glass and "Incan" was decorated with black and gold on crystal. The fourth, "Pizarro," was made of amber glass and decorated with satin yellow. Each was made in three sizes.

PICKLE DISHES

A staple item in Imperial's early years, pickle dishes were typically part of extensive pattern glass sets. These were shown in Imperial's comprehensive 1907 catalog.

Pink Carnival glass

Imperial revived its production of iridescent ware in the 1960s, using the term "Carnival glass" in deference to collectors. Several of the first hues produced (e. g., Rubigold and Peacock) in the 1960s were original terms. As Imperial expanded its offerings of Carnival glass, new color treatments came on the scene. Pink Carnival glass (see p. 679) was introduced in 1979, and some new items were added in 1980. Imperial's 1980 catalog illustrated more than 30 different items.

Pink Satin

This color was first introduced in Imperial's 1980 catalogue, although Pink Carnival glass had made its debut some months earlier. The catalogue described Pink Satin as "the fragile color tones of a rose petal and the subtle texture of sherbet ice" (see pp. 679-681). Several other satin-finished colors (Blue Satin, Ivory Satin and Satin Crystal) were contemporaries of Pink Satin.

Pizarro

The same tumbler motif, Imperial's No. 996 Toltec, had four different names, depending upon the color of the glass and the decoration. "Pizarro," was made of amber glass and decorated with satin yellow. "Peruvian" was decorated with satin white on crystal, while "Aztec" consisted of matte black on crystal glass and "Incan" was decorated with black and gold on crystal. Each was made in three sizes.

Platinum Tile Tumblers

Three of these decorated tumblers, which date about 1964-66, were made on milk glass blanks (Platinum Tile, Colonial Tile and Golden Tile) and three others were made using opaque turquoise blanks (Aztec Tile, Inca Tile and Casa Tile).

Plum

This was one of the last colors made at Imperial, and more than a dozen pieces (almost all vases) were illustrated in the firm's 1982-83 catalogue. Many of the vase shapes can also be found in Blue Optics or Yellow Optics, two other giftware lines that were being produced at this time.

Pokal

Imperial often used this term to describe a covered candy box.

Posie Bowl, No. 46C

This 6" tall item was created by a skilled finisher who flared and crimped a No. 46 Hoffman House 12 oz. goblet. The result was an attractive container suitable for a small bouquet of flowers. The No. 46C Posie Bowl was available in these colors during 1963-64: Amber, Antique Blue, Heather, Mustard, Ruby and Verde (see Figs. 2976-2981).

Pura

This glass color was developed for lighting goods, probably about 1912-13, when Northwood's Luna and Jefferson's FerLux were in strong competition with Macbeth-Evans for a share of this growing market. Imperial's 100F catalog described the glass as follows: "Our Pura glass is a white, semi-opaque glass, of the highest value for commercial lighting and for all other occasions, where a soft mellow light is wanted. This glass is superior to most other similar creations, being nearly free from air bubbles and other imperfections."

Reeded, No. 701

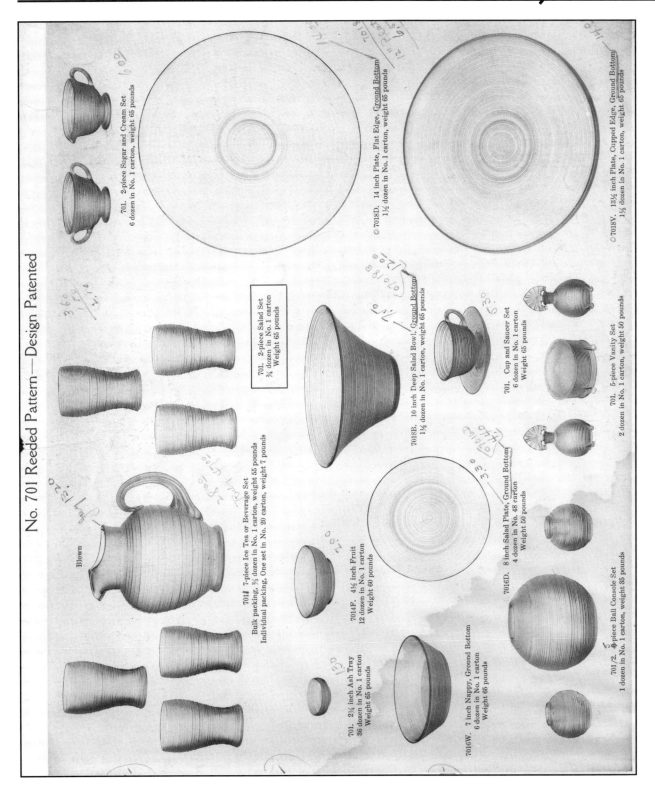

This pattern line dates from the mid-1930s. Two separate design patents (#96,622 and #96,623, dated August 20, 1935) were devoted to the pitcher and tumbler, respectively, but many other pieces were made. An Imperial listing dated April 3, 1936, indicates that the company was then marketing Reeded beverage sets in crystal, Stiegel Green, Ritz Blue, Amber and Tangerine, which was considerably more expensive than the others (see figs. 2430-2467). The sets were also available in crystal with colored feet on the highball tumblers and colored handles on the pitcher.

Reeded, No. 701

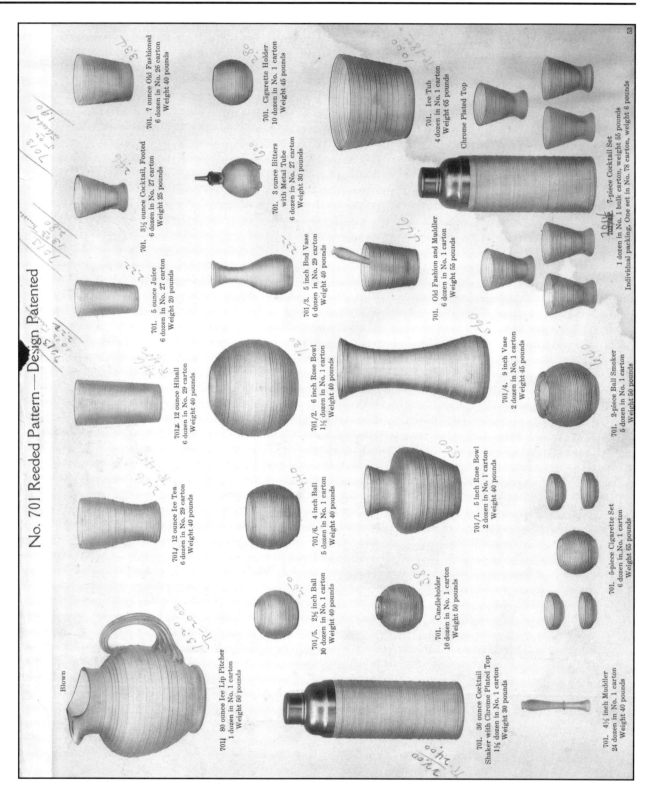

In the mid-1950s, a number of new Reeded moulds were put into service. The items were made in plain crystal as well crystal which was completely covered with bright gold. These latter pieces were called "Midas" (see p. 689 in this book and p. 463 in the previous volume of this series). About 1960, this pattern was further revived with a series of interesting items. These ranged from three sizes of Forester vases (in crystal, Mustard, Stiegel Green and Turquoise) to Dunce Cap decanters (crystal, Smoke and Turquoise) and a Tallboy cocktail shaker (crystal, Black and Smoke). A group of Whirlspool jars was also produced.

REVERE, NO. 1183

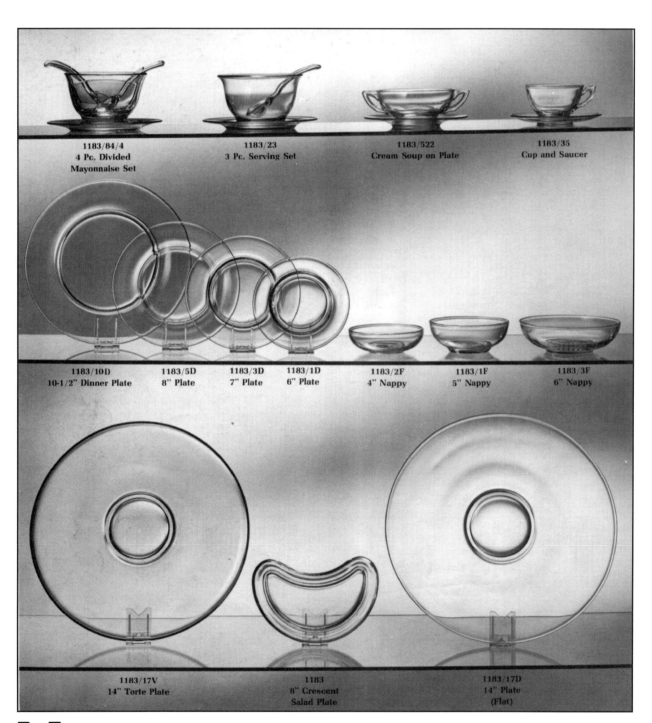

Made with moulds purchased from A. H. Heisey and Co. in 1958, this plain line in crystal glass was soon in Imperial price lists and catalogs. Imperial suggested to its dealers that Revere was "uncomplicated by design or decoration" and that it would go well "with contemporary and Scandinavian themes." Two of the Revere moulds were added to Imperial's No. 900 Intaglio line, which features a realistic fruit motif sandblasted on the underside of the items.

ROMAN KEY BEVERAGE WARE

This line of sandblasted crystal ware was introduced by Imperial in 1960, the same time that its Americana line was being marketed (see **Americana beverage ware** in the first volume of this series). The tumblers were purchased as blanks from the Federal Glass Company, and the pitcher and mug blanks were purchased from the West Virginia Glass Specialty Company.

R/MISCELLANEOUS

Radiant Star

RADIANT STAR

This cut decoration dates from 1909-1915 and is typically found on water sets or cream and sugar sets.

RAINBOW IRIDESCENT GLASS

This term comes up in Imperial's Bargain Book, where the color is described as "our latest addition to our iridescent lines." With few exceptions (such as the American Beauty 489 bowl), the articles shown in Rainbow do not appear in earlier assortments of Rubigold, Helios, Azur or Old Gold. Some nine pages of assortments in Rainbow were featured in Bargain Book 2, including water sets and other articles in the No. 682 Pillar Flute and No. 698 Monticello lines. Some articles, such as the No. 698 punch set, were offered in either Rubigold or Rainbow as well as in crystal glass. How wonderful it would be to be able to differentiate between Rubigold and Rainbow!! The term Rainbow does not appear in the supplement to the Bargain Books, nor in subsequent Imperial catalogs.

RANCH LIFE TUMBLER

Designated Imperial's No. 775, this tumbler dates from the early 1950s, when it was a contemporary of No. 777 Cow Brand, No. 779 Longhorn, and No. 778 Wee Scottie. The lower portion of the No. 775 Ranch Life tumbler resembles a coiled lariat, and there is a single strand near the top edge of the tumbler, too (see fig. 2820).

Ranch Life tumbler

Reflection

RED GLOW
GLASS COLOR
The supplement to Imperial's Bargain Books mentions this color along with Blue Glow, describing them, respectively, as "similar to Nuruby and Saphire." Items from the No. 682 Pillar Flute line were made in these colors, but probably not for long, as they are hard to find today (see figs. 3138-3139).

REFLECTION
Although not "stemware" in the traditional sense, Imperial's contemporary-styled Reflection line, which was designed by Lenox, first appeared in the company's 1977 catalog. The four items then available (7 oz. dessert, 12 oz. goblet, 10 oz. wine, and 16 oz. iced beverage/pilsner) were produced in crystal as well as four colors—Nut Brown, Sunshine Yellow, Ultra Blue and Verde. A 12 oz. double on-the-rocks was soon added to the line along with a four-piece cordial set (this set, which came in a gift box, was available only in crystal).

RIBBON BOW
CUTTING
Designated C901, this cutting on Imperial's No. 220 stemware is shown in Catalog 53.

RITZ BLUE
This Imperial color was probably developed in the early 1930s, for it appears in a price list dated February 17, 1932. The color was used for both Cape Cod and Candlewick articles, and some of these are illustrated in the previous volumes of this series. See pp. 689-690 in this book for some Ritz Blue items from Imperial's No. 701 Reeded line.

ROLY POLY
This phrase was commonly used in the glass trade to describe tumblers and pitchers such as Imperial's No. 785 (see **Lunar Dot** in the second volume of this series). Imperial offered these in crystal with gold decoration in its Catalog 53.

R/MISCELLANEOUS

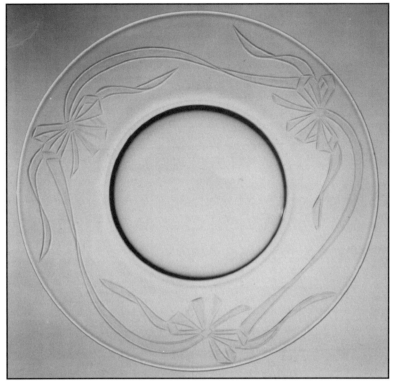

Ribbon bow cutting

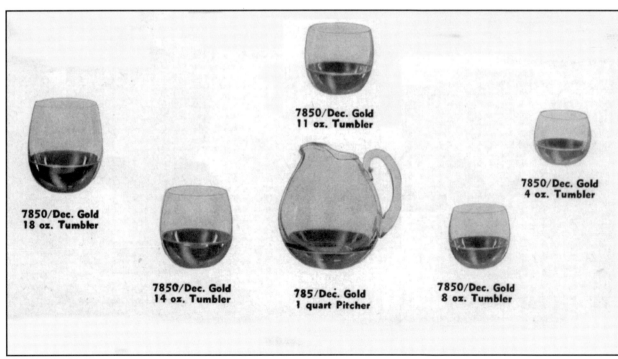

Roly Poly

R/MISCELLANEOUS

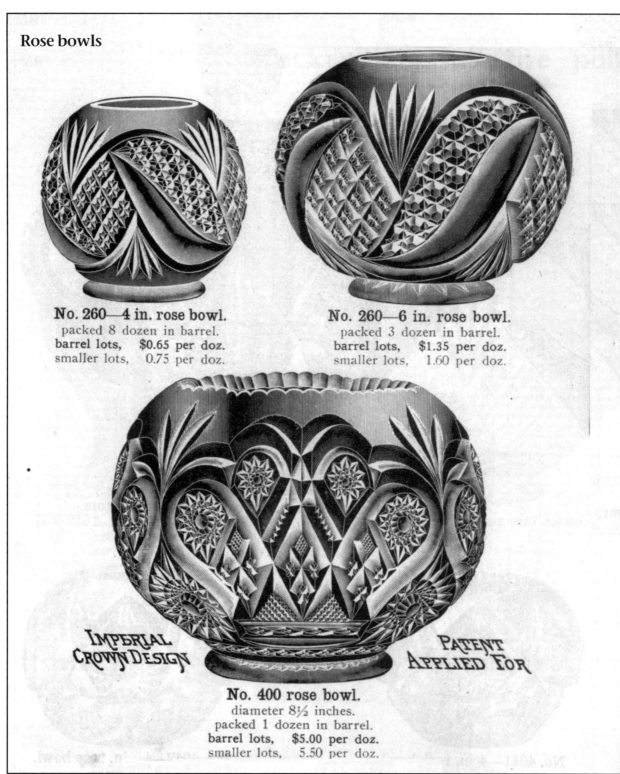

Rose bowls

No. 260—4 in. rose bowl.
packed 8 dozen in barrel.
barrel lots, $0.65 per doz.
smaller lots, 0.75 per doz.

No. 260—6 in. rose bowl.
packed 3 dozen in barrel.
barrel lots, $1.35 per doz.
smaller lots, 1.60 per doz.

IMPERIAL CROWN DESIGN   PATENT APPLIED FOR

No. 400 rose bowl.
diameter 8½ inches.
packed 1 dozen in barrel.
barrel lots, $5.00 per doz.
smaller lots, 5.50 per doz.

ROSE BOWLS

Some of these popular pressed ware items are shown in Imperial's first catalog, which was published in 1904.

ROSE ETCHING

This deep plate etching, enhanced by ruby stain, appears on a few vases and cordial sets in an Imperial catalog from the early 1940s. The etching plates may have been among those acquired by Imperial when it purchased moulds and other assets from the Wheeling-based Central Glass Company in 1940.

ROSE ICE

This iridescent ware was shown in Imperial's Supplement to the Bargain Book as well as in Catalog 200, both of which date from the mid- to late 1920s. Rose Ice was described as "pink crizzled on crystal glass" (see figs. 1758 and 1764 in the second volume of this series). Some items were shown with hand-cut decorations in Imperial's 201 catalog.

ROSE MARIE AND ROSE PINK

Designated color 91, the Rose Marie hue was introduced with considerable fanfare in 1926, along with Imperial Green, Amber and Golden Green. Rose Marie pieces were made with NUCUT moulds, too, particularly during the late 1920s. The successor to Rose Marie was Rose Pink (color 64) which appears in Imperial's Catalog 400 along with Green (color 81). Both Rose Marie and Rose Pink were difficult to produce consistently, and the intensity of the color will vary from item to item (see figs. 1552-1574 in the second volume of this series).

RUAMBER

This short-lived color is sometimes called "amberina" by glass collectors. The distinctive Ruamber hue is really a variation of Imperial's Vintage Ruby color, which contains selenium and cadmium. When the glass is struck to make Vintage Ruby as planned, each item is a uniform deep ruby color. At times, the glass is struck with variations in the color, such as orange with traces of ruby around the top or bottom as well as in thick areas of the item. Four pieces of Ruamber, all numbered 1854, are shown in Imperial's Catalog 53. According to Imperial's records, the Ruamber color was discontinued on January 1, 1955.

RUBIGOLD

This was the first of Imperial's iridescent treatments (these are popularly known as "Carnival glass' today) and it lasted for many years although the company's descriptions of it vary somewhat from catalog to catalog. Rubigold is mentioned first in an Imperial catalog which is dated October, 1909, on its front cover. The company noted that it had "not yet been able to secure illustrations which do justice to the beauty of this ware," but readers were informed that Rubigold Iridescent "is one of the most important novelties that ever appeared in the glass market."

Rubigold was described as "changeable colors in all the shades of the rain bow," and it was compared to "the high priced glasswares ... which were sold for a number of years in jewelery stores and other stores where expensive goods are being featured ..." An assortment of 20 dozen assorted Rubigold Iridescent pieces was offered for $14.40 plus $1.00 for the container in which it was packed.

By May, 1911, Rubigold was joined by a short-lived Amethyst iridescent treatment (this became Azur). In Imperial's 100B catalog, Rubigold was described as follows; "crystal glass, with a deep ruby iridescence on a ground of gold. Red and gold predominate in this color, though there are hints of other colors." The same description appeared in catalogs 101B and 103B, but the two Bargain Books described it as "our famous dark red iridescent glass." The supplement to the Bargain Books added "with hints of other colors" to this line. Rubigold was the only iridescent hue mentioned in Imperial's catalog 300; the color was described as "Crystal glass with a Deep Ruby Iridescence on a ground of Gold. Red and Gold predminate, though there are flashes of many other colors."

Along with Peacock Blue, Rubigold was one of the "new" Carnival glass colors of the 1960s and 1970s when Imperial decided to re-issue this popular ware. The Grape pattern No. 473 10 oz. goblet was the first item to appear, without any fanfare, in Imperial's 1962 catalog. For more information, see the discussion of **Carnival glass** and the many illustrations in the second volume of this series. In its 1975-76 catalog, Imperial offered a special Rubigold water set with satin-finished panels (see p. 147 of the first volume in this series for an illustration of this set).

RUBY SLAG

Also called End O'Day Ruby, this was another of the popular "slag" lines introduced by Imperial in the 1960s. Today, it is very popular among collectors, as are Caramel Slag, Jade Slag and Purple Slag. More than a dozen pieces of Ruby Slag were illustrated in Imperial's catalogue 69, and the line proved to be both popular and long-lived. The 1975-1976 catalogue describes Ruby Slag as "the ultimate in slag glass" and goes on to relate that the glass combined "bright Ruby Glass with White Milk Glass." Items were available in either the glossy finish or a satin finish (see figs. 2486-2548).

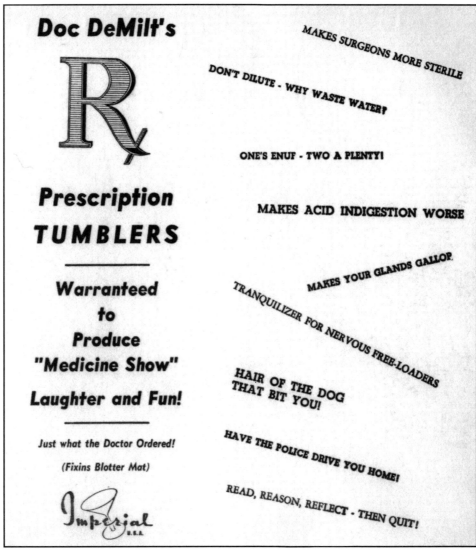

Rx MEDICINE TUMBLER

Also called "Prescription tumblers," these No. 71 tumblers (purchased as blanks from the Federal Glass Co.) were silk-screen decorated with witty one-liners designed to appeal to those who took their alcoholic drinks very seriously. A "blotter mat" (reproduced in part here) came with each set of eight tumblers. "Doc DeMilt" was D. Milton Gutman, a longtime friend of Imperial president Carl Gustkey, who headed the Gutman Advertising Agency in Wheeling, West Virginia.

Satin Crystal

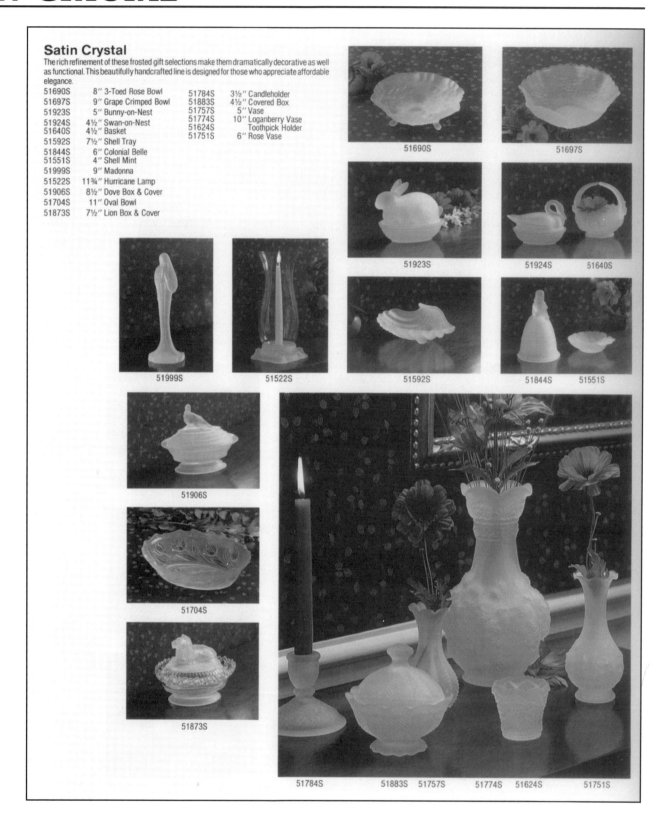

Satin Crystal

The rich refinement of these frosted gift selections make them dramatically decorative as well as functional. This beautifully handcrafted line is designed for those who appreciate affordable elegance.

51690S	8" 3-Toed Rose Bowl	51784S	3½" Candleholder
51697S	9" Grape Crimped Bowl	51883S	4½" Covered Box
51923S	5" Bunny-on-Nest	51757S	5" Vase
51924S	4½" Swan-on-Nest	51774S	10" Loganberry Vase
51640S	4½" Basket	51624S	Toothpick Holder
51592S	7½" Shell Tray	51751S	6" Rose Vase
51844S	6" Colonial Belle		
51551S	4" Shell Mint		
51999S	9" Madonna		
51522S	11¾" Hurricane Lamp		
51906S	8½" Dove Box & Cover		
51704S	11" Oval Bowl		
51873S	7½" Lion Box & Cover		

In 1980, Imperial was marketing several satin-finished colors (Blue Satin, Ivory Satin, Mint Green Satin, and Pink Satin) along with a line of some 19 items in satin-finished crystal. Offered as "giftware," these pieces were described as "dramatically decorative as well as functional." Lemon Frost was made about two years later.

Sculptured Rose

These dramatic articles represent the epitome of Imperial's decorating department. The sandcarving technique was pioneered by Imperial's Franz Hess, who developed the carving for the Celestial centerpiece and the Pavilion tray in the Cathay line (see pp. 260-261 of the first volume in this series).

Semi-Colonial, No. 666

666/1. SPECIAL LOT, contains 1 dozen each of the ten different pieces shown below, or a total of 10 dozen assorted, packed in one barrel.

666. 6½ inch Oval Comport
666. 8½ inch Oval Celery Tray
6666S. 6½ inch Square Bowl
6665. 5½ inch Two-handled Bowl
666. 6½ inch Oval Pickle
666. 6 inch Bouquet
6661. 4 inch Small Covered Butter
6666B. 7½ inch Salad Bowl
6660. Open Sugar
6660. Cream

Shown in Imperial's 300 catalog, this was an extensive line of crystal glassware. Some articles were also made in Imperial's iridescent colors from the 1920s.

Skanda, No 530 and No. 531

SKANDA
DIAMOND OPTIC

Imperial's handcrafted SKANDA sets the scene for sales with its fresh, clear, light look. SKANDA is available in lead Crystal, Amber, Antique Blue, Verde and new Nut Brown. Enrich your Spring profit picture with Imperial's nationally advertised SKANDA . . . drop us a note for details.

Imperial Glass Corporation
BELLAIRE, OHIO 43906

First shown in early 1964, Imperial's Skanda was a popular line of stemware for about eight years. As the name implies, these initial items were plain blown ware in distinctive Scandinavian-style shapes with hand drawn stems and a cast-on foot. They were available in crystal as well as crystal decorated with platinum or gold bands in 1964. In Imperial's Catalog 66A, No. 530 Skanda is shown in crystal, Amber, Antique Blue, Azalea and Verde. The 1969 Imperial catalog shows items in both Skanda No. 530 and No. 531; the latter have a "diamond optic" motif imparted by a spot mould during the production process (see figs. 2586-2605 to differentiate between the plain and Diamond Optic versions of Skanda).

Smart Alec tumblers

These silk screen decorated tumblers from the late 1950s were done on blanks purchased from the Federal Glass Company. This advertisement appeared in the June, 1959, issue of the trade publication *China, Glass and Tableware*.

SMITHSONIAN INSTITUTION

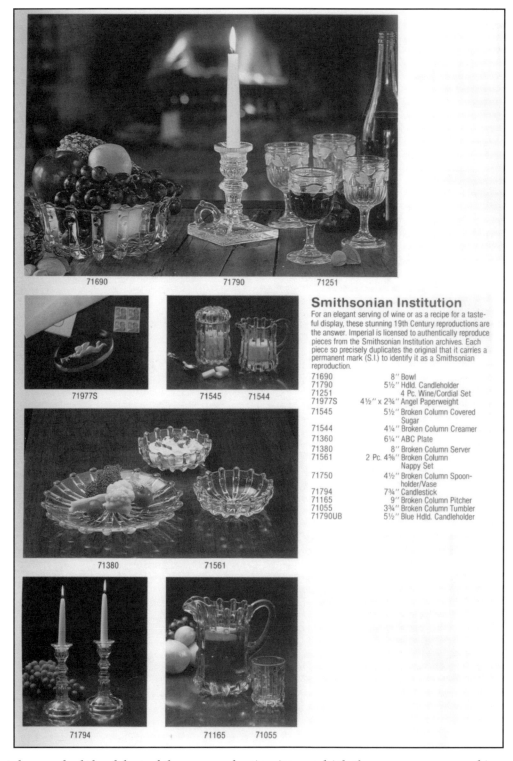

Smithsonian Institution

For an elegant serving of wine or as a recipe for a tasteful display, these stunning 19th Century reproductions are the answer. Imperial is licensed to authentically reproduce pieces from the Smithsonian Institution archives. Each piece so precisely duplicates the original that it carries a permanent mark (S.I.) to identify it as a Smithsonian reproduction.

71690	8" Bowl
71790	5½" Hdld. Candleholder
71251	4 Pc. Wine/Cordial Set
71977S	4½" x 2¾" Angel Paperweight
71545	5½" Broken Column Covered Sugar
71544	4¼" Broken Column Creamer
71360	6¼" ABC Plate
71380	8" Broken Column Server
71561	2 Pc. 4⅝" Broken Column Nappy Set
71750	4½" Broken Column Spoonholder/Vase
71794	7¾" Candlestick
71165	9" Broken Column Pitcher
71055	3¾" Broken Column Tumbler
71790UB	5½" Blue Hdld. Candleholder

Imperial's 1977 catalog marked the debut of three reproduction items which the company was making for the Smithsonian Institution in Washington, D. C.: 71250 wine/cordial 4-pc. set; 71360 ABC plate; and 71790 candleholder. The 1980 catalog showed these same items (the 71790 candleholder was available in Ultra Blue), along with the 71794 candlestick, the 71977S Angel paperweight and the following items in the Broken Column pattern: 71690 8" bowl; 71544 and 71545 creamer and sugar, 71380 8" server, 71561 4⅝" nappy, 71750 spoonholder/vase, 71165 pitcher, and 71055 tumbler. These items were made in moulds owned by Imperial, and all bear the mark "SI" (see also **Metropolitan Museum of Art** and **Old Sturbridge Village** earlier in this volume).

Southern Highlands

IMPERIAL GLASS CORPORATION
Bellaire, Ohio

11" Carbuncle Vase
SH/1 Crystal
SH/65/1 Cranberry
SH/85/1 Green

11" Vase, Plain Gourd Shape
SH/2 Crystal
SH/65/2 Cranberry
SH/85/2 Green

7½" Ring Handle "Little Brown Jug"
SH/3 Crystal
SH/65/3 Cranberry
SH/85/3 Green

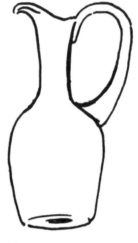

9½" 1 Hld. Lipped Jug or Pitcher Type Vase
SH/4 Crystal

11" Vase, Pinched, Festoon Base, Coil Neck
SH/5 Crystal

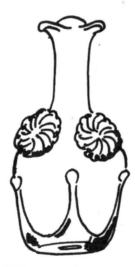

11" Vase, Festoon Base, 3 Rosettes
SH/6 Crystal

Tall Pitcher, Pinched
SH/65/1819 Cranberry
SH/85/1819 Green

12 oz. Tumbler Pinched
SH/65/1819 Cranberry
SH/85/1819 Green

These Imperial items were made in conjunction with a promotional effort for *House and Garden* magazine in May, 1942. These original line drawings and accompanying captions provide Imperial's numerical designations and the colors in which the pieces were produced.

SPRINGERLE SWEETSDISH

Introduced in the fall of 1963, this is the No. 618 footed bowl and cover. Imperial's POPA (Point-Of-Purchase-Aids/Assistance) tag explained that this design was "inspired by a wooden cookie roller and a metal reproduction of a still existing cookie mould used over 300 years ago." Advertising appeared in *China, Glass and Tablewares* (September, 1963) and *House and Garden* (November, 1963). The Springerle Sweetsdish was made in Antique Blue, Azalea, crystal, Flask Brown, Milk Glass, and Verde (see also **Butterpat Sweets Server** in the first volume of this series).

Square, No. 760

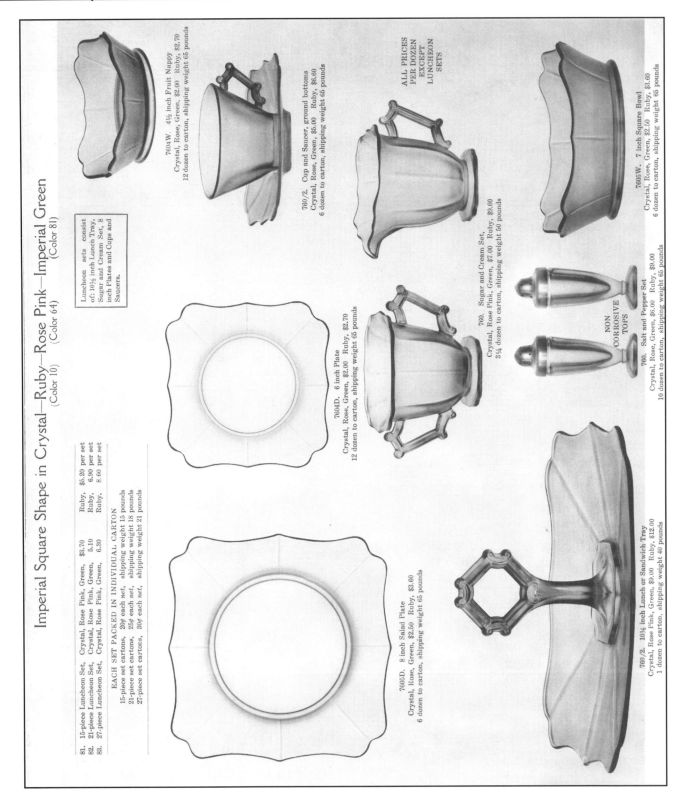

Imperial's No. 760 Square was introduced in the mid-1930s.

STAR HOLLY

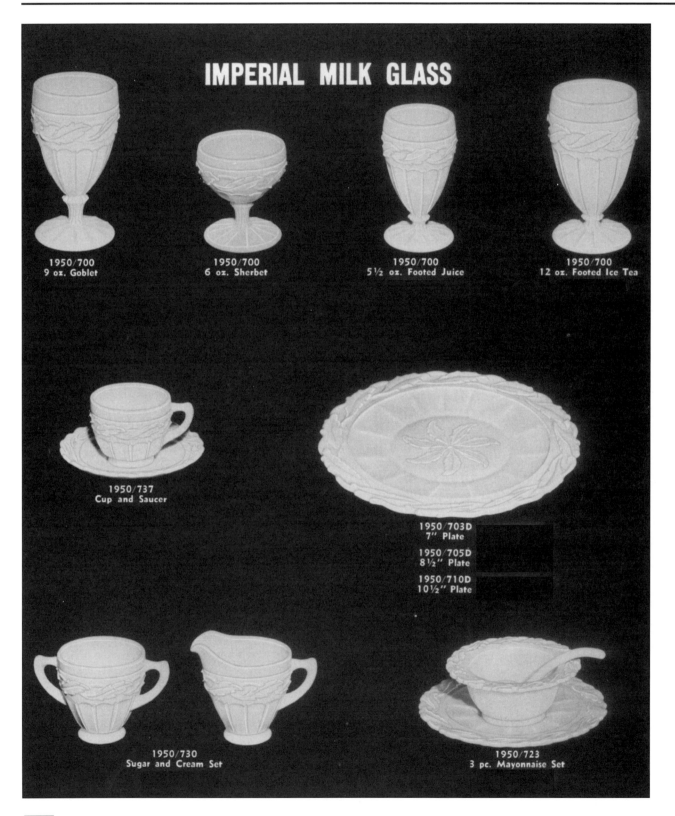

These items in Imperial's milk glass date from 1952. A note in one of salesman Ed Kleiner's notebooks says that the pattern was "first made for Sears Roebuck & Company in crystal only." Many different pieces are pictured in Imperial's catalogs. An error-filled article in *Hobbies* magazine (December, 1959) spread considerable misinformation about this line, but the authors, Ralph and Terry Kovel, issued a more correct version about 13 years later (*Hobbies*, January, 1973).

Star Holly

IMPERIAL MILK GLASS

1950/775X 9" Bowl
1950/759 6½" Candy Box and Cover
1950/765 9" Candy Box and Cover
1950/780 3½" Low Candleholder
1950/752 6½" Fruit
1950/766 11" Float Bowl with 3 Candle-Sockets
1950/767X 11" Footed Fruit Bowl
1950/767D 13" Cake Stand

STEMWARE, CUT

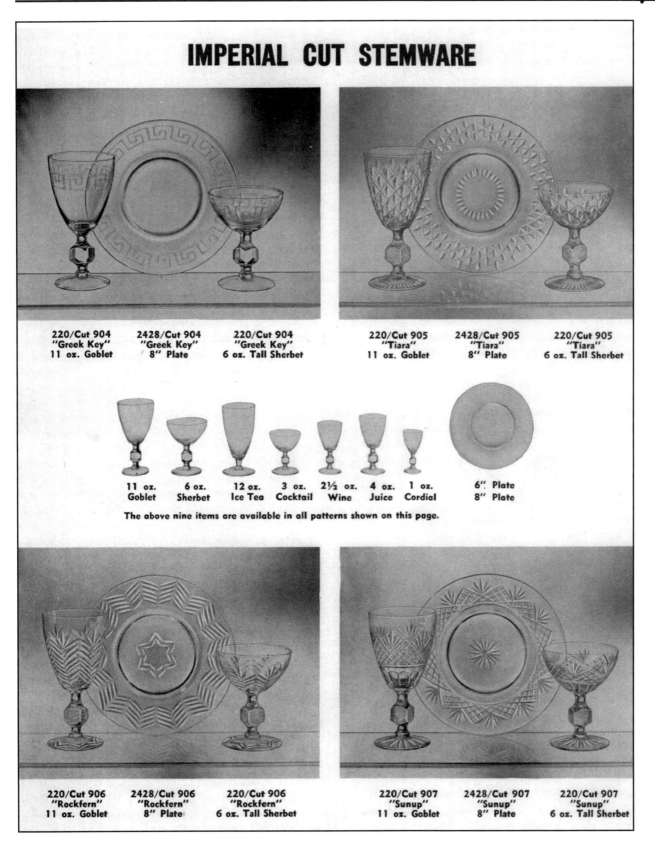

Imperial's General Catalog No. 53 contains a number of pages devoted to cut stemware. Blanks from various Imperial lines (No. 115, No. 220, No. 440, No. 3600 and No. 5300) were used.

IMPERIAL CUT STEMWARE

115/C553
"Holyoke"
11 oz. Goblet

115/C553
"Holyoke"
8 oz. Sherbet

115/C553
"Holyoke"
13 oz. Tumbler

115/550
"Wellesley"
11 oz. Goblet

115/C550
"Wellesley"
8 oz. Sherbet

115/C550
"Wellesley"
13 oz. Tumbler

| 11 oz. Goblet | 8 oz. Sherbet | 4½ oz. Cocktail | 6 oz. Footed Juice or Wine | 13 oz. Footed Ice Tea | 7 oz. Footed Juice or Parfait | 13 oz. Tumbler | 10 oz. Tumbler | 11 oz. Old Fashion |

The above nine items are available in all patterns shown on this page.

115/C551
"Vassar"
11 oz. Goblet

115/C551
"Vassar"
8 oz. Sherbet

115/C551
"Vassar"
13 oz. Tumbler

115/C552
"Radcliffe"
11 oz. Goblet

115/C552
"Radcliffe"
8 oz. Sherbet

115/C552
"Radcliffe"
13 oz. Tumbler

IMPERIAL CUT STEMWARE

440/Cut 954	2428/Cut 954	440/Cut 954
"Valencia"	"Valencia"	"Valencia"
11 oz. Goblet	8" Plate	6 oz. Tall Sherbet

440/Cut 955	2428/Cut 955	440/Cut 955
"Variant"	"Variant"	"Variant"
11 oz. Goblet	8" Plate	6 oz. Tall Sherbet

440/Cut 956	2428/Cut 956	440/Cut 956
"Vanessa"	"Vanessa"	"Vanessa"
11 oz. Goblet	8" Plate	6 oz. Tall Sherbet

440/Cut 957	2428/Cut 957	440/Cut 957
"Valerie"	"Valerie"	"Valerie"
11 oz. Goblet	8" Plate	6 oz. Tall Sherbet

5300/Cut 958	5300/Cut 958	5300/Cut 958
"Leehouse"	"Leehouse"	"Leehouse"
11 oz. Low Goblet	8" Plate	7 oz. Low Sherbet

5300/Cut 959	5300/Cut 959	5300/Cut 959
"Laureate"	"Laureate"	"Laureate"
11 oz. Low Goblet	8" Plate	7 oz. Low Sherbet

Stemware, Decorated

IMPERIAL DECORATED STEMWARE

440/Dec.
Encrusted Minton Band,
Gold or Palladium
11 oz. Goblet

440/Dec.
Encrusted Minton Band,
Gold or Palladium
6 oz. Sherbet

2428/Dec.
Encrusted Minton Band,
Gold or Palladium
8" Plate

440/Dec.
1/8" Band & Hair Line,
Gold or Palladium
11 oz. Goblet

440/Dec.
1/8" Band & Hair Line,
Gold or Palladium
6 oz. Sherbet

2428/Dec.
1/8" Band & Hair Line,
Gold or Palladium
8" Plate

5300/Dec.
Encrusted Minton Band,
Gold or Palladium
11 oz. Goblet

5300/Dec.
Encrusted Minton Band,
Gold or Palladium
7 oz. Low Sherbet

2428/Dec.
Encrusted Minton Band,
Gold or Palladium
8" Plate

5300/Dec.
1/8" Band & Hair Line,
Gold or Palladium
11 oz. Goblet

5300/Dec.
1/8" Band & Hair Line,
Gold or Palladium
7 oz. Low Sherbet

2428/Dec.
1/8" Band & Hair Line,
Gold or Palladium
8" Plate

Imperial's General Catalog No. 53 contains a few pages devoted to decorated stemware. The decorations range from gold or palladium bands to handpainted motifs. Blanks from various Imperial lines (No. 176, No. 440 and No. 5300) were used.

STEMWARE, DECORATED

IMPERIAL DECORATED STEMWARE

176/Dec. Western Rose
7 oz. Sherbet

176/Dec. Western Rose
12 oz. Goblet

176/Dec. Western Rose
14 oz. Tumbler

176/Dec. Western Apple
7 oz. Sherbet

176/Dec. Western Apple
12 oz. Goblet

176/Dec. Western Apple
14 oz. Tumbler

176/Dec. Yellow Poppy
7 oz. Sherbet

176/Dec. Yellow Poppy
12 oz. Goblet

176/Dec. Yellow Poppy
14 oz. Tumbler

176/Dec. Susan
7 oz. Sherbet

176/Dec. Susan
12 oz. Goblet

176/Dec. Susan
14 oz. Tumbler

176/Dec. Narcissus
7 oz. Sherbet

176/Dec. Narcissus
12 oz. Goblet

176/Dec. Narcissus
14 oz. Tumbler

176/Dec. Hawthorne
7 oz. Sherbet

176/Dec. Hawthorne
12 oz. Goblet

176/Dec. Hawthorne
14 oz. Tumbler

STEMWARE, DECORATED

IMPERIAL DECORATED STEMWARE

176/Dec. Bamboo
7 oz. Sherbet

176/Dec. Bamboo
12 oz. Goblet

176/Dec. Bamboo
14 oz. Tumbler

440/Dec. Magnolia
6 oz. Sherbet

440/Dec. Magnolia
13 oz. Goblet

4412/Dec. Magnolia
12 oz. Tumbler

440/Dec. Thistle
6 oz. Sherbet

440/Dec. Thistle
13 oz. Goblet

4412/Dec. Thistle
12 oz. Tumbler

440/Dec. Golden Harvest
6 oz. Sherbet

440/Dec. Golden Harvest
13 oz. Goblet

4412/Dec. Golden Harvest
12 oz. Tumbler

STIEGEL BOWLS

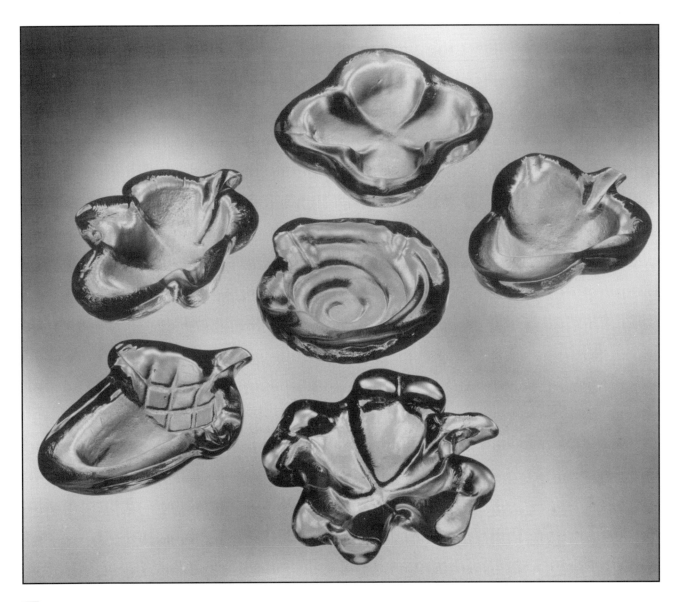

Introduced in the early 1950s, these items were intended to imitate the look and feel of eighteenth century glass. Imperial's publicity suggested that the bowls could be used for ash trays or for flowers as well as tidbits, salads and fancy desserts. Shown here are the following: Acorn (Flask Brown), Oak Leaf (Aquamarine), No. 6032 Petal (Smoky Chartruese), No. 6030 Shamrock (Bead Green), Snail (Olde Flint), and No. 6033 Spade (Heather). A No. 6031 Scallop was also made.

Sunset Ruby

This vivid Carnival glass color was introduced in 1968 with a dozen items. The initial advertising described the color as "a rich blend of oranges, reds and gold" and called it "new, alive and exciting." More than 20 articles were in the 1969 catalog, but Sunset Ruby was out of the Imperial line within about two years (see **Carnival glass** in the second volume of this series and figs. 2723-2742 in this book).

Sunshine Yellow

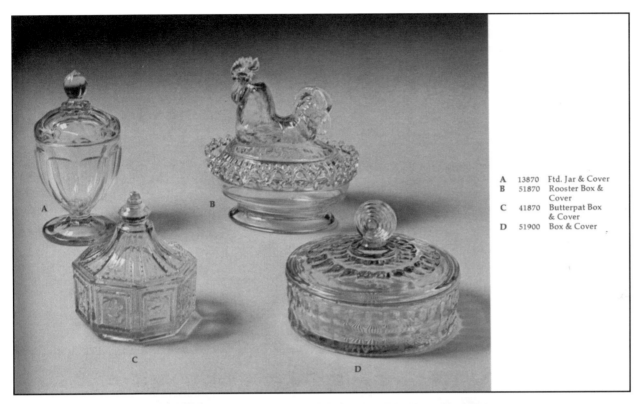

A	13870	Ftd. Jar & Cover
B	51870	Rooster Box & Cover
C	41870	Butterpat Box & Cover
D	51900	Box & Cover

A	41735	7" Crimped Compote
B	41737	10" Crimped Compote
C	41670	12" Cake Stand

The first appearance of this color was in Imperial's 1974-75 catalog, where a few items were shown. An extensive giftware section in the 1975-1976 catalog shows numerous pieces in Sunshine Yellow, but only a few are in Imperial's 1982-83 catalog. A satin finished version of this hue, called Lemon Frost, is in the 1982-83 Imperial catalog, as is an iridescent hue called Sunburst Carnival. The regular Sunshine Yellow was featured in a collection of optic vases.

Svelte, No. 330

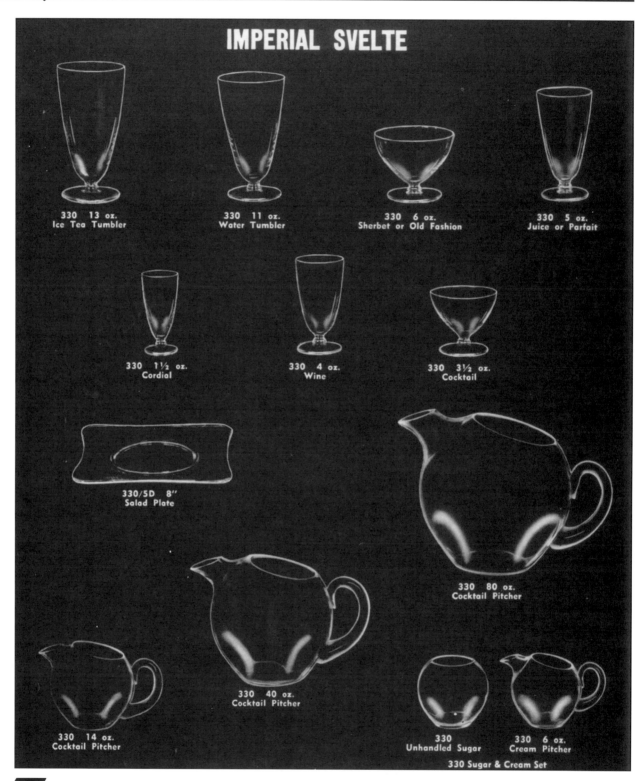

This line dates from the 1950s, and 13 crystal pieces were shown in Imperial's Catalog 53. A c. 1952 listing mentions these colors: Violet Heather (color 15), Forest Green (color 67), and Driftwood Brown (color 68). In the May, 1953, issue of *House and Garden* magazine, Svelte items were shown as table service with Stangl Pottery's "Golden Harvest" dinnerware line. During 1957, Svelte items were available in Champagne, Clover Pink and Dresden Blue. Five pieces of stemware (footed ice tea, footed on-the-rocks, goblet, sherbet and wine/juice) were re-issued as Imperial's No. 3300 Dawn line in the late 1960s (see **Dawn, No. 3300** in the second volume of this series).

SWEDISH PINCHED CRYSTAL, NO. 220

This line of crystal drinkware is shown in a 1943 folder which includes the shorter La France (No. 2600), Mardi Gras (No. 176), and Twisted Crystal (No. 100) lines. A three-piece console set was included in this line. This photo shows No. 2201 decanter set.

SWEENEY SWEETSBOWL, NO. 64

This 12" tall covered candy dish is a miniature version of the famed "Sweeney punch bowl" which now resides in the new Carriage House Glass Museum at Oglebay Park in Wheeling, West Virginia. When Imperial first undertook this project in 1963, the Sweeney punch bowl, which had been made about 1844, was on display at the Mansion Museum at Oglebay Park. This photograph of Imperial's Sweeney sweetsbowl replica appeared in the 1964 Directory Issue of *Gift and Tableware Reporter*, and a publicity story appeared in *Home Furnishings Daily* (August 24, 1964). This article was first made as one piece and marked IG. Later, the bowl and foot were made as separate pieces and were joined by epoxy (these may be marked IG, LIG or ALIG). This mould, which was owned by the Oglebay Institute, was used at the Viking Glass Company after Imperial closed its doors.

SWUNG VASES

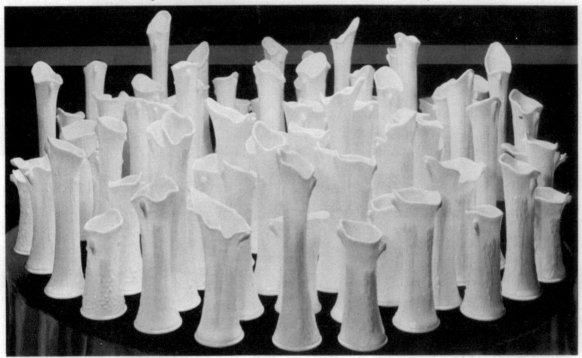

This elongated vase form begins with the production of an ordinary pressed item, typically a small vase, spooner or celery holder. After the item has been removed from the mould, it is placed in a tool called a "snap" which grips the base. The top area is then heated to a near molten state in a glory hole furnace, and the glassworker then swings the snap in motions not unlike those of a drum major with a long baton. Centrifugal force does the rest, and the glass object becomes a swung vase! These vases can be found as early as Imperial's 1907 catalog, and many of them were made in iridescent ware between 1909 and the late 1920s. Examples can also be found in Imperial's milk glass (see above), and several swung vases, some using original moulds, were produced when Imperial revived Carnival glass in the 1960s.

Swung vases

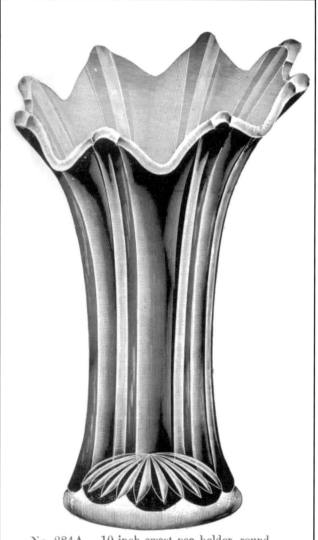

No. 284A. 10 inch sweet pea holder, round.
about 2½ dozen in barrel.
above vase being hand made, varies from
8 to 10 inches in height.

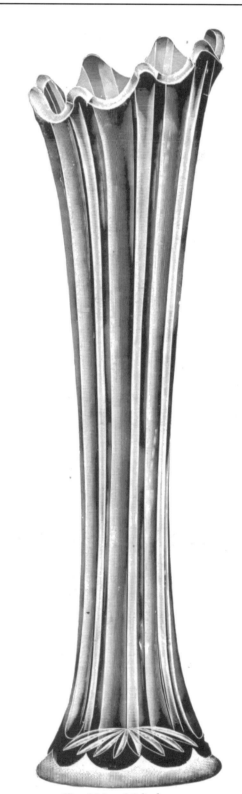

No. 284. 16 inch vase.
about 2½ dozen in barrel.
above vase being hand made, varies from
12 to 16 inches in height.

Symmetry

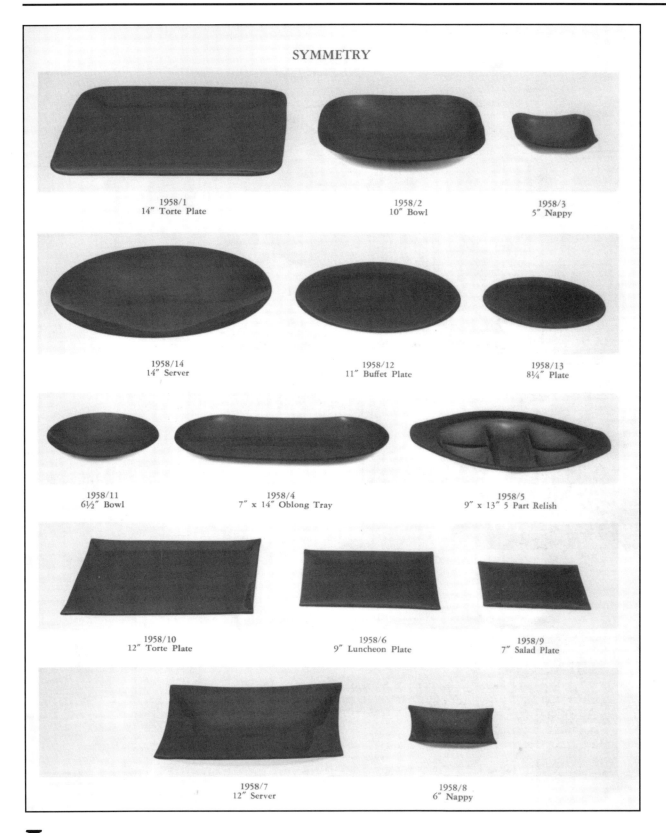

In the late 1950s, this plain, charcoal colored glass in contemporary shapes became part of Imperial's line. The glass was made by the H. J. Houze Glass Company of Point Marion, Pa., and shipped to Bellaire. The items shown here appeared in Imperial's Catalog 62 (see **Elysian** and **Grecian Key decoration** in the second volume of this series).

S/MISCELLANEOUS

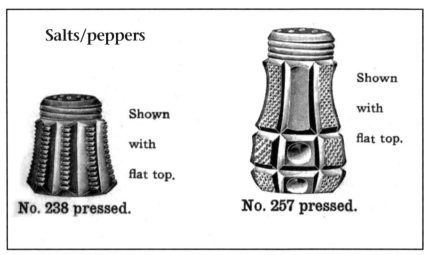

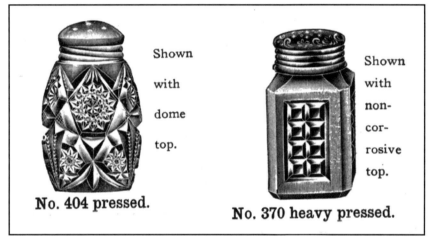

SALTS/PEPPERS

These were important staple products during the early years of Imperial's life, and most pattern glass sets included a pair of salt and pepper shakers.

SANDBLASTED GLASSWARE

Sandblasting is a form of decorating which requires less skill and time than engraving, but it can produce similar effects, such as floral motifs. In its 1904 catalog, the Imperial firm showed six different designs (Nos. 1-6) available in sandblasted ware. Two floral motifs, No. 4 and No. 6, were available on stemware, tumblers and tableware lines. Sandblasted glassware was produced for many years by Imperial.

SCROLL

(see **Atterbury Scroll Crystal** in the first volume of this series)

SCULPTURESQUE, NO. 55

Available in the mid-1950s, Imperial's Sculpturesque was a 7" oval bowl in cased glass, combining Milk Glass with one of these colors: Bead Green, Blue Mist, Flask Brown, Heather, Mustard, Pink, Stiegel Green, or Turquoise (see figs. 3032-3033).

S/MISCELLANEOUS

Sandblasted glassware

0134. pressed table tumbler, sandblast No. 1.
capacity 9 ounces.
ground bottom, hand finished.
price per dozen, $0.37. 37

0138. pressed table tumbler, sandblast No. 2.
capacity 9 ounces.
ground bottom, hand finished.
price per dozen, $0.37. 37

0136. pressed table tumbler, sandblast No. 4.
capacity 9 ounces.
ground bottom, hand finished.
price per dozen, $0.37.

0138. pressed table tumbler, sandblast No. 5.
capacity 9 ounces.
ground bottom, hand finished.
price per dozen, $0.37. 37

S/MISCELLANEOUS

Sekai Ichi, No. 103

SEKAI ICHI TUMBLERS

The translation from Japanese means "The Best"—"Tops"—"Finest"—and this exclusive Imperial Design is such and as such, will wed beautifully with ANY Decor; Oriental, Americana, Victorian or Spanish. Hand patterned Crystal, with 22 carat fired Gold on the bas-relief! Sets of Six of the Tall 16 oz. Tumblers, or of the NEW Short 13 oz. Ones are $9 per Set, gift-boxed, prepaid.

Old Hay Shed Gift Shop
P. O. Box 563
Bellaire, Ohio, U.S.A.

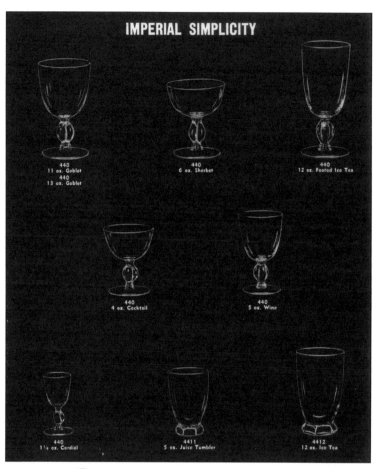

SEKAI ICHI, NO. 103

These gold decorated tumblers were popular from their inception in the 1960s to the mid-1970s. In addition to the 13 oz. on-the-rocks and the 16 oz. tumbler, two other items were made: 5 oz. cocktail and a Hospitality Bowl for pretzels or similar snacks.

SERVERS, BRASS HANDLED

The old saying that "necessity is the mother of invention" certainly rings true when one considers these unusual pieces, which appear in Imperial's Supplement One to Our Catalog Number 62, which was issued on January 1, 1964 (see figs. 2970-2975). In each case, one of the brass handles typically used for Imperial's tid-bit trays has been affixed to create a "server."

SHAEFFER

This is Weatherman's name for Imperial's No. 451 line.

SIMPLICITY, NO. 440

Popular in the 1950s, this line of eight relatively plain stemware items was available in plain crystal, with various cuttings (see **Stemware, cut** in this volume), or with handpainted decorations such as Golden Harvest, Magnolia and Thistle (see **Stemware, decorated** in this volume).

SLAG GLASS

This term is commonly used for glass which combines two colors, typically opaque white with a contrasting hue. Slag glass was made in England during the 1880s and in America in the late nineteenth and early twentieth centuries. The Fenton Art Glass Company made some slag colors in the 1940s and 1950s for the L. G. Wright Glass Co. of New Martinsville, West Virginia, and Westmoreland also produced slag. Imperial's slag colors began in the 1960s. See **Caramel Slag** and **Jade Slag** in the second volume of this series and **Purple Slag** and **Ruby Slag** in this volume.

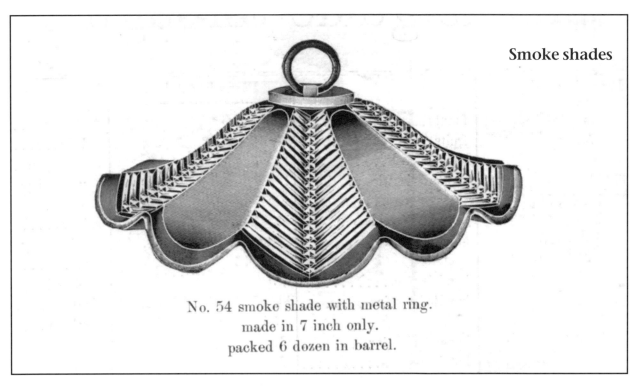

Smoke shades

No. 54 smoke shade with metal ring.
made in 7 inch only.
packed 6 dozen in barrel.

SMOKE SHADES

Also called smoke bells, these were among Imperial's earliest products.

SORTIJAS DE ORO

These tumblers were available in crystal with gold decoration as well as two-tone crystal in the 1960s.

SOUTH JERSEY ASSORTMENT

First appearing in Imperial's September 1, 1957 price list, this assortment consisted of twelve vases and six pitchers in assorted colors: Stiegel Green, Madeira, Ruby, Bead Green, Burgundy and Blue (see figs. 2647-2664). These were in the line less than a year before being discontinued.

Sortijas de Oro

SOUTHERN HIGHLANDS DECORATION

This decorated assortment was available on pitchers, goblets and other items from Imperial's No. 176 line in January, 1943. An original Imperial price list records the following decoration codes and descriptions: SH/1 Fruit; SH/2 Jonquil; SH/3 Aster; SH/4 Lilac; and SH/5 Tulip. The price list also notes that these decorations "are excellent to tie in the flat lines of Southern Potteries." For the glassware shapes on which these decorations may appear, see **Continental, No. 176** in the second volume of this series.

SPANGLED BITTERSWEET

(see **Bittersweet, Spangled** in the first volume of this series)

SPANISH WINDOWS, NO. 124

These two gold decorated tumblers (16 oz. and 13 oz. on-the-rocks) were made in the 1960s and 1970s.

SPUN

This is Weatherman's name for Imperial's No. 701 pattern, which was first in production during the mid-1930s (see **Reeded, No. 701** earlier in this volume).

STAMM HOUSE DEWDROP OPALESCENT

This large assortment of hobnail-patterned glassware brought together numerous Imperial articles in this motif (see figs. 2665-2672 in this book and figs. 1512-1551 in the second volume of this series). Imperial's president, Carl Gustkey, lived on Stamm Lane in nearby Wheeling, and both the glassware and his address derived their names from the Stamm House, a lodging and dining tavern east of Wheeling on the old Cumberland Road which dated from 1818.

STAR MEDALLION

This was Imperial's No. 671 line, first made in the 1920s (see **Amelia** in the first volume of this series).

STIEGEL GREEN

This vibrant green color was first made in the mid-1930s when it was associated with No. 701 Reeded, but some articles were also produced many years later.

STIRRUP COCKTAIL SET

Designated No. 120, this crystal set combined Imperial's No. 176 Continental 40 oz. pitcher with a half dozen 5 oz. cocktail glasses. The cocktail glasses feature an unusual "stirrup" stem and foot; these were produced from moulds acquired by Imperial from A. H. Heisey and Company.

Spanish Windows, No. 124

Stirrup Cocktail Set

Sugar Dusters

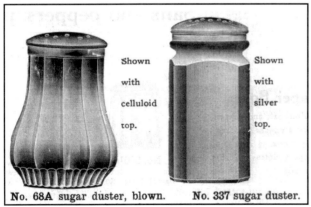
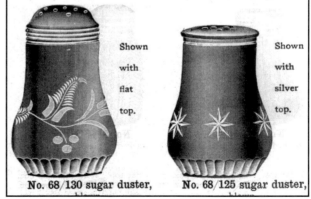

SUGAR DUSTERS

These utilitarian items were among the Imperial Glass Company's first products, and several are illustrated in the firm's first catalog, which was issued in 1904. Some of these moulds were used more than a half-century later, when sugar shakers were part of the Collectors Crystal assortments.

Sunburst Carnival

One of Imperial's last colors, this iridescent ware was produced by spraying Sunshine Yellow items with metallic salts. Imperial's 1982-83 catalog pictures more than two dozen items (see figs. 2698-2722).

Sunburst engraving

The Sunburst engraving, designated No. 199, was one of the Imperial Glass Company''s first ventures into the area of decorated goods. The motif consisted of a six- or eight-pointed star (depending upon the size of the object) and some thin rays to increase the visual impact. A 1904 catalog devoted exclusively to the Sunburst engraving described it as "so deep that they may be called cut, though the prices are not higher than those of the old style, common engravings." The Sunburst No. 199 engraving was available on some of the lines (such as No. 4 which had been introduced in the firm's first catalog (issued in 1904) as well as other articles, including stemware such the No. 11 Hoffman House shape.

Sunburst engraving

No. 2831 pressed pitcher.
engraved 199.
Imperial mirror bottom.

Sunburst engraving

No. 83A ½ gallon optic blown pitcher.
engraved 199.

TERRACE TUMBLERS, No. 990

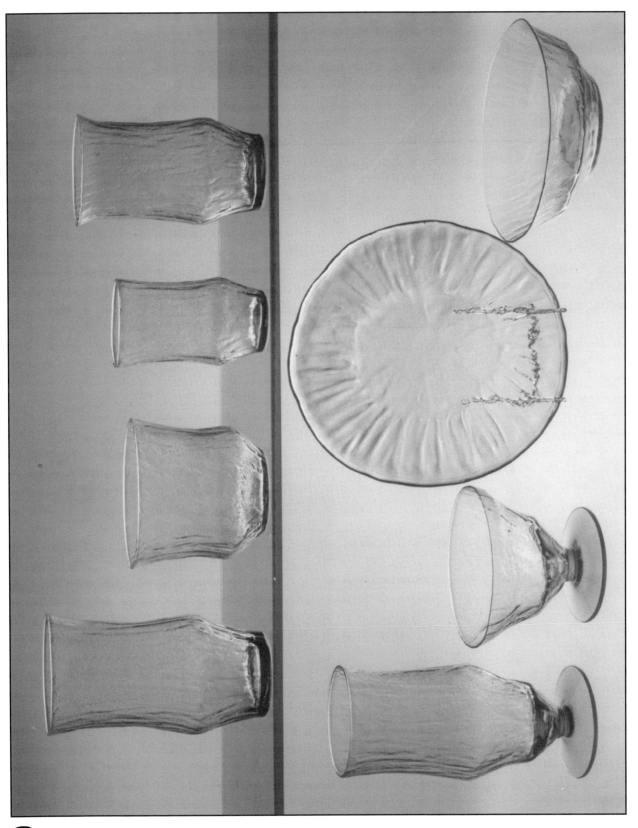

Shown in Blue Haze, Nut Brown and Verde in Imperial's 71R catalog, these items were previously part of the Kallaglas No. 990 line, which had been introduced in 1961 (see **Kallaglas** in the second volume of this series). Terrace tumblers, top row (l. to r.): 15 oz. tumbler, 13 oz. on-the-rocks, 6 oz. juice tumber and 11 oz. tumbler: bottom row (l. to r.): 12 oz. footed ice tea, 6 oz. footed sherbet, 7½" plate and 5½" nappy.

Tiara

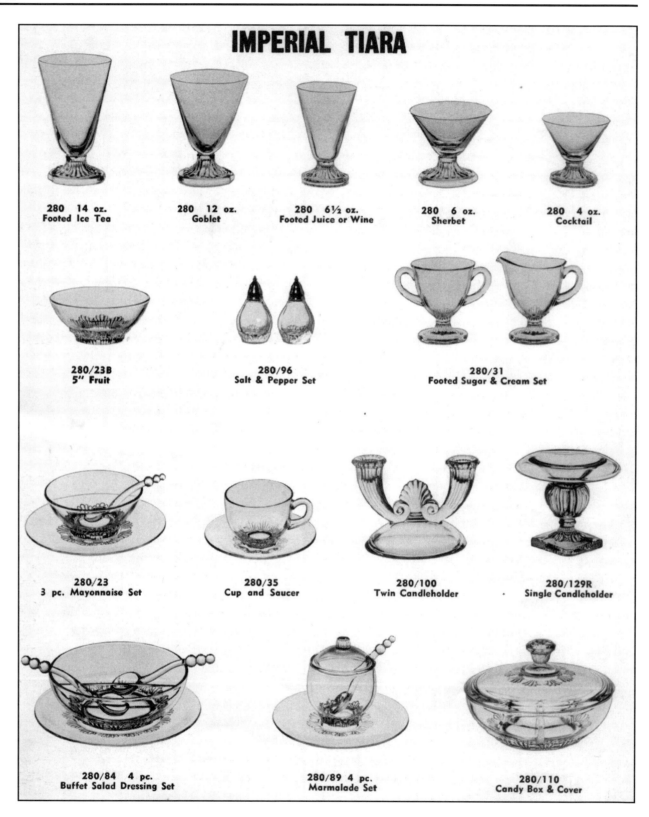

Originally called No. 280 Crystal Shell in 1940, this patented line was designed by Onnie Mankki of Cleveland, Ohio. The name was changed to Corinthian in September, 1940. The Corinthian line was phased out by the end of 1945. In the early 1950s, the line was renamed Tiara, and two full pages were devoted to it in Imperial's Catalog 53. Nudes were added to the No. 280 urns, and they were renumbered as 132 (later, the nudes were removed, and the urn was produced by Imperial for the Smithsonian Institution).

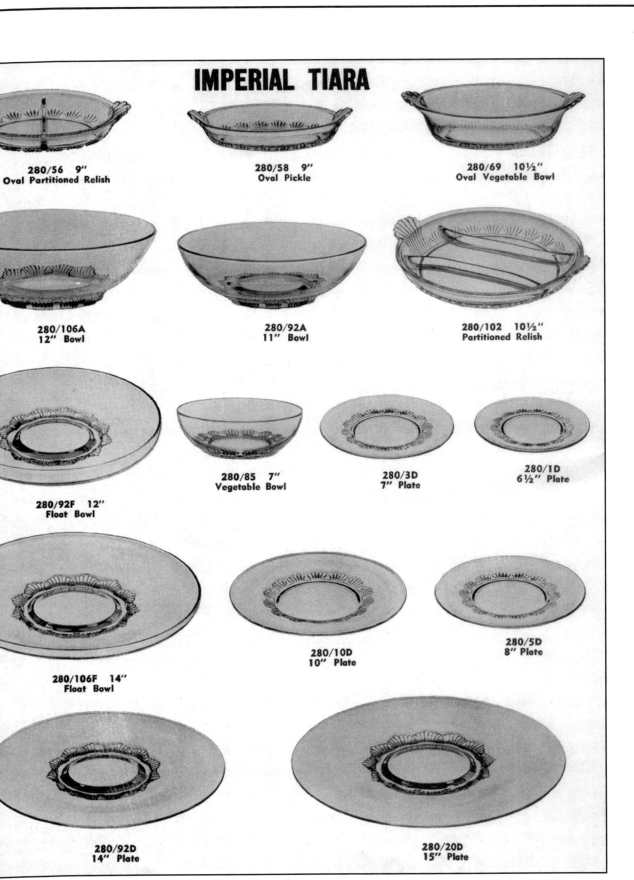

TIARA CUTTING

Designated Imperal's C905, this cutting was done on the No. 220 stemware line. Illustrated here are the following: 220/C905 3 oz. cocktail, 220/C905 12 oz. ice tea, 220/C905 6 oz. sherbet and the 220/C905 11 oz. goblet.

TOMORROW, NO. 760

This graceful line of seven beverage items in crystal glass is shown in Imperial's Catalog 53. The line was discontinued in 1957, but the pitcher and tumbler were used in 1969 to honor former President Dwight D. Eisenhower after his death (see **Eisenhower pitcher and tumblers** in the second volume of this series).

Tradition, No. 165

Production of this Imperial pattern began in the 1930s, when it was a contemporary of Cape Cod and Candlewick. The Tradition line was not nearly as extensive as either Cape Cod or Candlewick, however, but more than a dozen different items were shown in this 1942 brochure. No. 165 Tradition bears some resemblance to both No. 134 Olive and No. 166 Old English. Tradition items were made in a variety of colors (see figs. 2780-2801).

Twist, No. 110

Seven pieces of stemware for beverages were shown in a 1943 folder, along with a small compote and a finger bowl. Other beverage lines, such as La France (No. 4600), Mardi Gras (No. 176), and Swedish Pinched Crystal (No. 220) were being made at this time. The No. 110 Twist line continued throughout the 1950s, when it was called "Imperial Twist." The articles shown here appeared in Imperial's Catalog 53. Some items were still available in Imperial's 1962 catalog.

Twist, No. 110

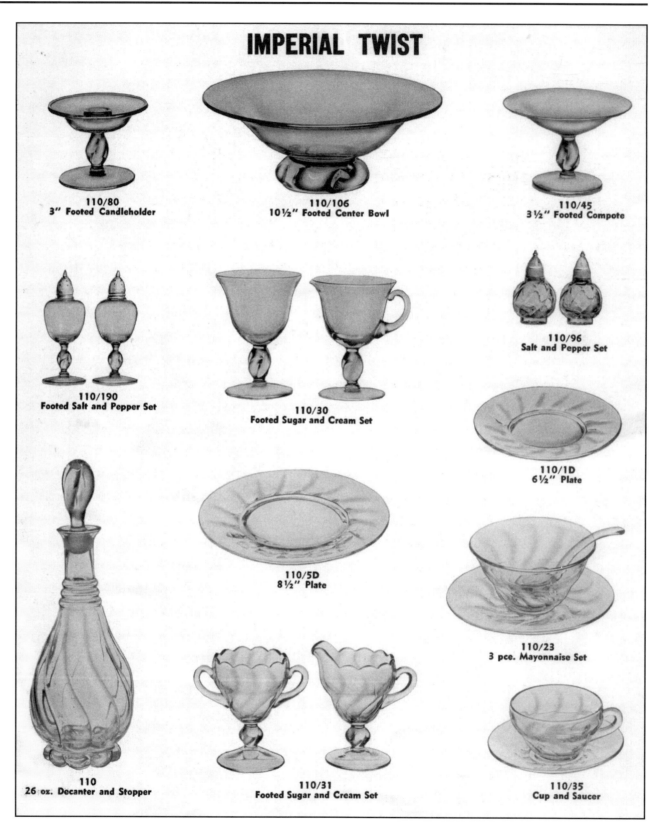

Twisted Optic

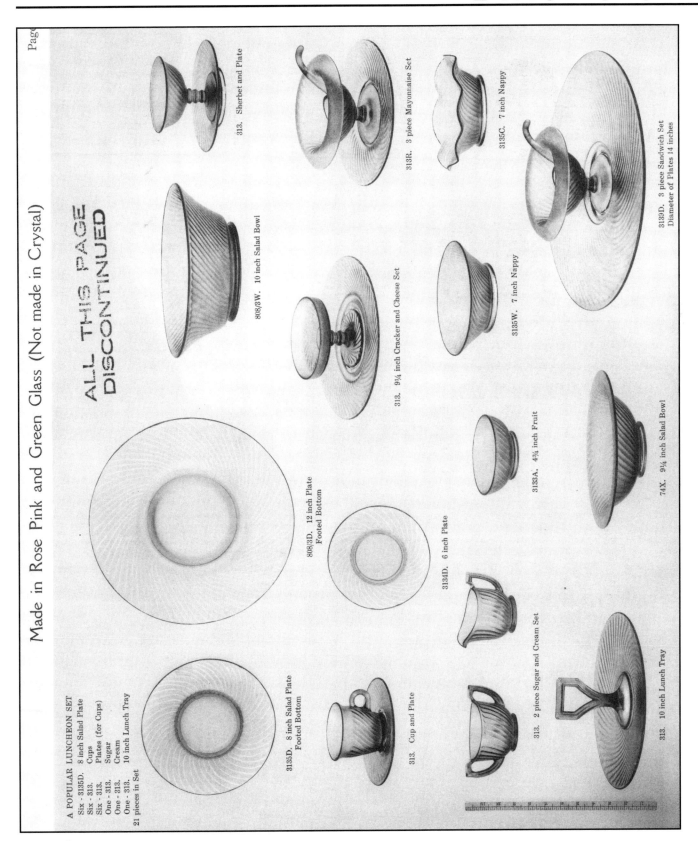

This is Weatherman's name (adopted by Gene Florence) for Imperial's No. 313 line. Neither Weatherman nor Florence seem to be aware of the many different items available in this extensive line, which was produced in the mid- and late 1920s.

T/MISCELLANEOUS

Tahitian tumblers

TAHITIAN TUMBLERS

These are shown as No. 788 in Imperial's Catalog 53. Four sizes (14 oz., 10 oz., 6 oz. and a 14 oz. double old fashion) were then available. The moulds were changed in the late 1950s by removing much of the texture, and these items were re-issued as No. 789 Woven in Imperial's Supplement One to Our Catalog 62.

TERRACE TUMBLERS, No. 855

(see **Pacesetter tumblers** earlier in this volume)

TERRA COTTA DECORATION

These three decorations—Aspen Green, Terra Cotta and Denim Blue—on 1950/700 Leaf items in Milk Glass were first mentioned in an Imperial memo dated June 2, 1952 (see figs. 2045-2046 and 2050).

TILE TUMBLERS

Some of these decorated tumblers (see figs. 2821-2825) were made on milk glass blanks (Platinum Tile, Colonial Tile and Golden Tile) and others were made using opaque turquoise blanks (Aztec Tile, Inca Tile and Casa Tile).

TOLTEC TUMBLERS

This was the general name for a series of four tumblers made c. 1960-64 from the same blanks but decorated differently. "Pizarro" was made of amber glass and decorated with satin yellow. "Peruvian" was decorated with satin white on crystal, while "Aztec" (see p. 43 in the first volume of this series) consisted of matte black on crystal glass and "Incan" was decorated with black and gold on crystal. Each was made in three sizes.

Tropical tumblers

TOM AND JERRY SET

This plain punch bowl and mugs with "Tom and Jerry" in gold decoration can be found in Imperial records as early as 1943. The No. 792 set was being marketed by Imperial, but they were produced for Imperial by the nearby Rodefer Glass Company, another Bellaire-based firm which had made milk glass for many years. When Imperial produced milk glass in the 1950s, the phrase "Tom and Jerry set" was used for the 1950/420 14 pc. set even though it was a grape pattern and had no writing.

TOPAZ COLOR

Designated as Imperial's color 2 in a price list dated February 12, 1932, this hue was used primarily for the No. 727 and No. 728 lines.

TORIL DE ORO

Made in two tone crystal and crystal decorated with gold, these tumblers were popular in the mid-1960s. The ad shown here appeared in *House Beautiful* ((March, 1965).

TRADER VIC

Imperial made items for Trader Vic restaurants, including nude stem cocktail glasses produced with Cambridge moulds.

TROPICAL TUMBLERS, NO. 787

Shown in four sizes (14 oz., 10 oz., 6 oz. and a 14 oz, double old fashion) in Imperial's Catalog 53, these tumblers were closed out in 1957. They reappeared in 1960 as part of the No. 787 Bambu line (see **Bambu** in the first volume of this series).

TULIP DECORATION
(see black glass)

TURQUOISE
This color, also called Turquoise Opaque, made its debut in 1956-57, a year after Midwest Custard, a light opaque blue called Forget-Me-Not Blue, and the short-lived Lichen Green. Turquoise was Imperial's color 89; when made with the doeskin satin finish, it was designated color 089. The No. 56 stemware shown here was made in the early 1960s (see also figs. 2217, 2221, 2227, 2229, 2231, 2233, and 2235).

Ultra Blue

- **A.** Lamp
- **B.** Spoonholder
  Sugar & Cream Set
- **C.** Rooster Box & Cover
- **D.** Bundling Lamp
- **E.** Dewey Box & Cover
- **F.** Boutique Lamp
- **G.** 9" Love's Request is Pickles

This strong blue color appears in Imperial's 1975-76 catalog. Just prior to this time, Imperial had been marketing a light color called Blue Haze and a medium blue named Antique Blue. Ultra Blue was used for Flower Fair and Hoffman House stemware, but Imperial's Old Williamsburg line (made from Heisey moulds) was probably the most noteworthy product in this color during 1974-75. Ultra Blue was used for a variety of novelty items over the next several years, and most of Imperial's final pattern lines were made in this color, too (see figs. 2857-2884).

Vases

Stiegel Green No. 967 16" vase.

Charcoal No. 970 18" vase.

Imperial made vases throughout its 80 year history. The exceptionally tall vases shown above and on the next page are from the mid-1960s. Those shown on the next two pages are from the mid-1920s. For many other vases, see figs. 2885-2969.

VASES

Heather No. 969
18" vase.

Verde No. 968
16" vase.

Vases

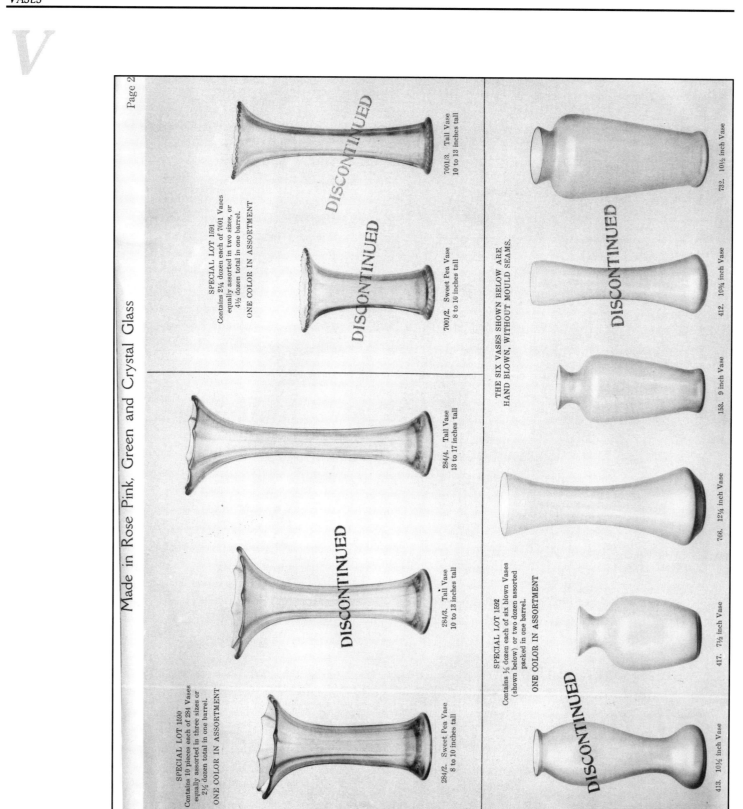

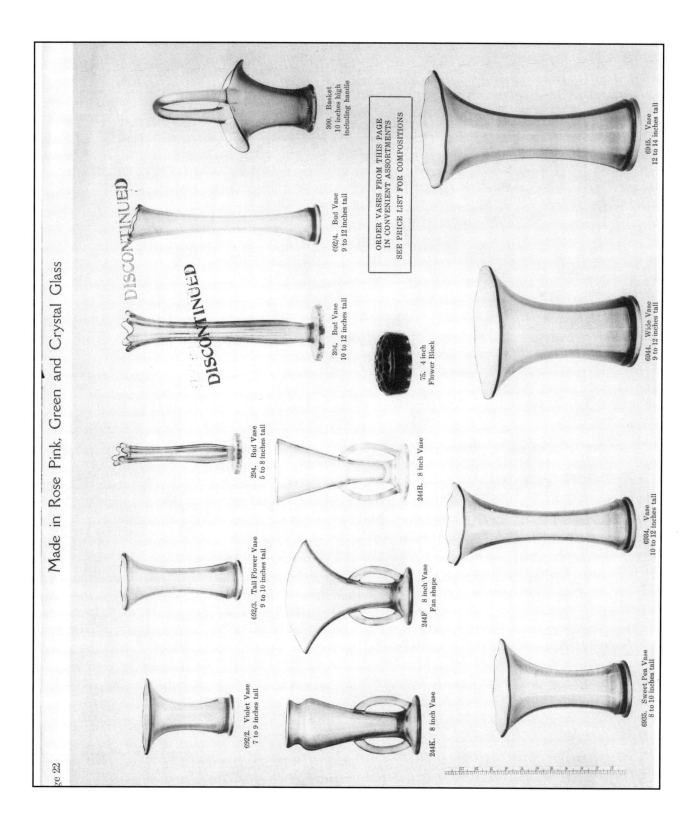

VASES

Made in Rose Pink, Green and Crystal Glass

300. Basket 10 inches high including handle

692/4. Bud Vase 9 to 12 inches tall — DISCONTINUED

304. Bud Vase 10 to 12 inches tall — DISCONTINUED

294. Bud Vase 5 to 8 inches tall

244B. 8 inch Vase

692/3. Tall Flower Vase 9 to 10 inches tall

244F. 8 inch Vase Fan shape

692/2. Violet Vase 7 to 9 inches tall

244K. 8 inch Vase

6945. Vase 12 to 14 inches tall

75. 4 inch Flower Block

6944. Wide Vase 9 to 12 inches tall

6934. Vase 10 to 12 inches tall

6935. Sweet Pea Vase 8 to 10 inches tall

ORDER VASES FROM THIS PAGE IN CONVENIENT ASSORTMENTS
SEE PRICE LIST FOR COMPOSITIONS

Page 22

Victorian Candy Jars

Shown in one of salesman Ed Kleiner's notebooks, these three plain covered candy jars (designated No. 685, No. 723 and No. 170) are similar in style to the No. 617 "Shaker shape" sweets jar which is shown elsewhere in this book (see figs. 2574-2576).

VICTORIAN, NO. 123

This pattern appears as No. 123 Coronet on a list which reflects the lines in Imperial's 1938 inventory, but its name was soon changed to Victorian. A January, 1941 price listing for No. 123 Victorian in Imperial's archives bears this handwritten note: "was Coronet." There were just eight items in the No. 123 Victorian line, which was discontinued in November, 1945. All of these items, except the salt/pepper shaker, were marketed under the name Chroma in the 1950s, although the No. 123 designation was retained (see **Chroma** in the second volume of this series).

Vintage Ruby

Two full pages are devoted to Vintage Ruby in the 1953 Imperial catalog. The name is actually a combination of "Vintage" (a common name for Imperial's No. 473 Grape pattern) and "ruby," a heat-sensitive glass color made with selenium and cadmium. Vintage Ruby was color 10 in Imperial's records (see figs. 3039-3052).

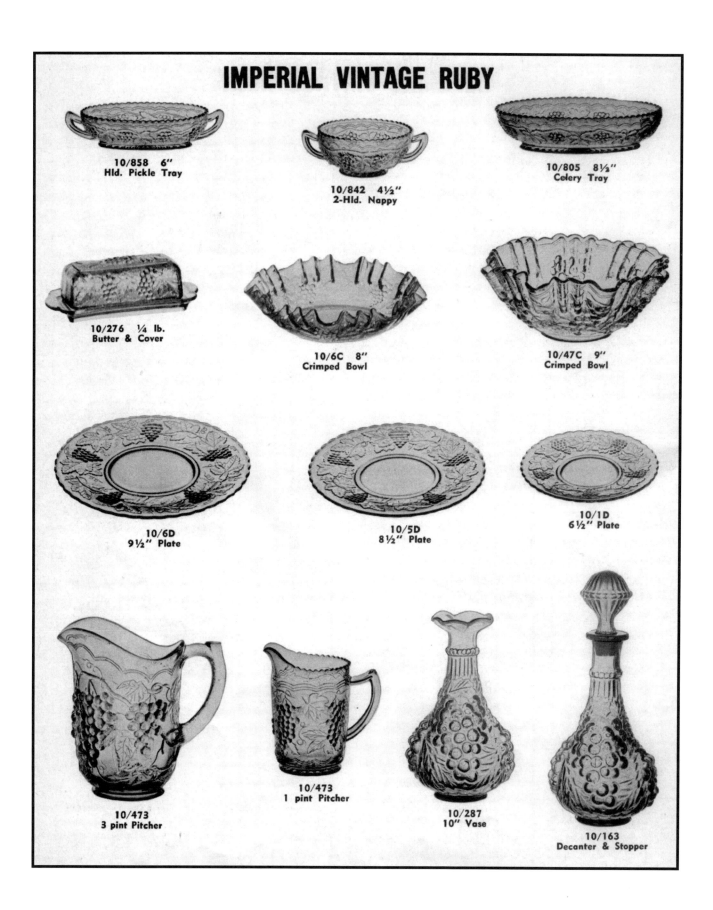

V/MISCELLANEOUS

VALENCIA

This was an etched and gold decorated assortment available in Rose Pink, Green and crystal in the early 1930s. No pictures are available, and the sole mention of the Valencia assortment in an Imperial price list (dated September 17, 1931).

VELVET PIE CRUST

These articles are shown in Imperial's Supplement One to Our Catalog Number 62 (issued January 1, 1964). They are sueded versions of the Pie Crust Bowls discussed earlier in this volume. The numerical designation was the same, No. 1592, as were the letters symbols for each style: CC (double crimped); F (shallow crimped); and B (flared and crimped). Each could be ordered in any of four colors—Gold (also called Mandarin Gold), Heather, Pink or Verde. See figs. 2982-2993.

VERDE

Sometimes called Verde Green, this glass color was developed by Imperial in the early 1960s, and designer Russel Wright was a major force in urging company executives to allow chemist Axel Ottoson to perfect the proper hue. Some Imperial documents refer to "Smoky Chartruese," and this was the early name for the Verde color which became a fixture in the Imperial line for some time (see figs. 2994-3022).

VIGNA VETRO

These interesting items date from the late 1950s, and they incorporated chips of colored glass called "frit" before the desired article was blown to its final shape in a mould. At this time, Imperial was producing several blown lines (called Murrhina and Spangled Bittersweet) using similar techniques. The Vigna Vetro pieces are all made from milk glass, and the typical colors of frit are yellow, blue and green (see figs. 3023-3025). The result is a vivid splash of color on the milk glass background, and no two pieces of Vigna Vetro are exactly alike! Just six Vigna Vetro items appear in Imperial's Price List No. 59 (January 1, 1959): No. 163 decanter and stopper; No. 180 7½" vase; No. 310 bud vase; No. 241 cruet and stopper; No. 287 10" vase; and No. 356 10" vase.

VINCENT PRICE NATIONAL TREASURES

Sold through Sears stores, these Imperial items feature a special logo—a large "S" with smaller initials (V, P, N and T) placed within its confines. The following items were produced by Imperial: No. 100 York River Captain's bottle (Jamestown Green); No. 1607 Jamestown wine bottle (Jamestown Green); No. 21 Brown's Indian Urb bottle (Flask Brown); No. 976 Rose-in-Snow jar (crystal); No. 3 Arch decanter (Blue); No. 169 Acanthus Leaf decanter (Blue); No. SD3 set of eight salt dips (crystal); No. 800 Owl jar (Purple Slag; see fig. 2554); No. 335 Owl sugar and creamer set (Purple Slag); No. 1950/228 Atterbury cream and sugar set (milk glass; see figs. 2552-2553); and No. 973 Bakewell Argus compote (crystal). The Fenton Art Glass Company of Williamstown, West Virginia, made some other items for this series.

VINELF

The Vinelf candleholder and compote (see figs. 2851-2855) were made in many of Imperial's colors, both transparent (Antique Blue, Cranberry, and Verde) and opaque (Forget-Me-Not Blue, Lichen Green, Midwest Custard, Milk Glass, and Turquoise Opaque).

VINTAGE STEMWARE

Made in 1970s at Lenox's Mt. Pleasant plant, these elegant shapes from Imperial's catalog would be difficult to isolate from the similar products of other companies making stemware with the paste mould/pulled stem technique. Five items were illustrated in Imperial's 1977 catalog: 34060 tulip wine; 34050 tulip goblet; 34090 brandy; 34080 red wine; and 34070 white wine.

V/MISCELLANEOUS

VOODOO TUMBLER

This was Imperial's No. 790 gold-decorated tumbler. Made first in the mid-1950s, this green tumbler was also marketed to specialty restaurants, such as Trader Vic's on the West Coast and in New York City and the Kahiki (Columbus, Ohio).

Voodoo tumbler

Washington, No. 699

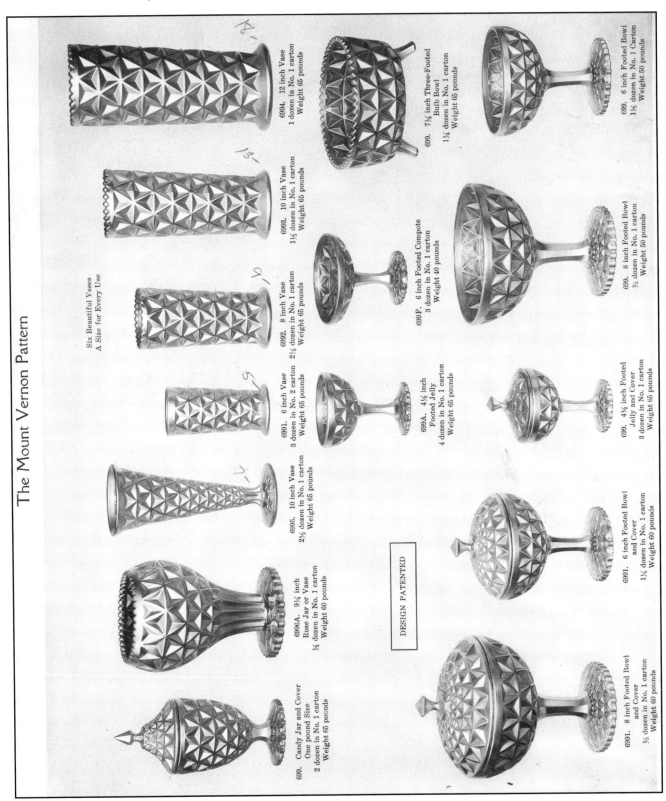

This pattern was first produced in the early 1920s under the name Prism Crystal. It was designed by Philip Ebeling, who also designed the famous American line for the Fostoria Glass Company. In one Imperial catalog from the mid-1920s, No. 699 was called Triangle. A note in one of salesman Ed Kleiner's notebooks indicates that it might have been known as Lincoln, too. In any case, No. 699 was called Mount Vernon during the

Washington, No. 699

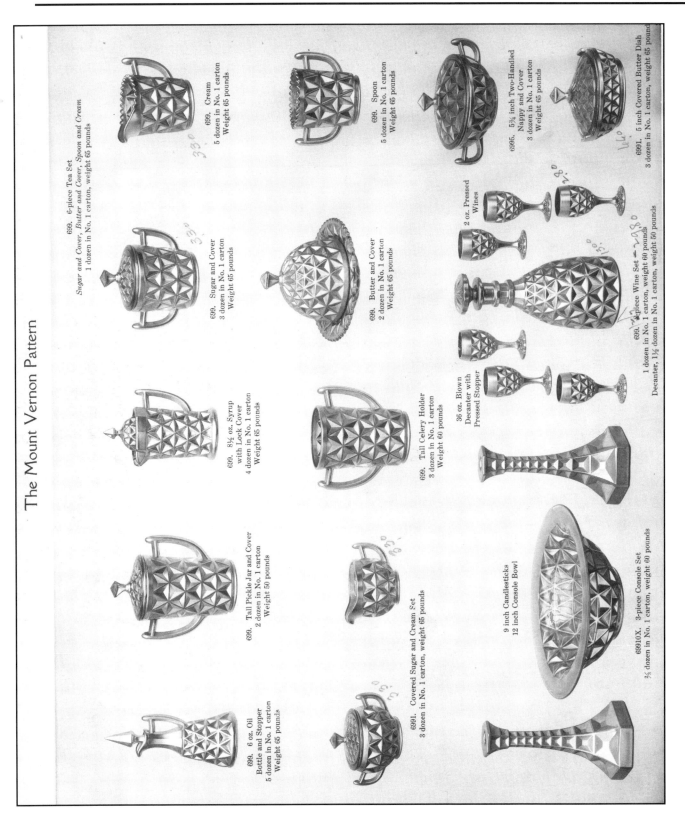

The Mount Vernon Pattern

1930s, and it was quite popular. Imperial's 1938 year-end inventory shows that No. 699 Mount Vernon was among the firm's best sellers during 1938, ranking second only to Cape Cod. In 1940, the Mount Vernon name was dropped due to a conflict with the Cambridge Glass Company, and No. 699 was marketed thereafter as Washington (see figs. 3054-3095).

Washington, No. 699

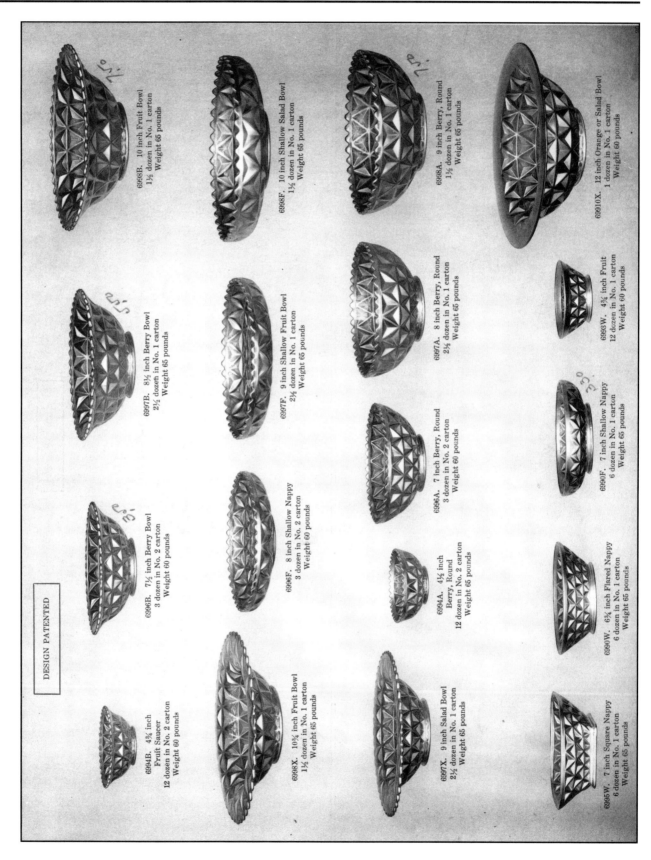

Washington, No. 699

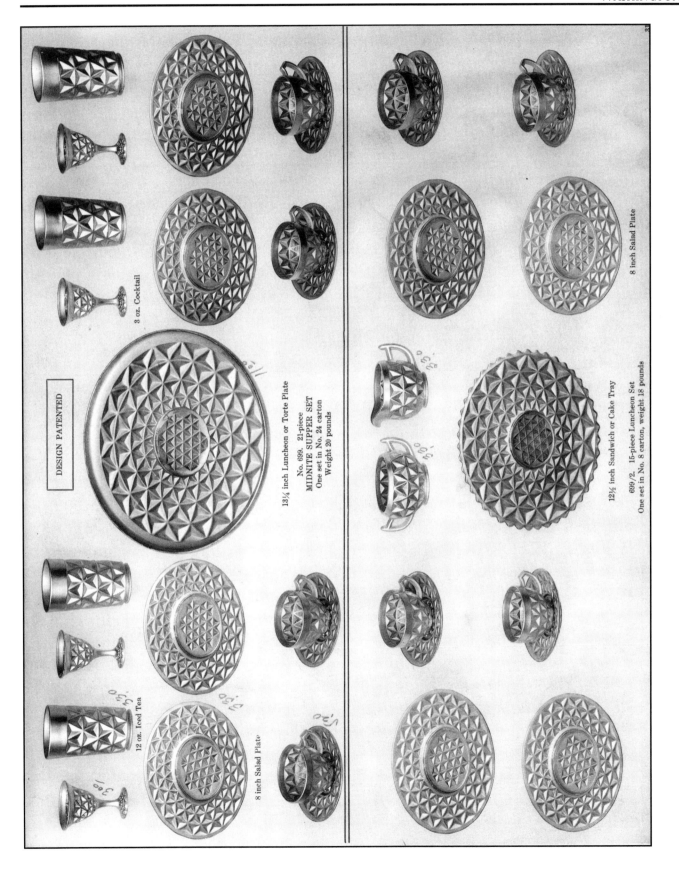

WAVERLY, NO. 1519

This line of relatively plain crystal ware was made with Heisey moulds which had been purchased by Imperial in April, 1958. About two dozen items were listed in Imperial's Price List No. 61 (issued January 1, 1960), and Waverly continued to appear in Imperial catalogs for the next several years.

Western Apple, Western Rose and Western Wild Flower

These three handpainted decorations, all of which were done on Imperial's No. 176 Continental line, are first mentioned in Imperial sales materials from 1943. The decorations were described as "excellent to tie in with ... Franciscan Dinner Ware" which was called Desert Rose and Desert Apple. The Western Wild Flower decoration was soon discontinued. Both Western Apple and Western Rose were shown in *Retailing* (May 27, 1948) and in *China, Glass and Decorative Accessories* (June, 1948) along with three new decorations: Brown-Eyed Susan, Hawthorne and Narcissus.

Whiskbroom Glass

Appearing in early 1964, these five items are reminiscent of the Victorian novelties made by such firms as Duncan and others. The No. 612 vase stands 8" tall. A smaller flower holder (No. 611/1) is 6" tall, and it can be fitted with a cover to create the No. 611 footed covered sweetsbowl. The flat whiskbroom was offered alone as the No. No. 910/1 server and in a covered version called the No. 910 covered broombox. These were produced in Autumn Amber and Heritage Blue in 1964, and most of them can also be found in milk glass.

White Carnival Glass

This short-lived iridescent hue was among Imperial's Carnival glass colors of the 1970s. The ad shown here appeared in *Gifts and Decorative Accessories*. Two full pages of White Carnival Glass appear in the 1975-76 Imperial catalog, but the color was discontinued at the end of 1975 (see figs. 1336-1358 and the discussion of Carnival glass in the second volume in this series as well as figs. 3096-3121 in this book).

WHITE ICE

This satin finished milk glass assortment was first shown in Imperial's 1977 catalog. The names—Barrow, Kodiak, Nome, Noorvik and Sitka—are cities from regions known for their cold climates. The eleven different articles were mould-blown, and the shapes were quite modern in design. The three vases designated Kodiak are similar in shape to pieces found in Imperial's mid-1920s Lead Lustre line.

W/MISCELLANEOUS

Wee Scottie tumbler

WATCH CANDY BOX

This interesting article is well-known in Imperial's milk glass (1950/260), but it can also be found in other colors, such as Amber, Antique Blue, Nut Brown, and Verde.

WEE SCOTTIE TUMBLER

Designated Imperial's No. 778, the Wee Scottie tumbler in the Kilt Green color was a contemporary of the Cow Brand, Longhorn and Ranch Life tumblers (c. 1953-54), each of which is pictured in other volumes in this series.

WEISS BEERS

In the early twentieth century, many glass companies made these utilitarian items for the saloon trade. Those pictured here are from Imperial's first catalog, which was published in 1904, but it would be difficult indeed to distinguish them from the products of other firms.

Weiss beers

No. 60 weiss beer.
capacity 15 oz, height 7⅜ inches.
6 dozen in barrel.

No. 61 weiss beer.
capacity 14 oz. height 7 inches.
6 dozen in barrel.

W/MISCELLANEOUS

WELSBACH GLOBES AND SHADES

(see **illuminating goods**)

Welsbach

No. 54 pressed Welsbach shade. 8 dozen in barrel.

WEST POINT GLASSWARE

A West Point cadet corps' catalogue from 1967 shows several Imperial-made items. These include Oxford No. 5024 plates, glasses and stemware (made from Heisey moulds) with a West Point crest along with Etiquette No. 554 stemware and several decanters.

WHIRLSPOOL JARS

These are related to Imperial's No. 701 Reeded pattern, a patented motif which debuted in the mid-1930s. The Whirlspool jars were available with a brass, chrome or wood knob and some of them feature a painted interior, giving the appearance of colored glass. The Gutman Advertising Agency designed a clever brochure to describe the Whirlspool jars (see p. 691).

WHITE FLYING GEESE DECORATION

The only mention of this in Imperial's records appears in a 1943 folder. The decoration was available on the No. 176 9" vase and on No. 176 stemware.

WINDMILL PATTERN, NO. 514

Edwards separates Windmill and Double Dutch, but they were, in fact, all part of the same line in iridescent glass in Imperial's 1912 catalog and its 1913 catalog supplement. Three sizes of pitchers (the largest accompanied by tumblers) were shown along with berry sets (both round and crimped) and oval plates. All were available in Azur, Helios and Rubigold at that time. When Imperial re-introduced Carnival glass in the 1960s, many of the No. 514 moulds were used (see figs. 1107, 1190, 1215-1217, 1276-1277, and 1280-1281 in the second volume of this series).

WOODBURY

This Weatherman's name for Imperial's No. 704 plate.

Woven tumblers

WOVEN TUMBLERS

These are shown as No. 789 in Antique Blue in Imperial's Supplement One to Our Catalog 62. These were called No. 788 Tahitian before the moulds were changed in the late 1950s (see **Tahitian** earlier in this volume).

WRIGHT, RUSSEL

A charter member of the American Society of Industrial Designers, Russel Wright was an influential figure in the history of this nation's ceramic dinnerware and glass accessories. Wright, who operated from a studio and business headquarters in Manhattan, did design work for quite a few Ohio Valley firms, including these: Sterling China Co., Steubenville Pottery Co., Fostoria Glass Co., Paden City Glass Manufacuring Co., and the Paden City Pottery Co.

Wright's relationship with Imperial began in late 1949. Over the next several years, he designed three lines of tumblers for the glass company—No. 670 Flare, No. 675 Pinch, and No. 680 Flame. Wright was particularly interested in the texture of glass, especially the "seed glass" made with flecks of mica or vermiculite which imperial used for the No. 670 Flare line. Wright was also influential in getting Imperial to develop the distinctive Verde color which was used for glass from Wright's designs and later became an important color in Imperial's regular line. Other Imperial glass colors used for the Russel Wright articles included Aquamarine, crystal, Hemlock (a deep forest green), Ripe Olive (a deep brown), and Sea Spray (light blue).

Regina Lee Blaszycyk, writing in vol. 4 (1993) of *The Acorn* (a publication of the Sandwich Glass Museum, provides an excellent summary of wright's career ("The Wright Way for Glass: Russel Wright and the Business of Industrial Design"). See **Flame, No. 680** and **Flare, No. 670** in the second volume of this series. Pinch No. 675, is shown here.

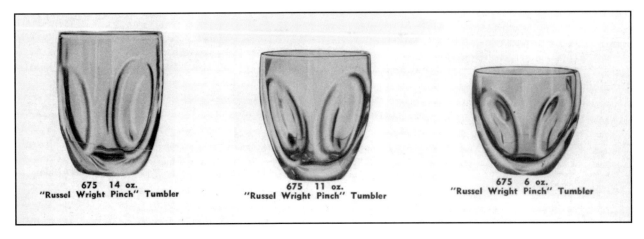

675   14 oz.
"Russel Wright Pinch" Tumbler

675   11 oz.
"Russel Wright Pinch" Tumbler

675   6 oz.
"Russel Wright Pinch" Tumbler

YELLOW OPTICS

This assortment of vases (and one bowl) made its appearance in Imperial's 1982-83 catalog, so these products were not produced for very long before Imperial closed for good. All of these items were offered in transparent Sunshine Yellow (Yellow Optics) and in transparent Ultra Blue (Blue Optics). Each item has a rib or swirl pattern, hence the term "optic" is used to describe them.

Yellow & Blue Optics*
A collection of timeless shapes and the richness of decorator colors combine to create a stunning display. The distinctive optic designs further enhance this superb collection of hand-blown vases.

51733	8" - 12"	Swung Vase
51734	8"	Bowl
51735	4"	Ball Vase
51736	9"	Ball Vase
51737	5¾"	Vase
51738	7"	Vase
51739	6½"	Vase
51740	6"	Rose Vase
51741	9"	Vase
51742	10"	Vase
51743	5"	Mei Vase
51744	6"	Meng Vase
51745	7½"	Li Po Vase
51746	6"	Bud Vase
51747	6"	Bud Vase
51748	4"	Vase
51767	6½"	Iris Vase

UB   Ultra Blue
SY   Sunshine Yellow
       *New Line

Yellow Optics

Yesterday tumblers

Two Imperial tumblers (530 and 913) were used as blanks for these attractive items which date from the early 1950s. One of salesman Ed Kleiner's notebooks tells the story that Imperial president Carl Gustkey "borrowed samples ... from some of his elderly friends' cupboards" in Preston County, West Virginia, and that the old cut glass tumblers served to inspire these Imperial creations: (top row, left to right) 913/C967, 913/C966, and 913/C965; (bottom row, left to right) 530/C961, 530/C960, and 513/C962.

You-Me-Us

This three-piece cocktail set in crystal glass, designated No. 7853 in Imperial's General Catalog 53, consists of two No. 785 "roly-poly" tumblers and an accompanying pitcher, all of which are decorated with simple cut letters. The tumblers bear separate pronouns ("You" and "Me"), while the pitcher says "Us".

Zodiac, No. 1590

This interesting line began with moulds purchased by Imperial from A. H. Heisey and Co. in 1958. The Zodiac line was composed of eighteen food service items and three ash trays, as shown in Imperial's 1969 catalog (the ash trays were made from Imperial's own moulds). Some of the larger items depict all twelve signs of the Zodiac, while the smaller items select just one or more, depending upon the space available on the article (see fig. 3012). Zodiac items were produced in crystal, Amberglo, and Verde.

Zodiac, No. 1590

It doesn't take a crystal ball to see that this timely pattern is destined to be a stellar attraction. The sales forecast is bright and all eighteen items are moderately priced to produce register results... and all dozen and one-half are beautifully handcrafted in Crystal, Verde and Amberglo. Influence your horoscope and find out about all of Imperial's News.

ZODIAC TUMBLERS, NO. 1234

The craze for astrological material and horoscope-related items in the 1960s was behind the creation of this set of twelve tumblers. Each depicts a separate sign of the Zodiac (Aquarius, Gemini, Taurus, etc.), complete with the appropriate symbols for that sign. These were made in Antique Blue only.

Z/MISCELLANEOUS

ZAK

This is Weatherman's name for Imperial's No. 600 wine set; unfortunately, she called the same pattern "Chesterfield" elsewhere in her book, and other writers, including Burns, have perpetuated the error, sometimes compounding it by insisting that Chesterfield was Imperial's original name for the line! In fact, the original name was simply No. 600 Colonial Crystal. The No. 600 line made its debut in Imperial's Catalog 104D (c. 1920-1922), and items were produced in Imperial's iridescent colors, such as Rubigold and Peacock, as well as in crystal (see **Colonial Crystal** in the second volume of this series).

Zipper Loop

No. 201 sewing lamp. made in size D only.

No. 201 hand lamp. made in 3 sizes.

ZIPPER LOOP

This is the name that today's collectors of Carnival glass have given to Imperial's No. 201 lamps. These are among the company's longest-lived products, for they are pictured in the very first catalog (issued in 1904) as well as in catalogs printed more than sixty years later when Imperial was re-issuing Carnival glass! (see **Lamps** in the second volume of this series)

ZOO LINE

(see **Animal decorated tumblers** in the first volume of this series)

COLOR PLATE DESCRIPTIONS

page 651
1921. Souvenir ashtray for the first All-American Glass Festival held in Bellaire in 1973 and box for ashtray (offered in satin-finished crystal as well as in limited quantities of a gold-decorated version that was not sold at retail). **1922.** Imperial glass logo with satin-finished background. **1923.** Imperial paperweight with blue/white interior. **1924.** Imperial glass logo with painted letters. **1925.** Imperial-Lenox glass logo with painted letters. **1926.** Imperial-Lenox plastic counter sign. **1927.** Candlewick satin-finished calendar sign with 1947 calendar. **1928.** White plastic car window coat hanger advertising novelty. **1929.** Iridescent change tray (note the various Imperial trade-marks: NUCUT, NUART and "iron cross"). **1930.** Crystal Candlewick calendar sign with metallic foil label and 1947 calendar. **1931.** Ruby "Save Imperial" miniature brick (made by the Viking Glass Co. for the "Save Imperial Committee").**1932.** Metallic foil sign. **1933.** Ceramic Jamestown Festival desk set (1958). **1934.** Crystal "Candlewick Crystal" sign. **1935.** Crystal paperweight with Imperial photo glued on backside. **1936.** Imperial sign (made by the Houze Glass Co., this is bent crystal glass with gold lettering on a black enamel background).

page 652
All of these are Horizon Blue Carnival glass, and old item numbers are given in parentheses. **1937.** 42320 HB Storybook mug (1591). **1938.** 42744 HB 10" Loganberry vase (356). **1939.** 42792 HB 9" Dolphin candleholder (90). **1940.** 42699 HB 9" crimped bowl (62C). **1941.** 42784 HB 3$^1/_2$" Rose candleholder (160). **1942.** 42162 HB Robin three-pint pitcher (670). **1943.** 42062 HB Robin tumbler (670). **1944.** 42474 HB salt and pepper set (474). **1945.** 42624 HB toothpick holder (505). **1946.** 42752 HB 5$^1/_2$" vase (661). **1947.** 42696 HB 9" Grape bowl (700B). **1948.** 42686 HB 7$^1/_2$" crimped bowl (389C). **1949.** 42844 HB 6" Colonial Belle (809). **1950.** 42724 HB 6" footed compote (671C). **1951.** 42610 HB covered butterdish (474).**1952.** 42885 HB 4$^1/_2$" covered box (475/2). **1953.** 42563 HB 6$^1/_2$" nappy (555/52). **1954.** 42930 HB 4" Swan (147).

page 653
This limited edition (750 sets) Horizon Blue Carnival glass punch set was offered as a sales incentive to Imperial dealers. **1955.** Horizon Blue punch cup. **1956.** Horizon Blue two-piece punch bowl.

page 654
All of these are Meadow Green Carnival glass, and old item numbers are given in parentheses. **1957.** 42050 LG 9 oz. tumbler (484). **1958.** 42152 LG 3 pt. pitcher (484). **1959.** 42150 LG 1 pt. pitcher, Grape (473). **1960.** 42788 LG 3" candleholder (3800/72; Cambridge mould). **1961.** 42707 LG 7" 4-Toed bowl (3800/49B; Cambridge mould). **1962.** 42725 LG 5" Crimped Compote (3800/42C; Cambridge mould). **1963.** 42693 LG 8" 3-Toed bowl, Rose (74C). **1964.** 42615 LG butter & cover, Rose (161). **1965.** 42555 LG 4$^3/_4$" crimped bowl, Grape (899C). **1966.** 42685 LG 7$^1/_2$" 3-toed bowl, Rose (489). **1967.** 42320 LG Storybook mug (1591). **1968.** 42926 LG Hen-on-nest (145). **1969.** 42528 LG 3" Cornucopia (123). **1970.** 42576 LG 5" handled nappy (568).

page 655
All of these are Meadow Green Carnival glass, and old item numbers are given in parentheses. **1971.** 42772 LG 9$^1/_2$" Vase, Grape (287C). **1972.** 42765 LG 4$^1/_2$" Vase (662). **1973.** 42774 LG 10" Loganberry vase (356). **1974.** 42754 LG 6" Loganberry vase (109). **1975.** 42686 LG 7$^1/_2$" crimped bowl (3897/3C). **1976.** 42640 LG 4$^1/_2$" basket (73). **1977.** 42932 LG 8" Swan (400). **1978.** 42563 LG 6$^1/_2$" nappy (555/52). **1979.** 42645 LG 6$^1/_2$" bell (404). **1980.** 42620 LG toothpick holder (1). **1981.** 42897 LG 4$^1/_2$" box & cover (156).

page 656
These articles were made by Imperial for the Metropolitan Museum of Art, although some were also available through regular Imperial retailers in the 1970s. **1982-1983** and **1985-1986.** 71755 6" Quilted Diamond Flip vases in Stiegel Green, Emerald Green, Amethyst and Sapphire. **1984.** Pair of 71762 10$^1/_2$" Dolphin candlesticks in opaque blue and milk glass (note gold decoration). **1987-1988-1989.** 71757 Bellflower pitchers in ruby (with milk glass interior), Stiegel Green, and ruby. **1990.** Opaque blue flower pot with tray. **1991.** Custard flower pot (MMA Tutankhamen Collection). **1992.** Metropolitan Museum of Art Catalogue. **1993-1994.** 71530 Magnet and Grape covered jar (Sapphire with crystal cover) and Sapphire creamer with crystal handle. **1995-1996-1997-1998.** 71155 4$^1/_4$" Diamond and Sunburst pitchers in Stiegel Green, Sapphire, Amber and Canary Yellow.

page 657
As indicated, most of these items were made by Imperial for various groups. **1999.** Sunset Ruby Carnival glass Santa bell, made in 1981 (marked LIG). **2000.** Ultra Blue Dresden Lady (Cambridge mould, 1981, marked LIG). **2001.** Pink Minuet Doll (Heisey mould, 1981, marked LIG). **2002.** Amber Lion bookend (Cambridge mould; made for National Cambridge Collectors). **2003.** Satin-finished black Scottie Dog

Color Plate Descriptions

bookend (Cambridge mould; made for National Cambridge Collectors). **2004.** Sunshine Yellow Empress No. 1401 candleholders (made for Collectors Guild of New York City). **2005.** Amber Lion trinket covered box, Waverly No. 1519 (made for Collectors Guild of New York City). **2006.** Ultra Blue Goose (wings halfway); Heisey mould, made for Mirror Images. **2007.** Ultra Blue Rabbit (head up); Heisey mould, made for Mirror Images. **2008.** Ultra Blue Rabbit (head down); Heisey mould, made for Mirror Images. **2009.** Ultra Blue Owl (on bust-off); made for Mirror Images. **2010.** Ultra Blue Gazelle; made for Mirror Images. **2011.** Satin-finished Sunset Ruby Venus Rising (Cambridge mould, made for Mirror Images, marked IG-81) **2012.** Ultra Blue Elephant; Heisey mould, made for Mirror Images. **2013.** Ultra Blue Standing Colt; Heisey mould, made for Dan Fortney, marked IG. **2014.** Ultra Blue Kicking Colt; Heisey mould, made for Dan Fortney, marked IG. **2015.** Ultra Blue Balking Colt; Heisey mould, made for Dan Fortney, marked IG. **2016.** Rubigold Cape Cod punch cup. **2017.** Rubigold Cape Cod cruet with stopper (limited edition of 300 for Levay Distributing Co. in 1976). **2018.** Pink Carnival Loving Mice, made in 1981 for PeeGee Glass of Ft. Wayne, Indiana. **2019.** Amber Owl covered jar, made for Star Exclusives of New Orleans, Louisiana, in 1977. **2020.** Black "Rocky" rocking horse, made for Guernsey Glass of Cambridge, Ohio, in 1982, marked with B-in-triangle. **2021.** Sunshine Yellow Standing Duckling, made for Heisey Collectors of America (HCA) from a Heisey mould in 1981, marked IG). **2022.** Sunshine Yellow Wood Duck, made for HCA from a Heisey mould in 1981, marked IG. **2023.** Sunshine Yellow 3" Fish matchholder, made for HCA from a Heisey mould in 1982, marked IG. **2024.** Sunshine Yellow Floating Ducking, made for HCA from a Heisey mould in 1981, marked IG. **2025.** Emerald Green Pony Stallion, made for HCA from a Heisey mould in 1982, marked IG. **2026.** Rose Pink Pony Stallion, made for HCA in 1978, marked IG. **2027.** Light Blue Pony Stallion, made for HCA in 1981, marked IG. **2028.** Satin-finished Heather Pony Stallion, made for HCA, marked IG. **2029.** Sunshine Yellow Pony Stallion, made for HCA in 1979, marked IG. **2030.** Heather Pony Stallion, made for HCA, marked IG.

page 658
This original color photo was included in the Imperial salesmen's binders in 1964. **2031.** 1950/613 6" bud vase. **2032.** 1950/736 Butterpat box and cover. **2033.** 1950/615 footed Hobnail box and cover. **2034.** 1950/610 Whiskbroom wall vase. **2035.** 1950/612 Whiskbroom 8" footed vase. **2036.** 1950/5 punch cup. **2037.** 1950/5 punch bowl. **2038.** 1950/618 Springerle sweets server. **2039.** 1950/81 footed, handled candleholder.

page 659
This advertisement for Imperial's Milk Glass and Golden Brass combination appeared in *House and Garden* magazine.

page 660
Decorated milk glass items, as described; those marked * were not in Imperial's regular retail line. **2040.** 1950/79 11$\frac{1}{2}$" hurricane lamp*. **2041.** 1950/203 10" footed fruit bowl*. **2042.** Iridescent 1950/3227 8" Scroll plate*. **2043.** 51770 White Ice 10" Sitka vase*. **2044.** 1950/191 Concord ivy with brass base*. **2045.** 1950/700 Leaf 12 oz. footed ice tea (Aspen Green). **2046.** 1950/700 Leaf 12 oz. footed ice tea (Terra Cotta). **2047.** 1950/473 Grape 10 oz. goblet*. **2048.** 1950/296 10$\frac{1}{2}$" tray*. **2049.** Iridescent 66C 5$\frac{1}{2}$" crimped compote*. **2050.** 1950/700 luncheon sherbet (Terra Cotta). **2051.** White enamel 792 tumbler, 14 oz. **2052.** E510 powder box with Dolly Madison decoration (made for Irving W. Rice, c. 1941). **2053.** E510 perfume bottles with Dolly Madison decoration (made for Irving W. Rice, c. 1941). **2054.** 1950/489 Rose tumbler*. **2055.** 1950/459 Rooster cocktail/toothpick holder/egg cup*. **2056.** 1950/266 iridescent Snow woman Salz*. **2057.** 1950/265 Snowman Pfeffer*. **2058.** Lunar Dot enamel decorated tumbler. **2059.** 1950/723 Closed Leaf mayonnaise bowl and ladle* (Aspen Green). **2060.** 1950/60 honey or jam jar with gold bees and black base and ribbon*.

page 661
These unique items were decorated by Ray Weekley, of Shadyside, Ohio, a longtime Imperial employee who served as manager of the decorating department. **2061.** 1950/524 10$\frac{1}{2}$" Mum plate. **2062.** 1950/7D 9" Windmill wall plate. **2063.** 1950/307 Grape 6 oz. footed tumbler. **2064.** 1950/306 Grape one quart pitcher. **2065-2068.** 1950/500 Parlor Pups set as follows: **2065.** Scottie Dog; **2066.** Bulldog; **2067.** Terrier (tail up); **2068.** Terrier (tongue out). **2069.** 1950/147 4" Swan mint. **2070.** 1950/335 Owl sugar. **2071.** 1950/800 Owl jar and cover. **2072.** 1950/335 Owl creamer.

page 662
These pieces of Mint Green Satin were shown in Imperial's 1981 Supplement. **2073.** 51751 LGS 6" Rose vase (108). **2074.** 51933 LGS small Elephant (Heisey mould). **2075.** 51744 LGS 10" Loganberry vase (356). **2076.** 51640 LGS 4$\frac{1}{2}$" basket (73). **2077.** 51847 LGS 4$\frac{3}{4}$" box and cover (1533, Heisey mould). **2078.** 51853 LGS 3" tray (1533, Heisey mould).

page 663
These pieces of Mint Green Satin were shown in Imperial's 1981 Supplement. **2079.** 51553 LGS 3" three-toed nappy (Cambridge mould, 1155N). **2080.** 51726 LGS 5" compote (Cambridge mould, 3800/42C). **2081.** 51690 LGS three-toed Rose bowl (1533, Heisey mould). **2082.** 51524 LGS 2$\frac{1}{2}$" puff box and cover

(1950/144). **2083.** 51854 LGS 4½" heart tray (294). **2084.** 51946 LGS 8" swan (400). **2085.** 51953 LGS 4" swan (147). **2086.** 51844 LGS 6" Colonial Bell (809). **2087.** 51628 LGS toothpick holder (402). **2088.** 51909 LGS duck on nest (146). **2089.** 51926 LGS hen on nest (145). **2090.** 51923 LGS bunny on nest (162).

page 664
All of these are from Imperial's No. 698 Monticello line. **2091.** Ruby 6987D 10½" round plate. **2092.** Rubigold M69810B deep bowl (also called four quart punch bowl) with separate foot. **2093.** Amber 6988D 12" plate. **2094-2095.** Imperial green 698 tumbler and 6988 pitcher. **2096.** Amber handled 698 basket. **2097.** Blue opalescent 698 tumbler. **2098.** Blue handled 698 basket. **2099-2100.** Rose Marie 698 tumbler and 6983 pitcher. **2101.** Rubigold 7½" 698 square bowl. **2102.** Ritz Blue 5" 698 deep bowl with chrome base. **2103.** Rubigold 4½" 698 compote. **2104.** Milk glass (Doeskin finish) 1952/699C 6½" crimped vase. **2105.** Rubigold 6987B 8½" salad bowl. **2106-2107.** Milk Glass 6980 open sugar and 6980 creamer. **2108.** Rubigold 6980 open sugar. **2109.** Rubigold 698 punch cup. **2110.** Imperial green 7½" square bowl. **2111.** Amber 6980 open sugar bowl. **2112.** Green opalescent 6985B 6¼" nappy. **2113.** Rubigold 6980 creamer.

page 665
These are excellent examples of Imperial's Murrhina line; measurements will vary on these items. **2114.** 604 8" vase. **2115.** 594 10" pitcher/vase. **2116.** 591 12" pitcher/vase. **2117.** Tumbler (not in line). **2118.** 606 8¾" vase. **2119.** 595/2 bottle (lacks stopper). **2120.** 597 7¼" pitcher. **2121.** 605 8¼" vase. **2122.** 595/2 bottle (lacks stopper). **2123.** 599 5¾" pitcher/vase. **2124.** 602 4¼" pitcher/vase. **2125.** Triangle crimp vase (not in line). **2126.** 600 4½" pitcher/vase. **2127.** 602 4¼" pitcher/vase. **2128.** Hatchet (not in line). **2129.** Hammer (not in line). **2130.** Hatchet (not in line).

page 666
All of these are from Imperial's "Nuart" line. Vases are marked on the outside with NUART in very small letters near the bottom of the vase. The green iridescent shown here is typical of most Nuart vases found today. **2131.** Nuart vase. **2132.** Nuart vase (note flared top). **2133.** Nuart vase. **2134.** Nuart vase in opaque white glass (perhaps "Pura") with light Rubigold iridescent finish. **2135.** Nuart vase (note pinched middle and flared top). **2136.** Nuart vase. **2137.** Nuart shade in opaque white glass (perhaps Imperial's Pura) with Rubigold iridescent finish (shades many be marked NUART in very small letters in the fitter area). **2138.** Nuart vase. **2139.** Nuart vase.

page 667
This original advertisement from the late 1930s shows Imperial's Nuart decorated assortment on Rose Pink glass.

page 668
Look carefully to distinguish the Old English and Olive pattern lines from one another. **2140.** Ruby No. 166 Old English 7" plate. **2141.** Pink No. 166 Old English 9 oz. tumbler. **2142.** Light blue No. 134 Olive 9" shallow bowl. **2143.** Ritz blue No. 134 Olive covered candy. **2144.** Ruby No. 134 Olive 9" banana bowl. **2145.** Green No. 134 Olive covered candy. **2146.** Amber No. 166 Old English mayonnaise bowl. **2147.** Ritz blue No. 166 Old English 9 oz. tumbler. **2148.** Ruby No. 166 Old English 6" nappy. **2149.** Ritz blue No. 166 Old English 12 oz. iced tea. **2150.** Amber No. 134 Olive 6½" flared bowl. **2151.** Pink No. 1346N Olive 7" flower bowl. **2152.** Ruby No. 134 Olive candleholder. **2153.** Viennese Blue No. 134 Olive candleholder. **2154.** Cobalt blue No. 166 Old English 4½" compote. **2155.** Amber No. 166 Old English 7" plate. **2156.** Green No. 134 Olive 6½" bowl. **2157.** Ruby No. 134 Olive 7" shallow bowl. **2158-2164.** No. 134 Olive 10 oz. mugs (l. to r.) in Light Smoke, Pink, Imperial Green, Heather, Viennese Blue, Amber and Smoke.

page 669
The Old Jamestowne pieces shown in this original advertisement were available in Olde Flint (crystal with a seedy quality to it), Bead Green, Chartreuse, Flask Brown or Heather.

page 670
All of these items are from Imperial's No. 341 Old Williamsburg line, which was made with moulds purchased from Heisey. **2165-2170.** 9 oz, tall goblets in Blue Haze, Nut Brown, Verde, Azalea, Antique Blue and Amber. **2171.** Blue Haze 9 oz. tall goblet. **2172.** Blue Haze 6 oz. tall sherbet. **2173.** Blue Haze 5D 8" plate. **2174.** Blue Haze 12 oz. ice tea. **2175.** Blue Haze 4½ oz. claret. **2176.** Blue Haze 12 oz. footed ice tea. **2177.** Nut Brown 66B 4½" compote. **2178-2179.** Nut Brown /902 sugar and cream set. **2180.** Nut Brown 96 salt and pepper. **2181.** Verde /58 9" pickle. **2182-2183.** Verde /122 individual sugar and cream set. **2184.** Nut Brown 7½" candleholder. **2185.** Nut Brown 67B 9" footed bowl. **2186.** Verde 105 13" celery tray. **2187.** Verde 56 three-partition relish. **2188.** Verde 75 9" salad bowl. **2189.** Verde 24 one quart pitcher. **2190.** Verde 354 7" footed jar and cover. **2191.** Verde 355 10" footed jar and cover.

page 671
Old Williamsburg goblets in a variety of colors, as shown in an Imperial advertisement. **2192.** Ruby. **2193.** Amber. **2194.** Verde. **2195.** Rose Pink. **2196.** Ultra Blue. **2197.** Sunshine Yellow. **2198.** Crystal. **2199.** Nut Brown. **2200.** Evergreen.

Color Plate Descriptions

page 672
All of these items are from Imperial's No. 341 Old Williamsburg line, which was made with moulds purchased from Heisey. **2201.** Ultra Blue 6 oz. tall sherbet. **2202.** Ultra Blue 9 oz. tall goblet. **2203.** Ultra Blue salt and pepper set. **2204.** Ultra Blue 4½ oz. claret. **2205.** Ultra Blue one quart pitcher. **2206.** Ultra Blue sugar. **2207.** Ultra Blue 12 oz. footed ice tea. **2208.** Ultra Blue cream. **2209.** Ultra Blue 12 oz. ice tea. **2210-2216.** 9 oz, tall goblets in Ruby, Nut Brown, Amber, Verde, Sunshine Yellow, Rose Pink, and Crystal.

page 673
2216A. Ruby 6 oz. tall sherbet. **2216B.** Ruby 9 oz. tall goblet. **2216C.** Ruby 4½ oz. claret. **2216D.** Ruby 12 oz. footed ice tea. **2216E.** Ruby 12 oz. ice tea.

page 674
2217. Turquoise 778 Dolphin comporte. **2218.** Forget-Me-Not Blue 180 7½" Grape vase. **2219.** Midwest Custard 132 urn. **2220.** Forget-Me-Not Blue 132 urn. **2221.** Turquoise 203D cakestand. **2222.** Forget-Me-Not Blue 282 covered jar. **2223.** Forget-Me-Not Blue 103 10" footed fruit bowl with leaf pattern. **2224.** Forget-Me-Not Blue 181 6½" Rose vase. **2225.** Forget-Me-Not Blue 125 Scroll footed bowl (lacks cover). **2226.** Ivory Satin 51755 6" Lovebird vase (143). **2227.** Turquoise 116 6" vase. **2228.** Ivory Satin 51784 3½" Rose candleholder (160). **2229.** Turquoise 629 salt/pepper shaker. **2230.** Ivory Satin 51690 8" three-toed Rose bowl (74C). **2231.** Turquoise 612 jar and cover. **2232.** Midwest Custard 116 6" decorated Rose vase. **2233.** Turquoise 893 Grape jar and cover with wicker handle. **2234.** Ivory Satin 51560 5½" Rose bowl (728N). **2235.** Turquoise 7243/1 Hobnail perfume bottle with stopper.

page 675
All of these are Imperial's No. 563 Parisian Provincial, which combined milk glass with various colors, as indicated. **2236.** Amber 12 oz. goblet. **2237.** Amber 8 oz. sherbet. **2238-2239.** Milk glass 7½" plate and amber 4¾" nappy. **2240.** Amber 7 oz. juice or wine. **2241.** Amber 16 oz. footed ice tea. **2242.** Heather 12 oz. goblet. **2243.** Heather 8 oz. sherbet. **2244-2245.** Milk glass 7½" plate and Heather 4¾" nappy. **2246.** Heather 7 oz. juice or wine. **2247.** Heather 16 oz. footed ice tea. **2248.** Verde 12 oz. goblet. **2249.** Verde 8 oz. sherbet. **2250-2251.** Milk glass 7½" plate and Verde 4¾" nappy. **2252.** Verde 7 oz. juice or wine. **2253.** Verde 16 oz. footed ice tea. **2254.** Ruby 12 oz. goblet. **2255.** Ruby 8 oz. sherbet. **2256-2257.** Milk glass 7½" plate and ruby 4¾" nappy. **2258.** Ruby 7 oz. juice or wine. **2259.** Ruby 16 oz. footed ice tea.

page 676
This original color photo of Imperial's new Peachblow was distributed to salesmen in 1964.

page 677
Unless otherwise indicated, these are Imperial's Peachblow, c. 1964-67 with finish as noted. **2260.** No. 4038 10½" vase (satin-finished amber with milk glass interior). **2261.** No. 4038 10½" vase (satin). **2262.** No. 4037 10½" vase (satin). **2263.** No. 4037 10½" vase (satin finished cobalt blue with milk glass interior). **2264.** No. 4037 10½" vase (satin). **2265.** No. P4038/1 decanter and stopper (glossy). **2266.** No. 287 vase with crimped top (glossy). **2267.** No. 287 vase, made into a pitcher shape (glossy). **2268.** No. 37 8¾" vase in Antique Blue with milk glass interior (glossy finish). **2269.** No. 4036 8¾" vase (satin). **2270.** No. 980/1 decanter and stopper (glossy). **2271.** No. 983 9½" vase (glossy). **2272.** No. 83 9½" vase in Antique Blue with milk glass interior (glossy finish). **2273.** No. 983 9½" vase (satin). **2274.** No. 83 9½" vase in Antique Blue with milk glass interior (satin finish). **2275.** No. P163 8" vase (satin). **2276.** Vase (ruby with milk glass interior, not in line). **2277.** Whimsey pear, glossy (not in line). **2278.** Satin-finished crystal Imperial logo. **2279.** Whimsey pear, glossy (not in line). **2280.** No. 980 7¾" vase, satin (not in line).

page 678
Pearl Venitian pieces, as shown in an original Imperial catalogue.

page 679
These Pink Satin (PKS) and Pink Carnival (PK) items were being produced in the early 1980s. **2281.** 51954 PKS candy box and cover (1533). **2282.** 51946 PKS Swan (400). **2283.** 42687 PK 10" banana bowl (496E). **2284.** 42726 PK 6" footed compote (474C). **2285.** 51690 PKS 8" three-toed Rose bowl (74C). **2286.** 51751 PKS 6" Rose vase (108). **2287.** 51774 PKS 10" Loganberry vase (356). **2288.** 42067 PK 9 oz. Windmill tumbler (239). **2289.** 42167 PK Windmill three-pint pitcher (239). **2290.** 42681 PK 8" Windmill bowl (52C). **2291.** 51844 PKS 6" Colonial Belle (809). **2292.** 51553 PKS three-toed nappy (Cambridge mould, 1155N). **2293.** 51640 PKS 4½" basket (73). **2294.** 51574 PKS 5½" Pansy handled nappy (478). **2295.** 42909 PK duck on nest (146). **2296.** 42563 PK 6½" nappy (555/52). **2297.** 51933 PKS 4½" elephant (Heisey mould). **2298.** 51854 PKS 4½" heart ashtray (294). **2299.** 51909 PKS duck on nest (146). **2300.** 42624 PK toothpick holder (505). **2301.** 42574 PK 5½" Pansy handled nappy (478).

page 680
All of these are Imperial's Pink Satin. **2301A.** 51592 PKS 7½" shell tray (297). **2302.** 51774 PKS 10" Loganberry vase (356). **2303.** 51524 PKS puff box and cover (1950/144). **2304.** 51937 PKS 6¾" jar and cover

Color Plate Descriptions

(975). **2305.** 51791 PKS Rose candleholder (160). **2306.** 51751 PKS 6" Rose vase (108). **2307.** 51640 PKS 4½" basket (73). **2308.** 51574 PKS 5½" Pansy handled nappy (478). **2309.** 51628 PKS toothpick holder (402). **2310.** 51854 PKS 4½" heart ashtray (294). **2311.** 51695 PKS 8½" Pansy crimped oval bowl (478C).

page 681
These items in Pink Satin (PKS), Blue Satin (BLS), and Satin Crystal (S) date from the early 1980s. **2312.** 51954 PKS candy box and cover (1533, Heisey mould). **2313.** 51954 BLS candy box and cover (1533, Heisey mould). **2314.** 51954 S candy box and cover (1533, Heisey mould). **2315.** 451946 PKS 8" swan (400). **2316.** 51909 BLS duck on nest (146). **2317.** 51909 S duck on nest (146). **2318.** 51947 S 3½" jewelry holder (1401). **2319.** 51946 S 8" swan (400). **2320.** 51947 PKS 3½" jewelry holder (1401). **2321.** 51909 PKS duck on nest (146). **2322.** 51524 BLS puff box and cover (1950/144). **2323.** 51524 S puff box and cover (1950/144).

page 682
2324. 51748 PL 4" vase. **2325.** 51745 PL 7½" Li Po vase. **2326.** 51743 PL 5" Mei vase.

page 683
2327. 51744 PL 6" Meng vase. **2328.** 51740 PL 6" Rose vase. **2329.** 51746 PL 6" vase. **2330.** 51741 PL 9" vase. **2331.** 51747 PL 6" vase. **2332.** 51742 PL 10" vase. **2333.** 51767 PL 6½" Iris vase.

page 684
These items in No. 1506 Provincial were shown in Imperial's Catalog No. 69 (the term "regular" is used to differentiate these items from "footed" versions such as those shown on the next page). **2334.** Verde 8" salad plate. **2335.** Verde 5 oz. regular juice. **2336.** Verde 8 oz. regular tumbler. **2337.** Verde 13 oz. regular tumbler. **2338.** Verde 80 oz. pitcher. **2339.** Amber 6" compote. **2340.** Amber covered jar. **2341.** Amber 5" vase. **2342.** Amber sugar. **2343.** Amber cream. **2344.** Amber salt and pepper set. **2345.** Amber 8" deep bowl. **2346.** Amber 4½" candleholder. **2347.** Amber 4½" nappy. **2348.** Amber 5½" nappy. **2349.** Amber 11½" bowl. **2350.** Amber 13" torte plate.

page 685
These No. 1506 Provincial items appeared in Imperial's 1972 catalogue. **2351.** Ruby 10 oz. goblet. **2352.** Ruby 5 oz. sherbet. **2353.** Ruby 3½ oz. wine. **2354.** Ruby 12 oz. footed tumbler. **2355.** Ruby 9 oz. footed tumbler. **2356.** Ruby 5 oz. footed juice. **2357.** Ruby 5 oz. regular juice. **2358.** Ruby 8 oz. regular tumbler. **2359.** Ruby 13 oz. regular tumbler. **2360.** Amber 10 oz. goblet. **2361.** Amber 5 oz. sherbet. **2362.** Amber 3½ oz. wine. **2363.** Amber 12 oz. footed tumbler. **2364.** Amber 9 oz. footed tumbler. **2365.** Amber 5 oz. footed juice. **2366.** Amber 5 oz. regular juice. **2367.** Amber 8 oz. regular tumbler. **2368.** Amber 13 oz. regular tumbler. **2369.** Verde 10 oz. goblet. **2370.** Verde 5 oz. sherbet. **2371.** Verde 3½ oz. wine. **2372.** Verde 12 oz. footed tumbler. **2373.** Verde 9 oz. footed tumbler. **2374.** Verde 5 oz. footed juice. **2375.** Verde 5 oz. regular juice. **2376.** Verde 8 oz. regular tumbler. **2377.** Verde 13 oz. regular tumbler. **2378.** Verde 5½" nappy and 8" salad plate. **2379.** Crystal 5½" nappy and 8" salad plate. **2380.** Amber 5½" nappy and 8" salad plate.

page 686
This original color photo of Imperial's No. 1506 Provincial was distributed to salesmen in the mid-1960s. **2381.** Crystal 80 oz. pitcher. **2382.** Verde 80 oz. pitcher. **2383.** Amber 80 oz. pitcher. **2384.** Heather 80 oz. pitcher.

page 687
These Purple Slag articles were shown in Imperial's Catalogue No. 69 (all of these have the glossy finish). **2385.** 5930 6" compote. **2386.** 727C footed compote. **2387.** 210 shaving mug planter. **2388.** 505 cruet with stopper. **2389.** 240 one pint pitcher. **2390.** 400 8" swan. **2391.** 147 swan mint whimsey. **2392.** 825 bee box and cover. **2393.** 159 lion box and cover. **2394.** 158 rooster box and cover. **2395.** 176 four-toed jar and cover. **2396.** 156 box and cover. **2397.** 156 basket. **2398.** 505 toothpick holder. **2399.** 104 miniature pitcher. **2400.** 780 6" covered bowl. **2401.** 461 eagle box and cover. **2402.** 641 8½" bowl. **2403.** 640 4½" nappy. **2404.** 1608/1 7" ashtray. **2405.** 74C three-toed crimped Rose bowl. **2406.** 62C 9½" crimped Rose bowl.

page 688
Unless otherwise indicated, these pieces of Purple Slag have the glossy finish. **2407.** 176 four-toed box and cover. **2408.** 780 punch cup. **2409.** 780 punch bowl. **2410.** 203F 10" footed fruit bowl. **2411.** 160 Rose candleholder. **2412.** 400 8" swan. **2413.** 823 duck box and cover. **2414.** 971 Flat Iron box and cover. **2415.** 157 rabbit box and cover. **2416.** 505 cruet with stopper (satin finish). **2417.** 191 partitioned box. **2418.** 822 dog box and cover. **2419.** 312 heart leaf covered box. **2420.** 661 5¼" vase. **2421.** 104 miniature pitcher. **2422.** Cape Cod 1602 piece used for cigarette lighter. **2423.** 1602 cigarette lighter. **2424.** 5390 6" compote (satin finish). **2425.** 60 honey or jam with cover (satin finish). **2426.** 156 5½" basket (satin finish) **2427.** 720 bell (satin finish). **2428.** 210 shaving mug planter. **2429.** 1560 box and cover.

Color Plate Descriptions

page 689
All of these items are from Imperial's No. 701 Reeded line (crystal items decorated with gold were called "Midas"). **2430.** Midas 8½" vase. **2431.** Ritz Blue 5" rose bowl. **2432.** Pink 6" rose bowl. **2433.** Ruby 9" vase. **2434-2435.** Midas shot glass (serves as top for decanter) and decanter. **2436.** Stiegel Green 6" bud vase. **2437.** Amber 6½" footed rose bowl with crystal foot. **2438.** Stiegel Green 12 oz. iced tea tumbler. **2439.** Stiegel Green ice lip pitcher. **2440.** Ritz Blue 6" rose bowl. **2441.** Midas 6" vase. **2442.** Ritz Blue 5" bud vase. **2443.** Ruby 7" nappy. **2444-2445.** Black/Milk Glass powder jar and perfume bottle. **2446.** Ruby 4" bowl. **2447.** Amber footed candleholder with crystal insert for candle. **2448.** Ritz Blue syrup.

page 690
All of these items are from Imperial's No. 701 Reeded line. **2449.** Blue vase with milk glass interior. **2450.** Pink 6" jar with brass handle. **2451.** Blue 7" jar. **2452.** Milk glass 5" jar with brass handle. **2453.** Ritz Blue ice lip pitcher with crystal handle. **2454.** Ruby rose bowl with crystal foot. **2455.** Ruby footed rose bowl. **2456.** Stiegel green rose bowl. **2457.** Crystal covered sugar bowl with gold and blue painted decoration. **2458.** Stiegel Green 6' bud vase. **2459.** Ritz Blue rose bowl. **2460.** Ruby 6" bud vase. **2461.** Milk glass perfume bottle with stopper. **2462.** Ritz blue tumbler. **2463.** Ruby cup and saucer. **2464-2465.** Ruby plate and mayonnaise bowl (note original label). **2466.** Crystal plate with painted pink underside. **2467.** Ruby plate.

page 691
Original advertising brochure for Imperial's Whirlspool jars.

page 692
Original catalogue sheet for Imperial's Rose Pink and Green No. 725 Octagon line.

page 693
All of these are Imperial's Ruby color. **2468.** No. 356 Loganberry 10" vase. **2469.** No. 473 7½" Grape plate. **2470.** No. 464 pokal. **2471.** No. 153 oval bowl. **2472.** 574B 9" crimped bowl (Cambridge mould). **2473.** No. 75 candelabrum. **2474.** No. 1575B 9½" bowl (Heisey mould). **2475.** No. 1506 Provincial 12 oz. footed tumbler. **2476.** No. 170 covered jar. **2477.** No. 791/dec Marine Lamp tumbler. **2478.** No. 563 6" crimped vase (Cambridge mould). **2479.** No. 13 6½" jar and cover. **2480.** No. 46 Hoffman House 5½" oz. sherbet. **2481.** Ruby glass color test disk, dated March 16, 1976. **2482.** No. 600 toothpick/cigarette holder. **2483-2484.** No. 4737 Grape cup and saucer. **2485.** No. 473 Grape sherbet.

page 694
This display of End O'Day Ruby Slag appeared in Imperial's Catalogue No. 69.

page 695
Unless indicated otherwise, these pieces of Ruby Slag have the glossy finish. **2486.** 132 8½" urn. **2487.** 300 9½" basket. **2488.** 524 Mum 10½" plate. **2489.** 43762 8½" tricorn vase (192). **2490.** 43770 10" footed vase (satin finish, S529). **2491.** 43699 Rose 9" crimped bowl (62C). **2492.** 43576 Grape handled nappy (satin finish, 851). **2493.** 43574 Pansy handled nappy (satin finish, S478). **2494.** 43681 7½" bowl (1605). **2495.** 43639 Rooster holder (459). **2496.** 43854 Heart ash tray (satin finish, S294). **2497.** 475 5½" basket. **2498.** 43060 Grape tumbler (satin finish, S473). **2499.** 43842 bell (720). **2500.** 43325 Robin mug (210). **2501.** 43320 Storybook mug (Heisey mould, 1591). **2502.** 1956 8" ashtray (Cambridge mould). **2503.** 154 eagle mug.

page 696
Unless indicated otherwise, these pieces of Ruby Slag have the glossy finish. **2504.** 965 10" footed vase. **2505.** S132 8½" urn (satin finish). **2506.** S47C Grape crimped bowl (satin finish). **2507.** 132 8½" urn. **2508.** 300 9½" basket. **2509.** 43681 7½" bowl. **2510.** 176 four-toed jar and cover. **2511.** 431C crimped compote. **2512.** 1608/1 ash tray. **2513.** 240 Windmill one-pint pitcher. **2514.** 1560 basket with milk glass handle (glossy). **2515.** 156 box and cover. **2516.** 154 eagle mug. **2517.** 43060 Grape tumbler (satin finish, S473). **2518.** 210 Robin mug. **2519.** S720 bell (satin finish). **2520.** 720 bell. **2521.** 475 5½" basket. **2522-2523.** 294 4½" Heart ash trays (note the color differences). **2524.** 1 toothpick holder. **2525.** 43320 Storybook mug (Heisey mould, 1591). **2526.** 123 3" cornucopia (Cambridge mould). **2527.** 61 salt dip (Cambridge mould). **2528.** 459 Rooster holder. **2529.** 160 Rose candleholder.

page 697
Unless indicated otherwise, these pieces of Ruby Slag have the glossy finish. **2530.** 43698 8½" footed bowl (satin finish, S737A). **2531.** 43910 covered jar (464). **2532.** S965 10" footed vase (satin finish). **2533.** 43699 Grape 9" crimped bowl (62C). **2534.** 176. four-toed jar and cover. **2535.** S431C 6½" crimped compote (satin finish). **2536.** 431C 6½" crimped compote. **2537.** 240 Windmill one-pint pitcher. **2538.** 759 box and cover. **2539.** 1608/1 ash tray. **2540.** 156 basket with milk glass handle. **2541.** 1560 box and cover. **2542-2543.** 43540 Owl sugar and cream set (glossy, 335). **2544.** 1 toothpick holder. **2545.** 61 salt dip (Cambridge mould). **2546.** S123 cornucopia (satin finish, Cambridge mould). **2547-2548.** S160 Rose candleholders (satin finish).

Color Plate Descriptions

page 698
2549. Madeira No. 123 Chroma ice tea. **2550.** Madeira No. 123 Chroma goblet. **2551.** Madeira No. 123 Chroma sherbet. **2552-2553.** 1950/228 milk glass Atterbury sugar and cream set (Vincent Price National Treasures series for Sears stores). **2554.** Purple Slag 800 owl covered jar (Vincent Price National Treasures series for Sears stores). **2555.** Purple Slag 335 owl creamer (Vincent Price National Treasures series for Sears stores). **2556-2573.** These thirteen bottles were made in 1981 for the Sons of the American Revolution (S. A. R.). The numbers and letters refer to various regiments of the Continental Army during the Revolutionary War. **2556.** Ruby bottle ("5 PA"). **2557.** Ruby bottle ("3rd NY"). **2558.** Cobalt blue bottle ("1st GA"). **2559.** Amethyst bottle ("Third NJ REGT."). **2560.** Cobalt blue bottle ("MASS IV REG."). **2561.** Green bottle ("NH 2d REGt"). **2562.** Nut Brown bottle ("2 RI"). **2563.** Amethyst bottle ("11d REGt South Carolina"). **2564.** Yellow bottle ("Sixth Virginia Regiment"). **2565.** Nut Brown bottle ("Smallwoods Maryland"). **2566.** Green bottle ("3rd Regt North Carolina"). **2567.** Amber bottle ("2nd Regiment Connecticut Light Dragoons"). **2568.** Blue bottle ("Delaware Blues"). **2569.** Mandarin Gold No. 1401 Jefferson 5 oz. footed juice (Cambridge mould). **2570.** 42749 Sunburst Carnival 8" swung bud vase (238). **2571.** 42707 Sunburst Carnival 7" four-toed bowl (Cambridge mould, 3800/49B). **2572.** 42749 Sunburst Carnival 6" swung bud vase (238). **2573.** Mandarin Gold No. 1401 Jefferson 10 oz. goblet (Cambridge mould).

page 699
This original color photo was distributed to Imperial's salesmen in the mid-1960s. **2574-2576.** No. 617 Shaker shape traditional sweets jars in Antique Blue, Verde and Amber.

page 700
2577. Nut Brown Dawn No. 3300 goblet. **2578.** Nut Brown Dawn No. 3300 sherbet. **2579.** Nut Brown No. 2428 plate. **2580.** Nut Brown Dawn No. 3300 footed on-the-rocks. **2581.** Nut Brown Dawn No. 3300 wine/juice. **2582.** Nut Brown Dawn No. 3300 footed ice tea. **2583.** Blue Haze Dawn No. 3300 goblet. **2584.** Verde Dawn No. 3300 goblet. **2585.** Nut Brown Dawn No. 3300 goblet. **2586.** Azalea Skanda No. 530 13 oz. goblet. **2587.** Amber Skanda No. 530 13 oz. goblet. **2588.** Antique Blue Skanda No. 530 13 oz. goblet. **2589.** Verde Skanda No. 530 13 oz. goblet. **2590.** Antique Blue Skanda No. 530 13 oz. goblet. **2591.** Antique Blue Skanda No. 530 10 oz. goblet. **2592.** Antique Blue Skanda No. 530 7 oz. sherbet. **2593.** Antique Blue Skanda No. 530 6 oz. wine. **2594.** Antique Blue Skanda No. 530 16 oz. footed ice tea. **2595.** Antique Blue Skanda No. 530 4½" nappy. **2596.** Antique Blue Skanda No. 46 7½" plate. **2597.** Verde Skanda No. 531 (Diamond Optic) 13 oz. goblet. **2598.** Verde Skanda No. 531 (Diamond Optic) 10 oz. goblet. **2599.** Verde Skanda No. 531 (Diamond Optic) 7 oz. sherbet. **2600.** Verde Skanda No. 531 (Diamond Optic) 6 oz. wine. **2601.** Verde Skanda No. 531 (Diamond Optic) 16 oz. footed ice tea. **2602.** Verde Skanda No. 531 (Diamond Optic) 4½" nappy. **2603.** Verde Skanda No. 531 (Diamond Optic) 7½ oz. on-the-rocks. **2604.** Verde Skanda No. 531 (Diamond Optic) 12 oz. on-the-rocks. **2605.** Verde Skanda No. 531 (Diamond Optic) 12 oz. tumbler.

page 701
Unless otherwise indicated, these pieces of Imperial slag have the glossy finish. **2606.** Caramel Slag 48 7" compote. **2607.** Jade Slag 43762 tricorn vase (satin finish, JSS192). **2608.** Ruby Slag 284 11-14" swung vase. **2609.** Purple Slag 203F 8¼" compote. **2610.** Ruby Slag 300 9½" basket. **2611.** Jade Slag 43770 vase (satin finish, JSS529). **2612.** Ruby Slag 431C crimped compote. **2613.** Caramel Slag sample vase. **2614.** Blue Slag 1605 bowl or ashtray. **2615.** Jade Slag 800 owl covered jar. **2616.** Caramel Slag sample basket with milk glass handle. **2617.** Blue Slag 1608/1 ashtray. **2618.** Ruby Slag S720 bell (satin finish). **2619.** Caramel Slag 43890 pie wagon box and cover (377). **2620.** Ruby Slag 176 four-toed jar and cover. **2621.** Blue Slag 62C Rose 9" crimped bowl (not in line). **2622.** Purple Slag 971 Flat Iron box and cover. **2623.** Blue Slag 41554 5" nappy (388, not in line). **2624.** Caramel Slag miniature vase (not in line). **2625.** Purple Slag 312 heart-shaped box with Blue Slag cover (not in line). **2626.** Blue Slag 400 toothpick. **2627.** Caramel Slag miniature vase (not in line). **2628.** Caramel Slag egg (not in line). **2629.** Jade Slag 156 basket.

page 702
Unless otherwise indicated, these pieces of Imperial slag have the glossy finish. **2630.** Caramel Slag 78 footed jar and cover. **2631.** Caramel Slag 809 Dresden Girl 7¾" bell (Cambridge mould). **2632.** Jade Slag 661 5" vase. **2633.** Ruby Slag 431C crimped compote (satin finish). **2634.** Ruby Slag 1591 storybook mug (Heisey mould). **2635.** Caramel Slag 5930 crimped compote (satin finish). **2636.** Not Imperial glass. **2637.** Jade Slag 1560 basket. **2638.** Purple Slag 19 toothpick/cigarette. **2639.** Ruby Slag 1776 Eagle holder. **2640.** Purple Slag 1602 Cape Cod lighter. **2641.** Ruby Slag 210 robin mug. **2642.** Caramel Slag 1591 storybook mug (Heisey mould). **2643.** Jade Slag 43630 toothpick (19). **2644.** Jade Slag 505 toothpick. **2645.** Caramel Slag 1560 box and cover. **2646.** Jade Slag 123 cornucopia (satin finish, Cambridge mould).

page 703
This original color photograph of Imperial's South Jersey assortment shows the same articles which were advertised in the May, 1958, issue of *Crockery and Glass Journal*. **2647.** Blue pitcher. **2648.** Ruby pitcher. **2649.** Bead Green pitcher. **2650.** Madeira pitcher. **2651.** Stiegel Green pitcher. **2652.** Burgundy pitcher. **2653.** Bead Green vase. **2654.** Burgundy vase. **2655.** Madeira vase. **2656.** Ruby vase. **2657.** Blue vase. **2658.** Stiegel Green vase. **2659.** Madeira vase. **2660.** Stiegel Green vase. **2661.** Blue vase. **2662.** Burgundy vase. **2663.** Bead Green vase. **2664.** Ruby vase.

Color Plate Descriptions

page 704
This original color photograph of Stamm House Dewdrop Opalescent Hobnail glassware was distributed to Imperial's salesmen in January, 1965. The cornice dated 1818 was from the old Stamm House hotel east of Wheeling. **2665.** 7423 $6^{1}/_{2}$" blown vase. **2666.** 1886 goblet. **2667.** 624 56 oz. pitcher/vase. **2668.** 642 10" bowl. **2669.** 188P 6" footed posie bowl. **2670.** 631 footed sugar. **2671.** 631 footed cream. **2672.** 635 $5^{1}/_{2}$" square box and cover.

page 705
These two patterns, No. 9 and No. 619, have a long history in Imperial's production. Collectors today often call them Star and File (No. 612) and Tulip and Cane (No. 9). **2673-2675.** No. 9 $8^{3}/_{4}$" Bundling Lamps in Antique Blue, Milk Glass and Amber. **2676.** Moonlight Blue No. 9 goblet. **2677.** Pink No. 612 Turn O' The Century goblet. **2678.** Antique Blue No. 612 decanter with stopper. **2679-2681.** Rubigold No. 612 celery holder, spooner and creamer. **2682.** Rubigold No. 9 footed jelly (note crystal stem and foot). **2683.** Rubigold No. 612 sherbet. **2684.** Purple Slag No. 9 candy bowl. **2685.** Pink No. 612 Turn O' The Century sherbet. **2686.** Milk glass No. 9 9" two-handled footed compote. **2687.** Rubigold No. 9 crimped berry bowl. **2688.** Pink No. 612 Turn O' The Century tumbler. **2689.** Moonlight Blue No. 612 Turn O' The Century cordial. **2690-2695.** No. 612 toothpick holders in Ultra Blue, Verde, Milk Glass, Amber, Nut Brown and Sunshine Yellow. **2696-2697.** No. 612 salt shakers in Milk Glass and Light Green.

page 706
These items in Sunburst Carnival were shown in Imperial's 1982-1983 catalogue. **2698.** 42643 SYC $5^{1}/_{2}$" handled basket (820). **2699.** 42732 SYC swung (will vary from 10" to 14" tall) vase (338). **2700.** 42795 SYC $3^{1}/_{2}$" oval candleholder or soap dish (715). **2701.** 42581 SYC puff box and cover (A-180). **2702.** 42958 SYC $8^{1}/_{2}$" handled mirror (M-167). **2703.** 42882 SYC four-toed candy jar and cover (176).

page 707
These items in Sunburst Carnival were shown in Imperial's 1982-1983 catalogue. **2704.** 42930 SYC 4" swan (147). **2705.** 42574 SYC $5^{1}/_{2}$" Pansy handled nappy (478). **2706.** 42926 SYC hen on nest (145). **2707.** 42904 SYC bunny on nest (162). **2708.** 42749 SYC swung (will vary from 6"-8" tall) bud vase (238). **2709.** 42155 SYC Rose three pint pitcher (24). **2710.** 42054 SYC Rose 9 oz. tumbler (489). **2711.** 42687 SYC 10" banana bowl (496E). **2712.** 42487 SYC cologne and stopper (M-123). **2713.** 42947 SYC $3^{1}/_{2}$" jewelry holder (1401). **2714.** 42707 SYC 7" four-toed bowl (Cambridge mould, 3800/498). **2715.** 42693 SYC 8" Rose three-toed crimped bowl (74C). **2716.** 42536 SYC lamb cream and sugar set (902/3). **2717.** 42725 SYC 5" crimped compote (Cambridge mould, 3800/42C). **2718.** 42844 SYC 6" Colonial Belle (809). **2719.** 42944 SYC terrier (5/4). **2720.** 42620 SYC toothpick holder (1). **2721.** 42943 SYC bulldog (5/1). **2722.** 42911 SYC lamb covered butter (905).

page 708
All of these are Imperial's Sunset Ruby Carnival glass. **2723.** 3800/57B 8" four-toed bowl (Cambridge mould). **2724.** 210 robin mug. **2725.** 494 9" pitcher/vase. **2726.** 494 9 oz. tumbler. **2727.** 505 8" footed vase. **2728.** 474 $6^{1}/_{2}$" vase. **2729.** 3800/42C 5" compote (Cambridge mould). **2730.** 474C $7^{1}/_{2}$" compote. **2731.** 975 jar and cover. **2732.** 5057 8" bowl. **2733.** 489C Rose 8" bowl. **2734.** 156 box and cover. **2735.** 3800/165 covered box (Cambridge mould). **2736.** 434N 7" bowl. **2737.** 3800/27 sugar and cream set (Cambridge moulds). **2738.** 402 toothpick holder. **2739.** 3800/72 3" candleholders (Cambridge mould). **2740.** 3800/165C 7" three-toed compote (Cambridge mould). **2741.** 147 swan mint. **2742.** 478 Pansy $5^{1}/_{2}$" handled nappy.

page 709
These "decorated ruby" Sweet Servers were pictured in a supplement to Imperial's Catalogue 62. **2743.** 974 jar and cover. **2744.** 975 jar and cover. **2745.** 176 four-toed jar and cover. **2746.** 976 jar and cover. **2747.** 780 Lace Edge 6" covered bowl. **2748.** 6990 Washington box and cover. **2749.** 1405 Ipswich covered pokal (Heisey mould). **2750.** 468 Grape $4^{1}/_{2}$" covered bowl. **2751.** 735 Grape hex box and cover. **2752.** C165 box and cover (Cambridge mould).

page 710
2753. No. 791 Green Marine Lights 15 oz. tumbler. **2754.** K-3 Amber "Big Keg" tumbler (note gold decoration and original label). **2755.** 454 Green 11 oz. trigger-handled Big Shot mug. **2756.** 1776 Sunset Ruby Eagle cigarette. **2757.** 27/267 Aurora Jewels Pfeffer. **2758.** 27/267 Aurora Jewels Salz. **2758-2766.** No. 505 toothpick holders in Amber, Peacock Carnival, Heather, Turquoise, Sunshine Yellow, Pink Carnival, Crystal (gold decoration) and Rubigold. **2767-2769.** No. 1 toothpick holders in Verde, Amethyst Carnival and Helios Carnival. **2770.** Aurora Jewels 27/19 toothpick holder. **2771.** 402 Sunset Ruby toothpick holder. **2772.** Aurora Jewels 27/1454 Top-Hat toothpick (Heisey mould). **2773.** 612 Sunshine Yellow No. 612 (Star and File) toothpick holder. **2774.** 612 Amberglo toothpick holder. **2775.** 123 Jade Slag (satin finish) cornucopia (Cambridge mould). **2776.** 505 Jade Slag toothpick holder. **2777.** 19 Purple Slag toothpick holder. **2778.** 19 Jade Slag toothpick holder. **2779.** 102 Ultra Blue urn.

COLOR PLATE DESCRIPTIONS

page 711
All of these are from Imperial's Tradition No. 165 line. **2780.** Heather 8" salad plate. **2781.** Nut Brown 72-hole birthday cake plate. **2782.** Bead Green 8" salad plate. **2783-2789.** Goblets in Green, Light Amber, Ruby, Aquamarine, Pink, Blue Mist, and Heather. **2790-2792.** Goblets in Topaz, Bead Green, and Mustard. **2793-2796.** Sherbets in Heather, Aquamarine, Pink and Green. **2797.** Amber baked apple. **2798.** Viennese Blue cocktail. **2799.** Ruby finger bowl. **2800.** Milk Glass tumbler. **2801.** Ruby $7^{3}/_{4}$" flared nappy.

page 712
These original photographs depicting Imperial's Voodoo, Marine Lights and Christmas Season tumblers appeared in the mid-1960s.

page 713
Tumblers were an important part of Imperial's production for many years. **2803.** Dusk No. 8401 Persian $10^{1}/_{2}$ oz. tumbler. **2804.** Dusk No. 8401 Persian 13 oz. tumbler. **2805.** Dusk No. 8401 Persian $5^{1}/_{2}$ oz. tumbler. **2806.** Vert No. 8401 Persian $10^{1}/_{2}$ oz. tumbler. **2807.** Vert No. 8401 Persian 13 oz. tumbler. **2808.** Vert No. 8401 Persian $5^{1}/_{2}$ oz. tumbler. **2809.** Pecan No. 8401 Persian 13 oz. tumbler. **2810.** Pecan No. 8401 Persian $5^{1}/_{2}$ oz. tumbler. **2811.** Mulberry No. 8401 Persian $10^{1}/_{2}$ oz. tumbler. **2812.** Mulberry No. 8401 Persian 13 oz. tumbler. **2813.** Mulberry No. 8401 Persian $5^{1}/_{2}$ oz. tumbler. **2814.** Trial decorated tumbler. **2815.** No. 124 Spanish windows 16 oz. tumbler, trial decoration. **2816.** No. 114 Toril de Oro 11 oz. on-the-rocks tumbler, trial decoration. **2817.** No. 104 Golden Shoji 15 oz. tumbler, trial decoration. **2818.** Trial decorated tumbler. **2819.** No. 322 Scroll tumbler, trial decoration. **2820.** Sage No. 775 Ranch Life tumbler. **2821.** Turquoise opaque Tile tumbler (14 oz., not decorated). **2822.** 71/dec. Mosaic Tile 12 oz. tumbler with fired multi-color decoration. **2823.** Iridescent milk glass Tile tumbler, trial decoration. **2824.** Milk glass 14 oz. Tile tumbler, trial decoration. **2825.** Casa Tile 14 oz. tumbler (red enamel decoration on Turquoise opaque). **2826.** No. 176 14 oz. tumbler, decorated "Panther P". **2827.** No. 71 tumbler, decal trial decoration. **2828.** No. 176 tumbler, enamel trial decoration. **2829.** No. 71 tumbler, trial decoration. **2830.** No. 71 tumbler, trial decoration. **2831.** No. 71 tumbler, trial decoration. **2832.** No. 71 tumbler, trial decoration. **2833.** No. 554 12 oz. hi-ball (black enamel decoration, "Have One on Imperial"). **2834.** Tumbler with trail gold decoration. **2835.** Green No. 780 decorated Voodoo tumbler. **2836.** Flask Brown No. 779 Longhorn 16 oz. tumbler with gold decoration. **2837.** Bead Green No. 996 Toltec 11 oz. tumbler. **2838.** Flask Brown No. 779 Longhorn $13^{1}/_{2}$ oz. tumbler. **2839.** No. 176/6 Blue Coil 10 oz. tumbler. **2840.** No. 176 Signature tumbler (etched and gold decorated). **2841.** No. 1950/113 light blue Trellis 15 oz. tumbler. **2842.** Kilt Green No. 778 Wee Scottie 14 oz. tumbler.

page 714
Imperial's Turn O' The Century items (figs. 2843-2850) were reissues of patterns made many years earlier. **2843-2844.** Amberglo 505 goblet and 505C compote. **2845-2846.** Verde 671 goblet and 671C compote. **2847-2848.** Azalea 612 goblet and 612C compote. **2849-2850.** Antique Blue 474 goblet and 474C compote. **2851-2852.** Satin finished Antique Blue 80 Vinelf candleholders and 67 Vinelf comporte. **2853-2854.** Satin finished Verde 80 Vinelf candleholders and 67 Vinelf comporte. **2855-2856.** Satin finished crystal 80 Vinelf candleholders and 67 Vinelf comporte.

page 715
All of these items are Imperial's Ultra Blue. **2857.** 51792 9" Dolphin candleholder (90). **2858.** 51796 7" candleholder (330). **2859.** 51757 5" vase (86). **2860.** 51774 10" Loganberry vase (356). **2861.** 51775 12" umbrella vase; also known as Poppy vase (488). **2862.** 41870 Butterpat box and cover (736). **2863.** 51934 Baltimore Pear jar and cover (974). **2864.** 51926 hen on nest (145). **2865.** 51844 6" Colonial Belle (809). **2866.** 51599 9"pickle dish, "Love's Request Is Pickles" (213). **2867.** 51410 $10^{1}/_{2}$" Rose plate (10D). **2868.** 51699 Rose 9" crimped bowl (62C). **2869.** 51690 8" Rose three-toed bowl (74C). **2870.** 51692 Daisy 9" bowl (464). **2871.** 51862 8" ashtray (Cambridge mould, 214/3). **2872.** 51861 6" ashtray (Cambridge mould, 214/2). **2873.** 51860 4" ashtray (Cambridge mould, 214/1). **2874.** 14853 6""ashtray (Candlewick 400/150). **2875.** 14852 5" ashtray (Candlewick 400/133). **2876.** 14851 4" ashtray (Candlewick 400/440). **2877.** 51852 duck ashtray (532). **2878.** 51851 6" ashtray (Cambridge mould, P-735). **2879.** 51850 Leaf $4^{1}/_{2}$" ashtray (293). **2880.** 51474 salt/pepper set (Heisey mould, $64^{1}/_{2}$). **2881.** 51477 salt/pepper set (Heisey mould, 1503/96). **2882.** 51470 salt/pepper set (698). **2883.** 51490 cruet with stopper (Heisey mould, 1503). **2884.** 51320 Storybook mug (Heisey mould, 1591).

page 716
This original color photograph was part of Imperial's sales literature in the mid-1960s. **2885.** Cranberry 488 crimped 12" umbrella vase. **2886.** Verde 488 crimped 12" umbrella vase. **2887.** Flask Brown 787 Bambu $10^{1}/_{2}$" vase. **2888-2889.** Cranberry and Verde 1620 11" footed vases (Heisey mould). **2890-2891.** Satin finished Verde and Cranberry 132 urns. **2892.** Verde 787 $10^{1}/_{2}$" Bambu vase. **2893-2894.** Satin finished Cranberry and Verde Everglade vases (Cambridge mould, 21).

647

Color Plate Descriptions

page 717
2895. Sunset Ruby Carnival glass 505 vase. **2896.** 41566 Verde heart nappy (541). **2897.** Amber 505C 7" crimped compote. **2898.** Turquoise 555 4½" footed compote. **2899.** Rubigold 474 punch cup. **2900.** Crystal 536 6" vase with gold decoration. **2901.** Peacock Carnival 536 6" vase. **2902.** 192 Peacock Carnival tricorn 8½" vase. **2903.** 486 Rubigold Carnival 8½" Masque/Drama vase. **2904.** Sunburst Carnival 6-8" swung bud vase (238). **2905.** Lichen Green 132 8½" urn. **2906.** 185 amber cased fiddle 9" vase with milk glass interior. **2907.** Satin finished Verde 132 urn. **2908.** Ruby Grape 6" vase (21). **2909.** Antique Blue 613 6" Whiskbroom vase. **2910.** Nugreen 698 Monticello basket. **2911.** Aurora Jewels 457 5" vase. **2912.** Rubigold 698 Monticello basket. **2913.** 51754 satin finished green 5" bud vase (308) **2914.** Stiegel Green 142 canape tray. **2915.** 51590 Bead Green horse shoe 8" relish (54). **2916.** 51590 Nut Brown horse shoe 8" relish. **2917.** Ruby 142 canape tray.

page 718
2918. 51746 Ultra Blue 6" bud vase (849). **2919.** 51747 Sunshine Yellow 6" bud vase (850). **2920.** 51746 Plum 6" bud vase (849). **2921.** 51736 Plum 9" ball vase (Heisey mould, 4045). **2922.** 51747 Ultra Blue 6" bud vase (850). **2923.** 51745 Sunshine Yellow 7½" Li Po vase (731). **2924.** 51744 Plum 6" Meng vase (618). **2925.** 51743 Sunshine Yellow 5" Mei vase (308). **2926.** Black Rose 6" satin-finished vase (108). **2927.** Black Grape 6" bud vase (310). **2928-2931.** Hobnail ivy ball in Stamm House Dewdrop Opalescent (1886/188), Ritz Blue (188), Black (188), and Stiegel Green (188). **2932-2937.** 86 vase in green, Amberglo, Verde, crystal with gold decoration, Ultra Blue and Heather. **2938-2940.** 699 vases in Mustard, green and blue. **2941.** 51735 Ultra Blue, 4" ball vase (Heisey mould, 4045). **2942-2946.** 100 boot in Smoke, cobalt blue, Amber, Turquoise and Mustard.

page 719
2947. Heather cased 12" umbrella vase with milk glass interior (488). **2948.** Vigna Vetro Loganberry 10" vase (356). **2949.** Amber with milk glass interior Loganberry 10" vase (356). **2950.** Green with milk glass interior 12" umbrella vase. **2951.** Stiegel Green 1483 Stanhope two-handled vase (made for Smithsonian Institution, 1980). **2952.** No. 969 Heather vase/lamp base. **2953.** Jonquil 1823 8" vase. **2954.** Pink Carnival what? **2955.** Azure Blue Carnival 16" swung vase (338). **2956.** Antique Blue cased with milk glass interior 185 fiddle bud vase. **2957.** Spangled Bittersweet 599 5½" vase. **2958.** Experimental 7243 Hobnail 6" vase. **2959.** Experimental optic bud vase. **2960.** Heather vase. **2961.** Jade 51758 JA 7½" Li Po vase. **2962.** Ruby bottle/vase. **2963.** Stiegel Green 6" bud vase (850). **2964.** Verde 980 pitcher/vase. **2965.** Lichen Green 181 Rose 6¼" vase. **2966.** Lead Lustre pulled feather vase. **2967.** Jonquil 848 6" bud vase. **2968.** Charcoal vase. **2969.** Green iridescent Nuart vase.

page 720
These articles were shown in a supplement to Imperial's Catalogue No. 62. Brass handles converted various items into "servers." **2970.** Mustard 511 server. **2971.** Amber 973 server. **2972.** Ruby 37/27 server. **2973.** Verde 972 server. **2974.** Antique Blue 727C server. **2975.** Milk glass 1950/749F server. **2976-2981.** 46C crimped posie bowls in Mustard, amber, ruby, Verde, Antique Blue and Heather. Imperial's "Velvet Pie Crust" items were made by satin-finishing various colors. **2982-2984.** Pink velvet pie crust 1592CC 8" double crimped bowl, 1592F 8½" shallow crimped bowl and 1592B 7½" flared crimped bowl. **2985-2987.** Verde velvet pie crust 1592CC 8" double crimped bowl, 1592F 8½" shallow crimped bowl and 1592B 7½" flared crimped bowl. **2988-2990.** Mandarin Gold velvet pie crust 1592CC 8" double crimped bowl, 1592F 8½" shallow crimped bowl and 1592B 7½" flared crimped bowl. **2991-2993.** Heather velvet pie crust 1592CC 8" double crimped bowl, 1592F 8½" shallow crimped bowl and 1592B 7½" flared crimped bowl.

page 721
All of these are Imperial's distinctive Verde color. **2994.** No. 1506 Provincial 11½" gardenia bowl. **2995.** No. 8 Grape decanter with stopper (satin finish) **2996.** No. 160/163 Cape Cod 30 oz. decanter with stopper. **2997.** No. 1506 Provincial 13" torte plate. **2998.** No. 8 Grape decante (no stopper). **2999.** No. 965 10" footed vase. **3000.** No. 341/67B 9" footed bowl. **3001.** No. 330 7½" candleholder. **3002.** No. 464 pokal. **3003.** No. 185 9" Fiddle vase. **3004.** No. 160/221/0 Cape Cod 9" basket (made for Star Exclusives in 1977). **3005.** No. 671 Turn O' The Century goblet. **3006.** Cape Cod 160/1112 divided relish, lacks dressing covered jar (made for Star Exclusives in 1977). **3007.** Blown bottle. **3008.** No. 530 7" Duck ashtray (532). **3009.** No. 473 3 oz. wine (satin finish). **3010.** No. 505 toothpick/cigarette holder. **3011.** No. 699 Washington covered butterdish (made for Star Exclusives). **3012.** Zodiac 3½" coaster (Heisey mould, 1590/78) **3013.** No. 86 5" vase.

page 722
This original color photograph of Imperial's Vintage Grape pattern in Verde dates from the early 1960s. **3014.** 473 10 oz. goblet. **3015.** 473 6 oz. sherbet. **3016.** 473 12 oz. tumbler. **3017.** 473 three-pint pitcher. **3018.** 8 decanter and stopper. **3019.** 473 3 oz. wine. **3020.** 3D 7½" plate. **3021.** 49 4½" nappie. **3022.** 47 8" bowl.

COLOR PLATE DESCRIPTIONS

page 723
3023. Vigna Vetro 287 Grape vase. **3024.** Vigna Vetro 241 Grape cruet with stopper. **3025.** Vigna Vetro 163 Grape decanter with stopper. **3026.** Iridescent milk glass Loganberry vase (1950/356). **3027.** Murrhina 596/1 8½" vase. **3028.** Aurora Jewels 27/3531 Ram's Head 6" candleholders (Cambridge mould). **3029.** Aurora Jewels 27/3525 Ram's Head 9" bowl (Cambridge mould). **3030.** Murrhina 597/1 7" vase. **3031.** Turquoise No. 56 Provincial 12 oz. goblet. **3032.** Sculpturesque No. 55 Turquoise cased 7" oval bowl. **3033.** Sculpturesque No. 55 Heather cased 7" oval bowl. **3034.** Iridescent milk glass Monticello No. 699 vase. **3035.** Lichen Green Grape decanter, no stopper (8). **3036.** Lichen Green 132 urn. **3037.** Trial vase, amber with mica. **3038.** Trial vase, green with mica.

page 724
Many of these pieces of Imperial's Vintage Ruby were shown in the company's General Catalog No. 53. Pieces in Ruamber (fig. 3053) are hard to find today. **3039.** 287 Grape 10" vase. **3040.** 163 Grape decanter and stopper. **3041.** 473 10 oz. goblet. **3042.** 473 Grape one pint pitcher. **3043.** 310 Grape bud vase. **3044.** 727C Grape crimped compote. **3045.** 831 Grape footed sugar. **3046.** 831 Grape footed creamer. **3047.** 899 Grape covered marmalade. **3048.** 858 Grape 6' handled pickle tray. **3049.** 47C Grape crimped 9" bowl. **3050.** 805 Grape 8½" celery tray. **3051.** 842 Grape 4½" handled nappy. **3052.** 276 Grape ¼ pound butter and cover. **3053.** Ruamber 1854 6 oz. sherbet.

page 725
No. 699 Washington pieces with this cranberry rim decoration were being made in the early 1940s. Beginning in the 1950s, this set was sold in crystal as the 69911 15-piece punch set. **3054.** Punch cup. **3055.** Punch bowl with underplate and ladle.

page 726
Items from Imperial's No. 699 Washington line. **3056.** Trial yellow/orange 6994 12" vase. **3057.** Verde 12" flared bowl (made for Star Exclusives). **3058.** Rubigold 6996B 7" flared berry bowl. **3059.** Verde covered butterdish (made for Star Exclusives). **3060-3062.** Amber, Ritz Blue and Stiegel Green 749 4½" twin candleholders. **3063.** Ruby 6992 goblet. **3064.** Ruby 699 7 oz. old fashioned. **3065.** Ritz Blue 6992 sherbet. **3066.** Ruby 699 9 oz. table tumbler. **3067.** Ruby 6992 sherbet. **3068.** Milk glass 6 oz. oil with stopper. **3069.** Milk glass 6992 sherbet. **3070.** Milk glass 6992 goblet. **3071.** Milk glass 6995D 8" square plate. **3072.** Milk glass 6994 finger bowl. **3073.** Milk glass 699 10½" covered candy jar with gold trim.

page 727
Items 3074-3075 and 3077-3083 were made by the Pioneer Glass Co., a venture which made glass for a short time in the old plant after Imperial had closed. The Pioneer pieces are often marked "SIC" (Save Imperial Committee). **3074.** Green 8" round plate. **3075.** Blue 8" berry bowl. **3076.** Ritz Blue 6995D 8" square plate. **3077.** Green 7½" crimped bowl. **3078.** Blue 12 oz. tumbler. **3079.** 7 oz. old fashion. **3080.** Green 8" berry bowl. **3081.** Green 7" lily bowl. **3082.** Blue Carnival glass 4" berry bowl. **3083.** Blue 9 oz. tumbler. **3084.** Topaz 5" bon bon. **3085.** Topaz 6994A 4" berry bowl. **3086.** Rubigold 699A 4½" compote. **3087.** Topaz 6990 sugar. **3088.** Topaz 6990 creamer. **3089.** Topaz goblet. **3090.** Peacock iridescent shade. **3091.** Rubigold shade. **3092.** Burgundy 699 5" square vase. **3093.** Cobalt Blue 699 5" square vase. **3094.** Mustard 699 7" square vase. **3095.** Stiegel Green 699 7" square vase.

page 728
All of these are Imperial's White Carnival glass. **3096.** Mum 10½" plate (524). **3097.** 42400 Homestead 10½" plate (525). **3098.** 42062 Robin tumbler (670). **3099.** 42162 Robin three pint pitcher (670). **3100.** 42150 Grape one pint pitcher (473). **3101.** 42774 Loganberry 10" vase (356). **3102.** 42685 Rose three-toed 7½" bowl. **3103.** 42784 Rose candleholder (160). **3104.** 42699 Rose 9" crimped bowl (62C). **3105.** 42786 three-toed candleholder (Cambridge mould, 1155). **3106.** 42701 10" three-toed bowl (Cambridge mould, 1152). **3107.** 42684 7" bowl (496). **3108.** 42844 Suzanne Bell (809). **3109.** 42615 Rose butter and cover (161). **3110.** Rose covered sugar (25). **3111.** Rose creamer (26). **3112.** 42725 5" compote (Cambridge mould, 3800/42C). **3113.** 42728 4¾" compote (505A). **3114.** 42754 Loganberry 6½" vase (109). **3115.** 42756 6" vase (536). **3116.** 42891 box and cover (975). **3117.** 42695 Pansy 8½" oval bowl (478C). **3118.** 42930 4" swan (147). **3119.** 42622 toothpick holder (7). **3120.** 42551 three-toed nappy (Cambridge mould, 1155N). **3121.** 42574 Pansy 5½" handled nappy (478).

page 729
3122. Ruby No. 330 (Diamond Block) 6½" relish. **3123.** Viennese Blue No. 330 (Diamond Block) bowl. **3124.** Topaz No. 779 Empire 9½" crimped bowl. **3125.** Ruby No. 779 Empire 9½" crimped bowl. **3126.** No. 582 Fancy Colonial Pink, 8½" Bowl. 3127. No. 104 Golden Shoji 6½" bud vase. **3128.** No. 104 Golden Shoji 2 oz. sake tumbler. **3129.** Stamm House Dewdrop Opalescent 1886/213 pickle dish ("Love's Request Is Pickles"). **3130.** Green No. 742 Hobnail cologne bottle with stopper. **3131.** Turquoise opaque Hobnail powder box (742). **3132.** Turquoise Opaque cologne bottle with stopper (741). **3133.** Stamm House Dewdrop Opalescent 1886/741 Hobnail cologne bottle with stopper. **3134.** Turquoise Opaque cologne bottle

649

with stopper (741). **3135.** Black Hobnail ivy ball (188). **3136.** No. 46 Amber Hoffman House goblet. **3137.** No. 46 Nut Brown Hoffman House goblet. **3138.** Red Glow No. 682 Pillar Flute bowl. **3139.** Red Glow No. 682 Pillar Flute plate.

page 730
3140. 71762 10$^{1}/_{2}$" Dolphin candlestick in Moonstone Blue and Moonstone White with gold decoration (made for Metropolitan Museum of Art). **3141.** Stamm House Dewdrop Opalescent 1886/201 footed lamp. **3142.** Crystal (doeskin) 10" swan (Cambridge mould, 1044). **3143-3145.** No. 699 Washington shades in Rubigold, Cobalt Blue (satin finished) and iridescent crystal (satin finished). **3146.** Viennese Blue No. 134 Olive bowl. **3147.** Moonlight Blue 3550/133 bowl (made from Cambridge mould). **3148.** Ruby No. 1346N Olive 7" flower bowl. **3149.** Amber No. 1346N Olive 7" flower bowl. **3150.** Old Williamsburg No. 341 Emerald Green 12 oz. footed ice tea. **3151.** Old Williamsburg No. 341 Antique Blue 12 oz. ice tea tumbler. **3152.** Old Williamsburg No. 341 Siamese Pink wine (LIG mark). **3153.** Old Williamsburg No. 341 Stiegel Green 6 oz. tall sherbet. **3154.** Siamese Pink 4$^{1}/_{2}$ oz. wine (LIG mark; top not flared and stem is satin finished). **3155.** Crystal No. 699 Washington 6 oz. cologne in metal holder (note decoration on stopper). **3156.** Crystal No. 699 Washington cigarette box and four individual ashtrays in metal holder. **3157-3158.** Crystal No. 699 Washington 6 oz. cologne bottles and puff box in metal holders.

BIBLIOGRAPHY

Archer, Douglas and Margaret. *Imperial Glass* (1978). Paducah, KY: Collector Books.

Burns, Carl O. *Imperial Carnival Glass* (1995). Paducah, KY: Collector Books.

Edwards, Bill. *The Standard Encyclopedia of Carnival Glass*, 6th ed. (1998). Paducah, KY: Collector Books.

Garrison, Myrna and Bob. *Imperial's Boudoir, Etcetera ... A Comprehensive Look at Dresser Accessories for Irice and Others* (1996).

Garrison, Myrna and Bob. *Imperial's Vintage Milk Glass* (1992).

Ross, Richard and Wilma. *Imperial Glass: Imperial Jewels, Free Hand and Pressed Glass* (1971). Des Moines, IA: Wallace-Homestead.

Logos, Signs and Paperweights

1921

1922 1923 1924 1925 1926

1929

1927 1928 1930 1931 1932 1933

1934

1935

1936

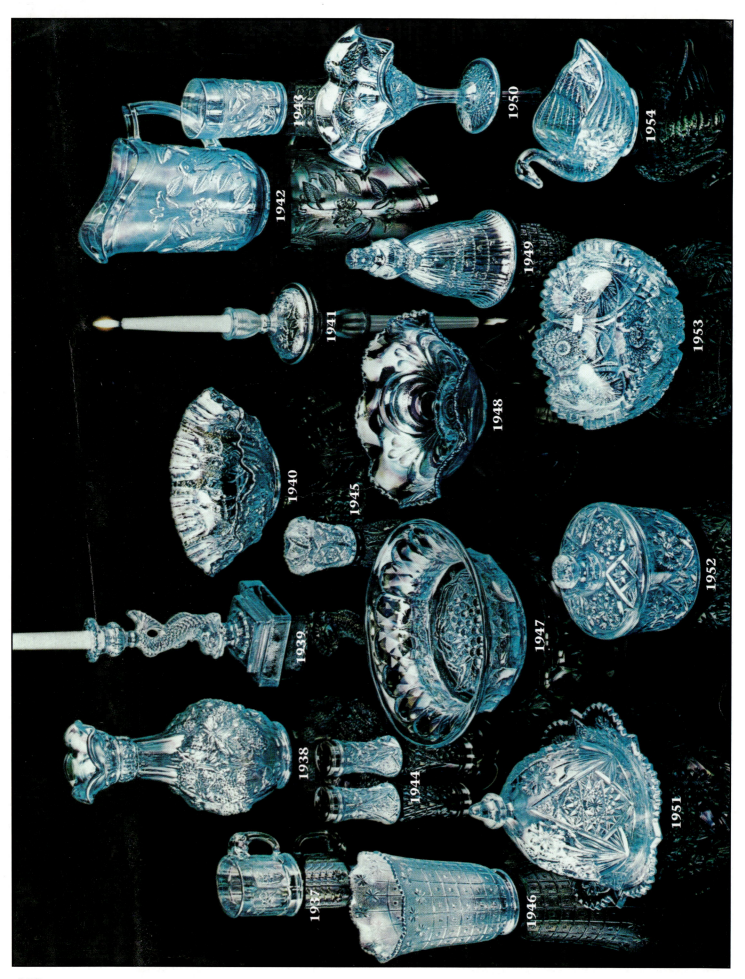

Horizon Blue Carnival

1956

1955

Meadow Green Carnival

Metropolitan Museum of Art

1982   1983   1984   1985   1986

1987   1988   1989

1990   1991   1992   1993   1994

1995   1996   1997   1998

"Made For ..."

657

Decorated Milk Glass

Decorated Milk Glass

2061 2062 2063 2064 2065 2066 2067 2068 2069 2070 2071 2072

661

Mint Green Satin

Mint Green Satin

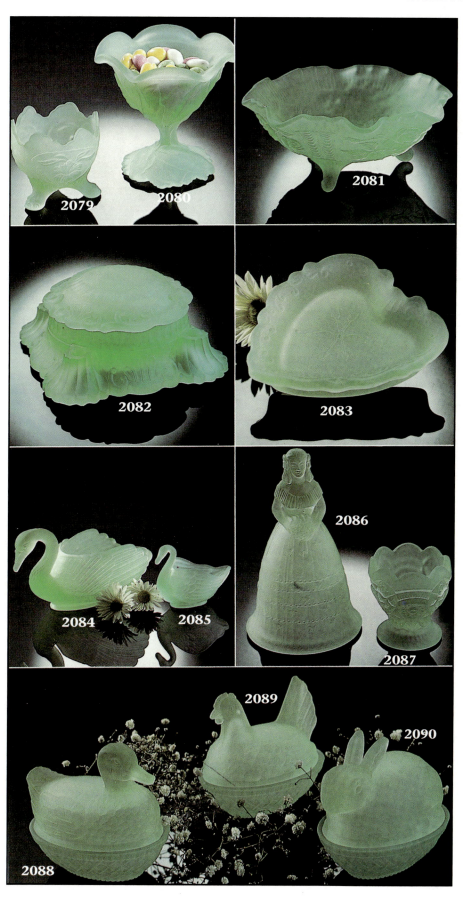

MONTICELLO, No. 698

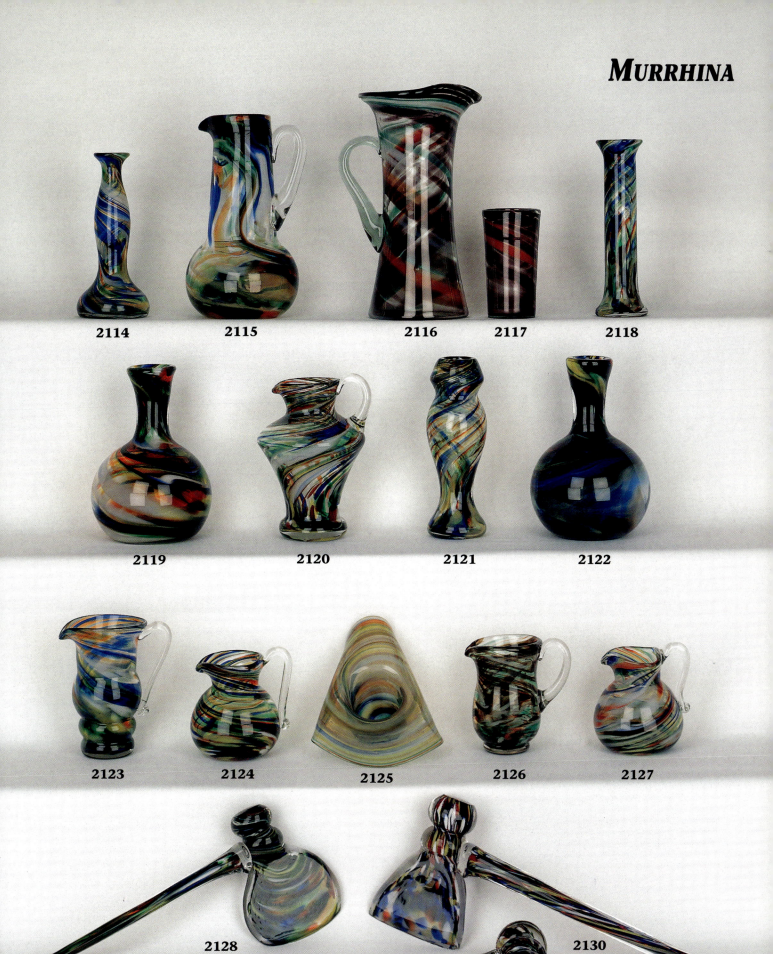
MURRHINA

Nuart Vases and Shades

666

Nuart Decorated

EASTER NUART DECORATED ASSORTMENT

consisting of 4 pieces of each item illustrated above, or 4 dozen total, packed in one barrel.

Price per dozen $7.00

Barrels $1.25 each extra.

Useful, ornamental glass articles that will fit every home and are particularly salable for card prizes or gifts.

The floral decoration is done in natural colors on Rose Pink Transparent Glass, and is fired into the glass at a high temperature. It will wear like china. Each piece is trimmed with real burnished gold.

Use ORDER BLANK enclosed for your convenience.

Old English, No. 166 and Olive, No. 134

Old Williamsburg, No. 341

OLD WILLIAMSBURG, NO. 341

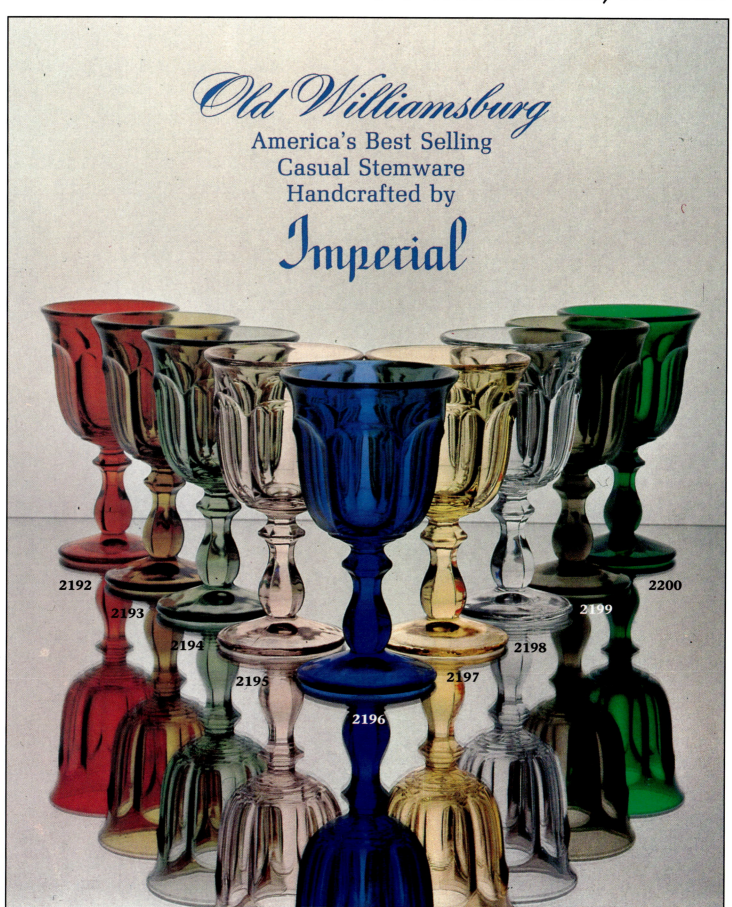

672

Old Williamsburg, No. 341

Opaque Colors

674

PARISIAN PROVINCIAL, No. 563

Peachblow

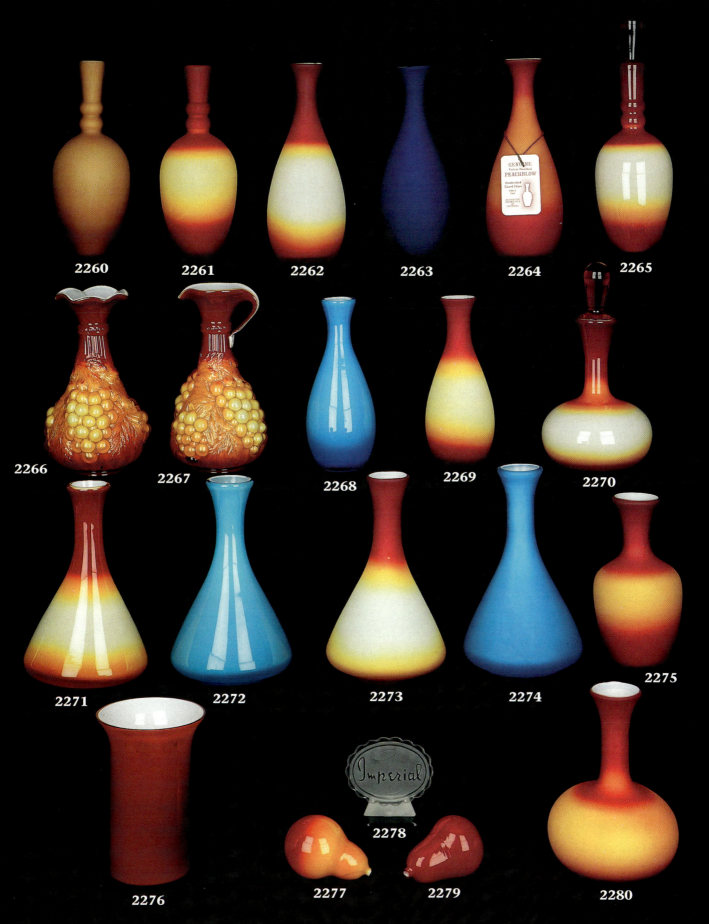

677

Pearl Venitian

Pearl Venitian Imperial Art Glass Assortment No 57

- x609/2 Jug
- x653/2 Tumbler
- x609/2 Cream
- x6933/2 Vase
- x609/2 Sugar
- x615/2 Pickle
- x602/2 Set
- x609/2 Olive
- x6154/2 B Berry
- x6674/2 P Bonbon
- x646/2 D Plate
- x646/2 B Salad
- x6157/2 B Berry
- x6935/2 Vase
- x648/2 F Bowl

Pink Satin and Pink Carnival

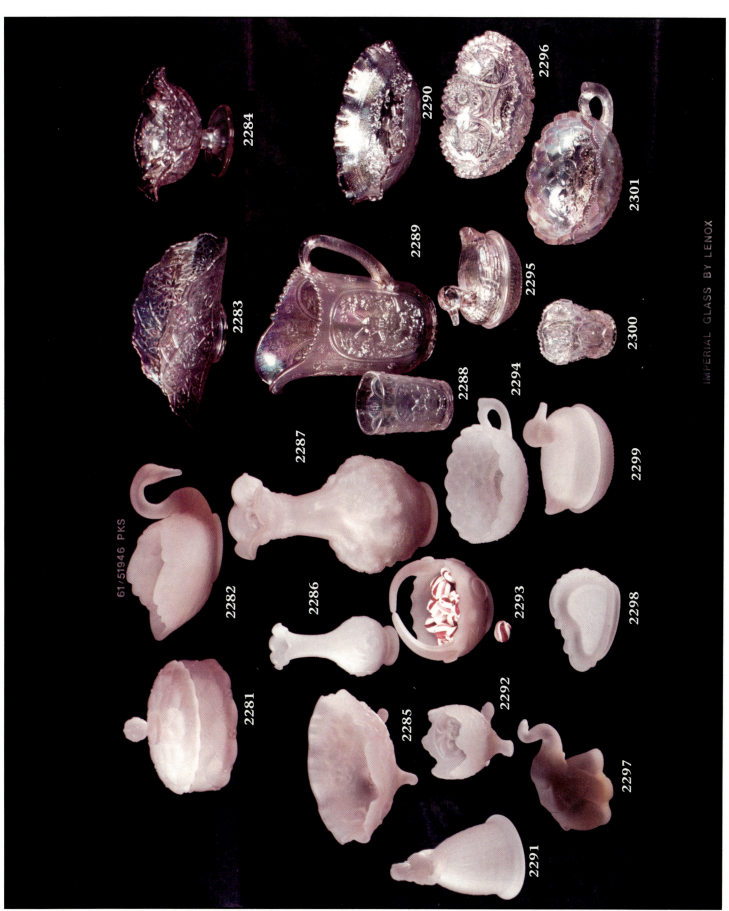

Pink Satin

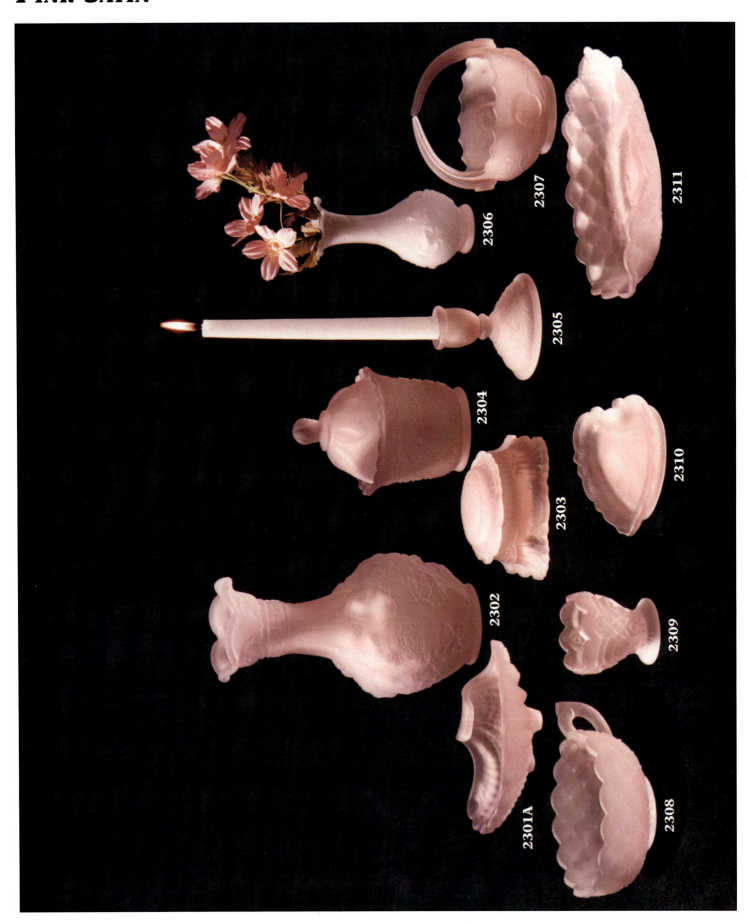

Pink Satin, Blue Satin and Satin Crystal

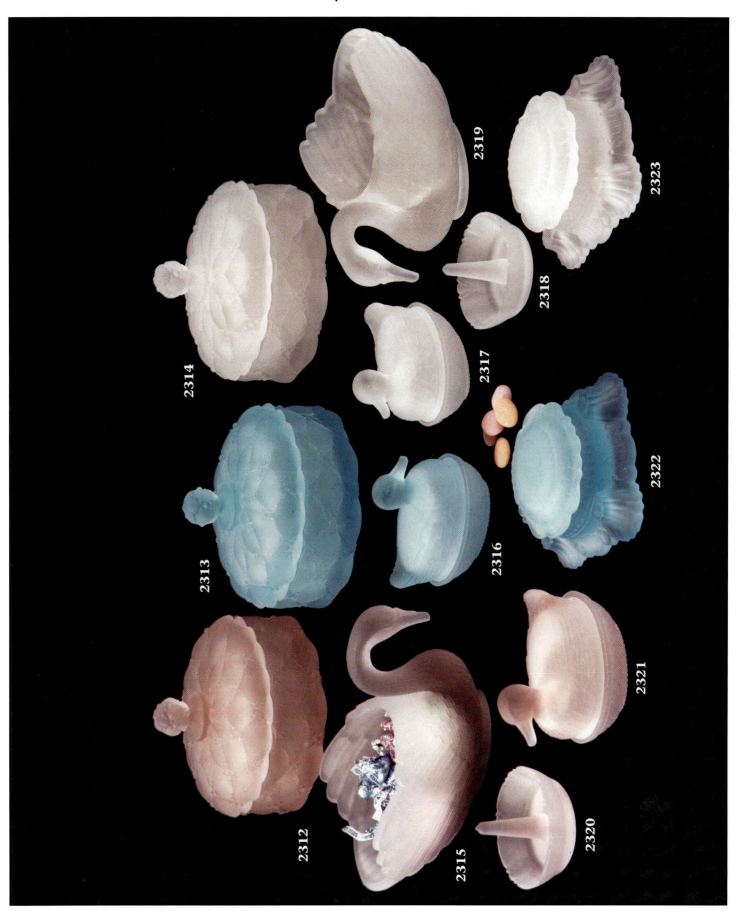

PLUM

683

PROVINCIAL, NO. 1506

Provincial, No. 1506

Purple Slag

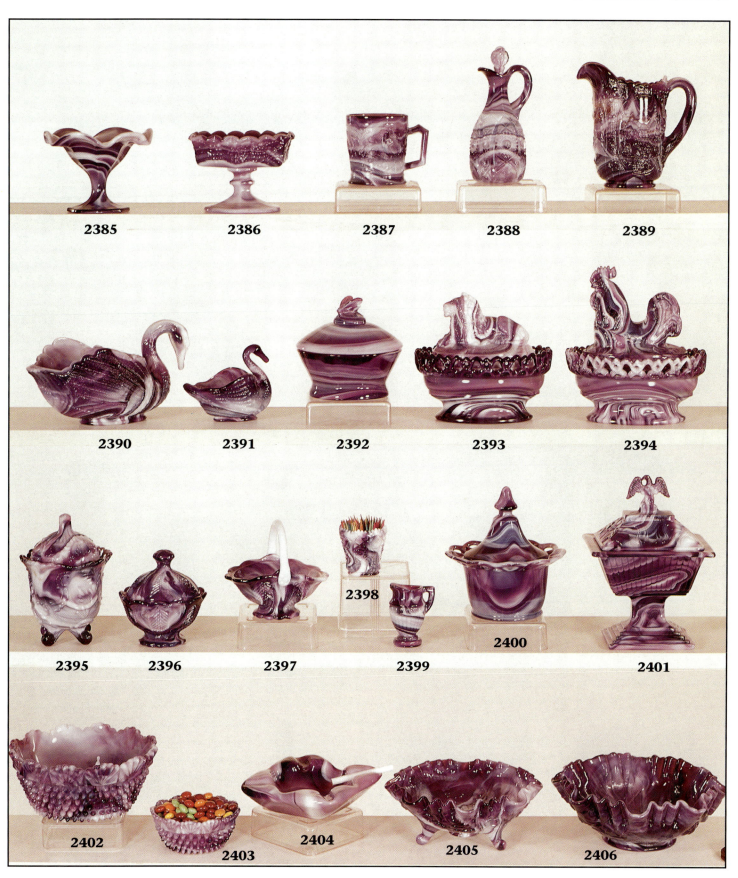

687

Purple Slag

Reeded, No. 701

Reeded, No. 701

REEDED, No. 701

Imperial

WHIRLSPOOL

Every room has a *Whirlspool* Spot....

BATH and NURSERY
Powder — Crystals — Soap
Cotton Puffs
Trinket Jar — Decoration

#704—7" Tall x 4¼" Wide—Retail $2.25*

ORDER 4 PC. SET
#7025 MUSTARD

KITCHEN
Tidbit Jar — Vase
All-purpose Cannisters
Cookie Jar

LIVING ROOMS
Candy, Nut, Snack Server:
Vase — Whatnot
Decoration — Humidor

#703—6" Tall x 4¼" Wide—Retail $2.00*

ORDER 4 PC. SET
#7025 TURQUOISE

JARS

691

Rose Pink

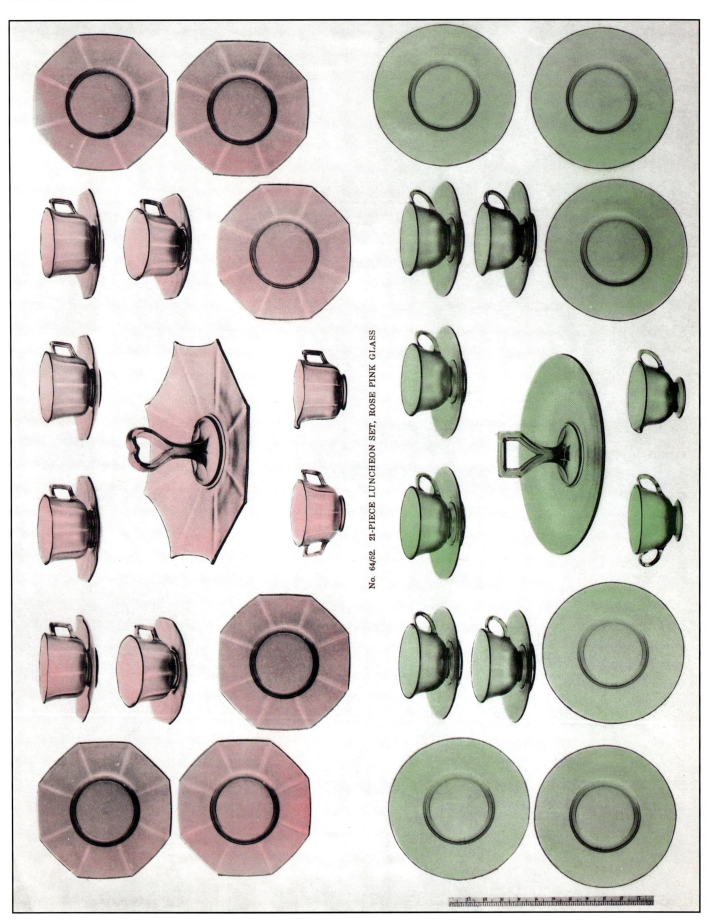

No. 64/52. 21-PIECE LUNCHEON SET, ROSE PINK GLASS

RUBY

2468　　2469　　2470　　2471

2472　　2473　　2474

2475　　2476　　2477　　2478　　2479

2480　　2481　　2482　　2483　　2484　　2485

Ruby Slag

Ruby Slag

695

Ruby Slag

696

Ruby Slag

2530 2531 2532 2533

2534 2535 2536 2537

2538 2539 2540 2541

2542 2543 2544 2545 2546 2547 2548

697

S. A. R. Bottles, Etc.

Skanda, No. 531 and Dawn, No. 3300

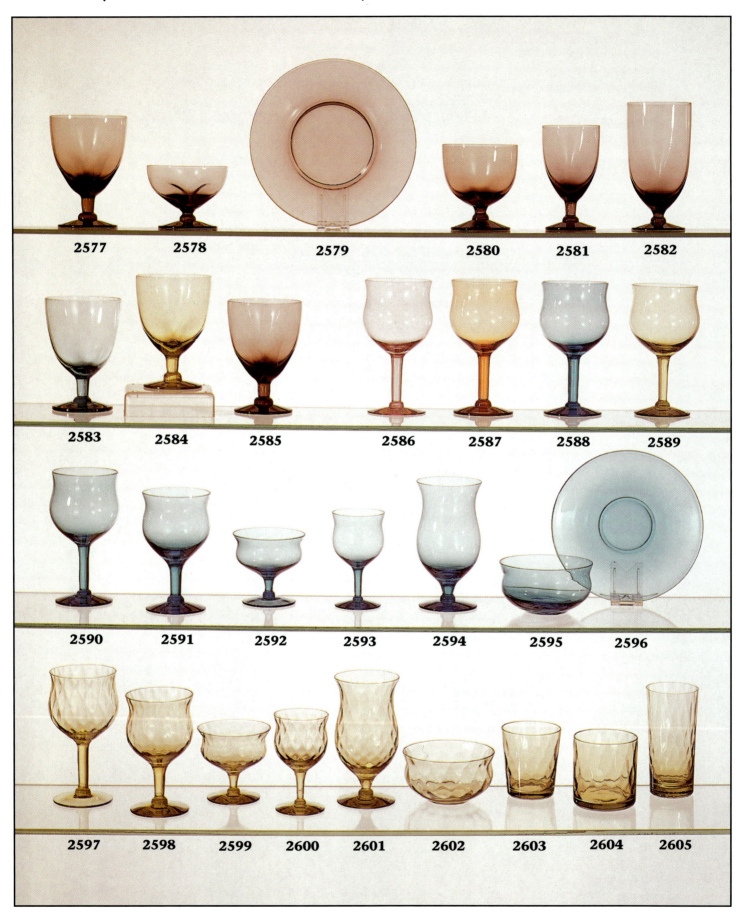

SLAG

701

South Jersey Assortment

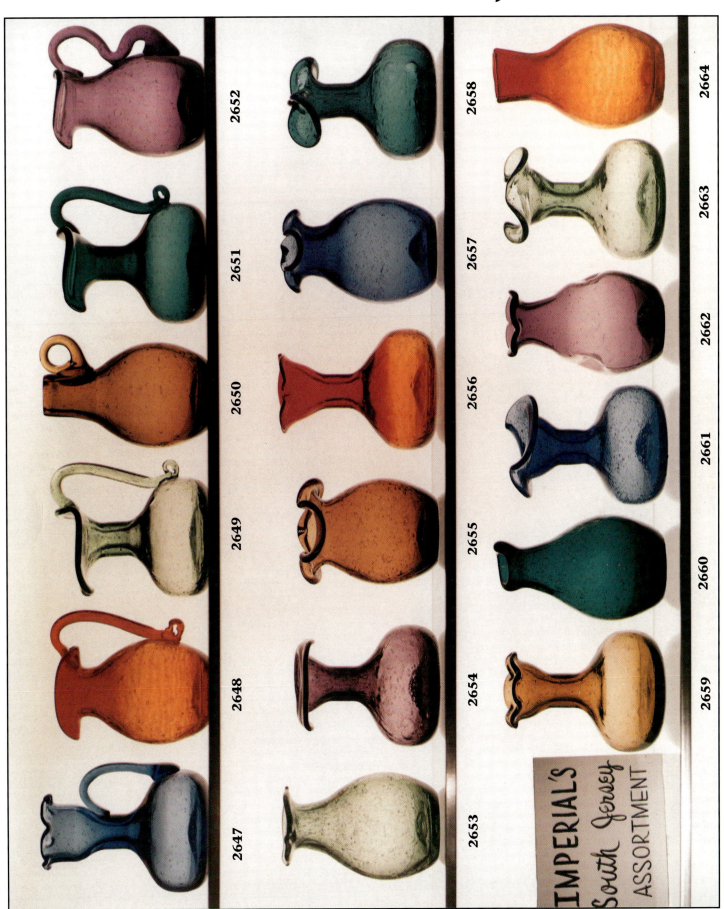

703

Stamm House Dewdrop Opalescent

2665

2666

2667

2668

2669

2670　2671

2672

Star and File & Tulip and Cane

2673   2674   2675   2676   2677   2678

2679   2680   2681   2682   2683

2684   2685   2686   2687   2688

2689   2690   2691   2692   2693   2694   2695   2696   2697

705

Sunburst Carnival

Sunburst Carnival

707

SWEET SERVERS

Tumblers and Toothpicks

710

TRADITION, No. 165

Tumblers

TUMBLERS

2803　2804　2805　2806　2807　2808　2809　2810　2811　2812　2813

2814　2815　2816　2817　2818　2819　2820　2821　2822　2823　2824　2825

2826　2827　2828　2829　2830　2831　2832　2833　2834

2835　2836　2837　2838　2839　2840　2841　2842

713

Turn O'Century and Vinelf

2843 2844 2845 2846
2847 2848 2849 2850

2851 2852 2853 2854 2855 2856

Ultra Blue

715

Vases

717

VASES

718

VASES

719

Velvet Pie Crust, etc.

VERDE

721

Verde Vintage Grape

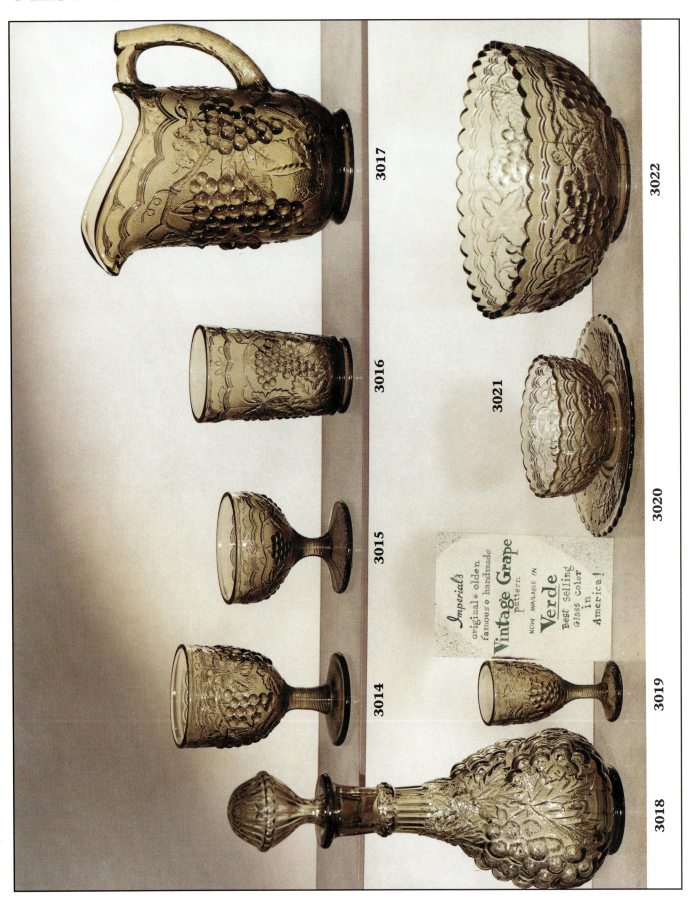

722

Vintage Ruby and Ruamber

3039 3040 3041 3042 3043
3044 3045 3046 3047
3048 3049 3050

3051 3052 3053

724

WASHINGTON, No. 699

3055

3054

WASHINGTON, No. 699

WASHINGTON, No. 699

MISCELLANEOUS

Miscellaneous

| 3140 | 3141 | 3142 | 3143 | 3144 | 3145 |

| 3146 | 3147 | 3148 | 3149 |

| 3150 | 3151 | 3152 | 3153 | 3154 |

| 3155 | 3156 | 3157 | 3158 | 3157 |

Milk Glass

Milk Glass items with the doeskin satin finish were sometimes combined with mat finish wrought iron frames to create interesting articles.
A. Five-pc. condiment set (wire frame, 1950/247 Grape salt/pepper set, and two 1950/241 Grape oil or vinegar bottles with stoppers).
B. W-1 Wall Lamp Ivy (1950/152 vase).
C. W-2 Lamp Stand Ivy (1950/182 vase).
D. Buffet Trio (two 1950/69 bowls and a 1950/259 covered bowl).
E. Twin Jar Server, Cape Cod (two 1950/94 covered jars).

Milk Glass

A. Rooster (Heisey mould).
B. Rabbit (Heisey mould).
C. 1950/158 covered Rooster.
D. 1950/149 Turkey.
E. 1950/149 Turkey.
F. 1950/147 Swan.
G. 1950/147 Swan.
H. 1950/800 Owl Jar.
I. 1950/146 Duck on Nest.
J. 1950/148 Swan on Nest.

K. 1950/459 Rooster Egg Cup.
L. Hen (Heisey mould).
M. Scotty (Heisey mould).
N. 1950/162 Bunny on Nest.
O. Chicks, head down (Heisey mould).
P. Bunny (Heisey mould).
Q. Rabbit Paper Weight (Heisey mould).
R. Bunny (Heisey mould).
S. Chicks, head up (Heisey mould).

MILK GLASS

A. 1950/356 10" Loganberry 10" vase.
B. 11/4732L vase.
C. 1950/486 Masque vase.
D. 1950/112 Jonquil 6" vase.
E. 1950/186 Banjo vase.
F. 1950/185 gold-flecked Fiddle vase.
G. 1950/699C Monticello 6 1/2" vase.
H. 1950/21 Grape vase.
I. 1950/111 Mum vase.
J. 11/538 footed bud vase.
K. 11/330 Diamond Block 6" vase.
L. 1950/612 Whisk Broom footed vase.
M. 1950/109 Loganberry vase.
N. 1950/109 Loganberry vase.
O. 1950/613 Whisk Broom bud vase.
P. 1950/457 5" vase.
Q. 1950/22 5 1/2" vase.
R. 1950/188 Hobnail 6 1/2" footed Ivy Ball.

Milk Glass

Milk Glass

Milk Glass

Milk Glass

Milk Glass

Milk Glass

Milk Glass

Milk Glass

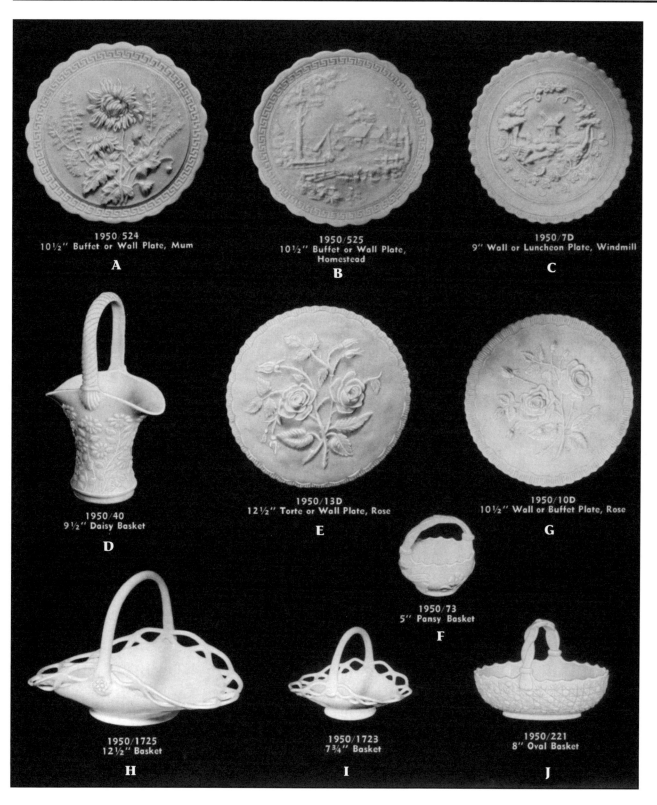

A. 1950/524 10½" Buffet or Wall Plate, Mum
B. 1950/525 10½" Buffet or Wall Plate, Homestead
C. 1950/7D 9" Wall or Luncheon Plate, Windmill
D. 1950/40 9½" Daisy Basket
E. 1950/13D 12½" Torte or Wall Plate, Rose
F. 1950/73 5" Pansy Basket
G. 1950/10D 10½" Wall or Buffet Plate, Rose
H. 1950/1725 12½" Basket
I. 1950/1723 7¾" Basket
J. 1950/221 8" Oval Basket

Milk Glass

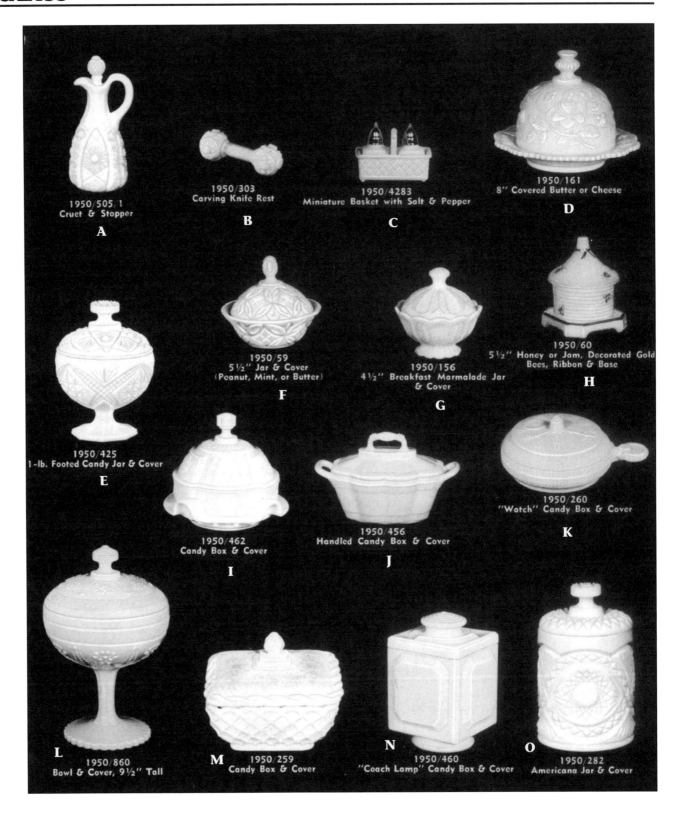

MILK GLASS

Milk Glass

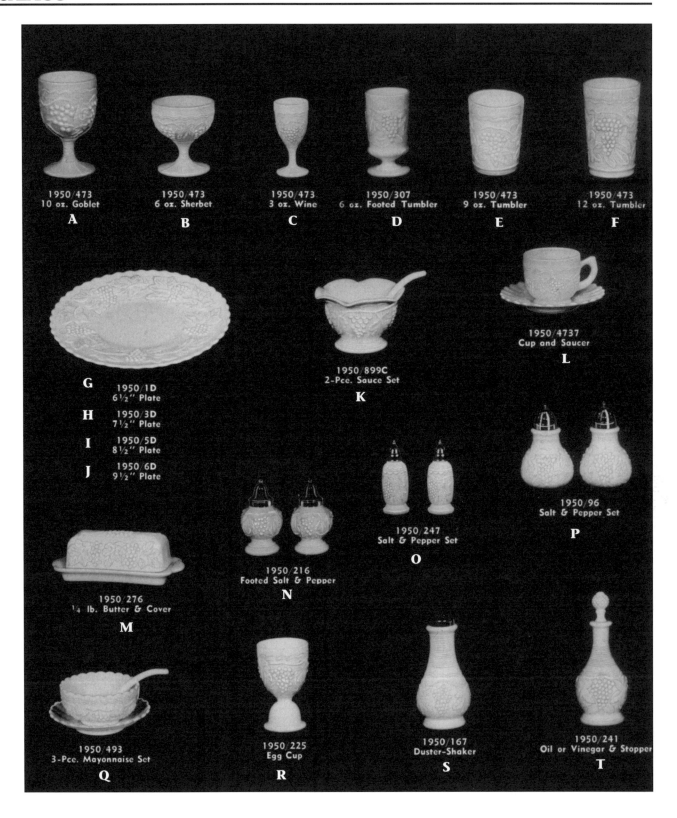

Milk Glass

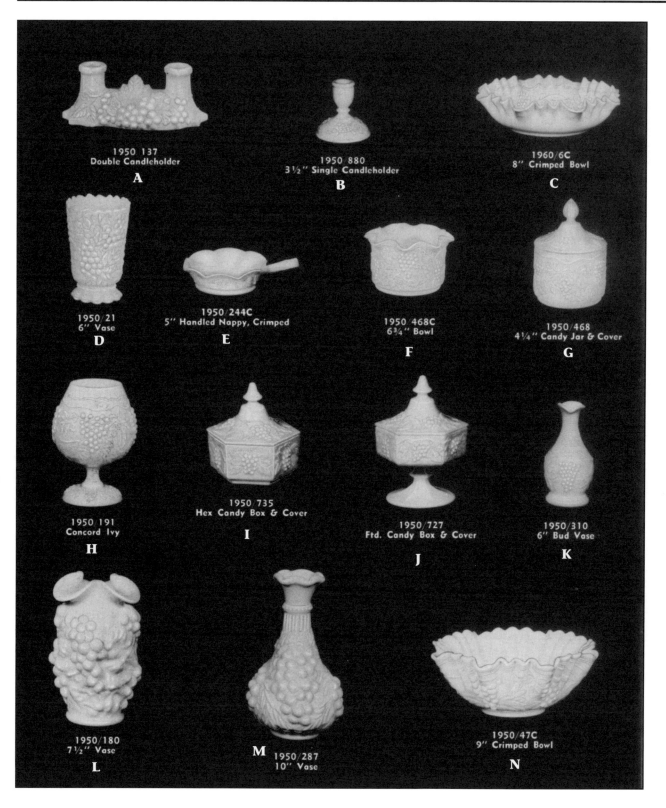

A. 1950/137 Double Candleholder
B. 1950/880 3½" Single Candleholder
C. 1960/6C 8" Crimped Bowl
D. 1950/21 6" Vase
E. 1950/244C 5" Handled Nappy, Crimped
F. 1950/468C 6¾" Bowl
G. 1950/468 4¼" Candy Jar & Cover
H. 1950/191 Concord Ivy
I. 1950/735 Hex Candy Box & Cover
J. 1950/727 Ftd. Candy Box & Cover
K. 1950/310 6" Bud Vase
L. 1950/180 7½" Vase
M. 1950/287 10" Vase
N. 1950/47C 9" Crimped Bowl

Milk Glass

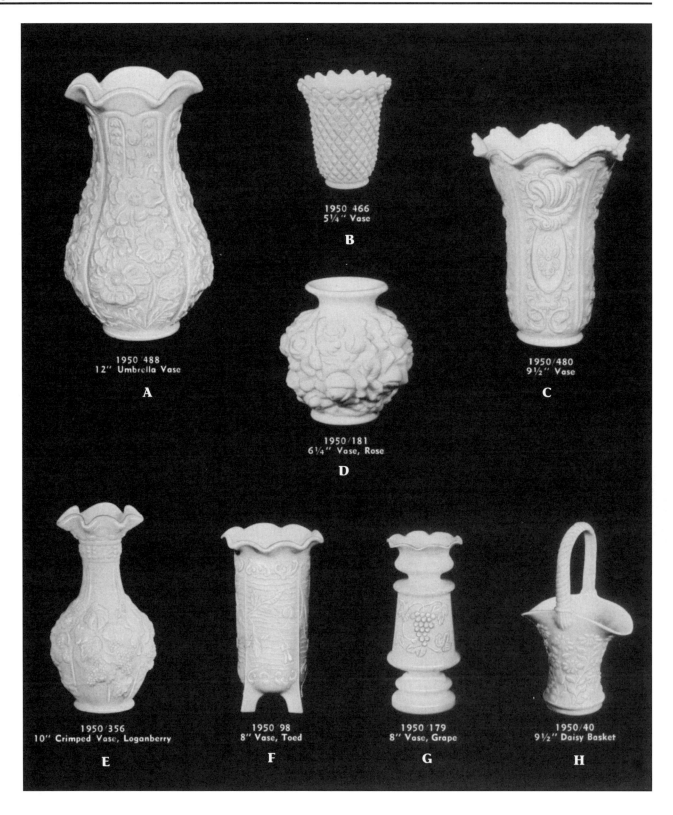

INDEX

Pages 1-226 are in volume 1; pages 227-494 are in Volume 2; pages 495-762 are in this book.

Acanthus 34 *illustrated* 34
acid-etched glass 1 *illustrated* 1, 147
Adobe Wall 34 *illustrated* 34
Advertising paperweights 34 *illustrated* 651
advertising signs 34 *illustrated* 651
ale glasses 34 *illustrated* 34
Allard cutting 35 *illustrated* 35
Aloha tumbler 35 *illustrated* 35
All-American Glass Festival paperweight *illustrated* 651
Allways tumblers 2 *illustrated* 2-3
Amber 36 *illustrated* 148-149
Amber Carnival glass 36 *illustrated* 150-151
Amberglo *illustrated* 174
Amberina tumblers 36
Amelia 4 *illustrated* 4-5, 152
America Always 6 *illustrated* 6
America the Beautiful Series *illustrated* 429
American Beauty Rose 7 *illustrated* 7-8, 153
American Way 36
Americana beverage ware 9 *illustrated* 9
Americana bottles 10 *illustrated* 10-11, 154
Americana decanters (see Americana bottles)
Americana Folk Vases 36 *illustrated* 155
Americana jars 36 *illustrated* 37, 149, 187
Americana lamps 12 *illustrated* 12-13
Americana Waffle 37 *illustrated* 37, 156
Amethyst 38
Amethyst Carnival glass 14, 38 *illustrated* 157
Anemone cutting 38, *illustrated* 38
Angry Cockerel (see Fighting Rooster)
Animal covered dishes 14, *illustrated* 14, 159
Animal decorated tumblers 15-17 *illustrated* 15-17
Animal figurines 18-20 *illustrated* 19, 160-166
Anniversary compote 21 *illustrated* 21
Anniversary cutting 38
Anniversary goblets 22, *illustrated* 22
Antique Blue 10-11, 21, 65, *illustrated* 188-189
Antique Buttons 23-24, *illustrated* 23-24
Apple Blossom 39
Aquamarine 39
Arcs 39, *illustrated* 39
Art Glass 25-27 *illustrated* 27, 169-172
ashtrays 28-30 *illustrated* 28-30, 63, 173-174, 196
Asiatic Pheasant 18 *illustrated* 19, 160
Aspen Green 40 *illustrated* 438, 660
Aster cutting 40 *illustrated* 40
Athele 40 *illustrated* 40
Athens 41
Atterbury 41-42
Atterbury animal covered dishes 41, *illustrated* 41, 158
Atterbury bowls 41 *illustrated* 175
Atterbury candleholders 41 *illustrated* 176
Atterbury footed bowls 42 *illustrated* 176
Atterbury Scroll 24, 42 *illustrated* 42
Aurora Jewels 31, *illustrated* 31, 177-178, 710, 723
Autograph Crystal Sales 32
Autumn Amber 21

Azalea 43
Aztec 43, *illustrated* 43
Azur 7, 33, 65, *illustrated* 33
Azure Blue Carnival 43, 65, *illustrated* 179, 188, 416

Baker's cakestands 44 *illustrated* 44
Bamboo decoration *illustrated* 578
Bambu 45-47 *illustrated* 45-47, 148, 716
banded ware 72 *illustrated* 72
Banjo vase (see Americana Folk Vases)
Barber Pole 72 *illustrated* 180
Barnyard tumblers 48 *illustrated* 48
Basket decoration 72
baskets 72 *illustrated* 73, 181
bathroom glassware 72
Bead Green 74
Beaded Acanthus 74 *illustrated* 74
Beaded Block/Frosted Block 49-51, 270
  illustrated 49-51, 182-183, 187
Beaded Bull's Eye 74 *illustrated* 74
Bear (see Little Pals)
bedroom glassware 75 *illustrated* 75
beer mugs 76 *illustrated* 76
Bel-Aire etching 52 *illustrated* 52
Belknap collection 76
Bellaire Key 76
Bellaire No. 505 53 *illustrated* 53, 710
Bellaire souvenir 76
bells 76 *illustrated* 180
Belmont Crystal 54 *illustrated* 54
Belmont Hills cutting 55 *illustrated* 55
Bennett, Harold 20
Bicentennial Coin Plate 77 *illustrated* 77
Big Cooler 77 *illustrated* 77
Big Shots 56 *illustrated* 56, 184, 710
Bird Feeder 57 *illustrated* 57
Bird No. 670 78 *illustrated* 78
Birthday Cake Plate 78
Bittersweet, Spangled 58 *illustrated* 187
Black Cosmos decorated assortment
  illustrated 195
black glass 28, 59, *illustrated* 30, 59, 185-186
black glass/crystal glass 78
black glass/milk glass 78
black glass with gold decoration 60,
  illustrated 60, 186
Black Pearl 45-46 *illustrated* 148
Black Suede 1, 61-64 *illustrated* 61-64, 186, 195
Blossom 79 *illustrated* 79, 171
Blossoms and Band 79
blown covered jars 79 *illustrated* 187
Blue 65
Blue Coil tumbler *illustrated* 713
Blue Glow 65
Blue Haze 65
Blue Ice 65
Blue Mist 10
Blue Optics 65
Blue Ridge Mountain Banjo vase

747

(see Americana Folk Vases)
Blue Satin 1, 14 *illustrated* 188, 681
Blue Slag 65 *illustrated* 188, 701
Bolt tumbler 79 *illustrated* 79
Booze Pot 66 *illustrated* 66
Bottle Collection 67
bottles, bar 80 *illustrated* 80
bottles, bitter 80 *illustrated* 80
bottles, ketchup 81 *illustrated* 81
bottles, water 81 *illustrated* 81
bottles, wine 82 *illustrated* 82
Boutique Lamp, No. 216 *illustrated* 13
bouquet holders 68 *illustrated* 68
Bowling Set 82 *illustrated* 186
Boxed Sunburst (see Amelia)
brandy glasses 82 *illustrated* 82
Bridal Wreath cut *illustrated* 287
Bridesmaid bowl (see Atterbury Scroll)
Bridge/Poker Set [ashtrays] *illustrated* 30
Broken Arches 83 *illustrated* 83
Broken Column 83 *illustrated* 83
Brown, Nut 14 *illustrated* 190
Brown-eyed Susan decoration 84 *illustrated* 200, 577
Bud Bottles 84 *illustrated* 84, 189
Bull 18 *illustrated* 160-161, 165
Bulldog 18 *illustrated* 19, 166
Bundling Lamp, No. 9 12-13, 84 *illustrated* 13
Bunny *illustrated* 166
Bunny-on-nest (see Rabbit, No. 162)
Burgundy 69-70 *illustrated* 69-70
Burnt Almond 50, 84
Burnt Orange 58, 71
Butterfly cutting 85 *illustrated* 85
Butterpat Sweets Server 85 *illustrated* 191, 658
Buzz Star cutting 85

Cabochon 86 *illustrated* 86
cakestands 87 *illustrated* 181
Calendar tumblers 88 *illustrated* 88
Cambridge Arms 89 *illustrated* 89
Cambridge by Imperial animals
  (see Animal figurines)
Cambridge Canoe ashtray (see No. 739 ashtray)
Cambridge Caprice 90, 288 *illustrated* 90-91
Cambridge Cascade ashtrays
  (see No. 214 ashtrays)
Cambridge moulds 31, 92 *illustrated* 652, 657
Cambridge Square 94 *illustrated* 94, 192
candelabra 95 *illustrated* 95-96
candlesticks 97 *illustrated* 97
candleholders 97
Candlewick 98-142 *illustrated* 98, 100-142, 193-209
Candlewick, cut 110-116 *illustrated* 110-115
Candlewick, etched 116, 118 *illustrated* 112-115, 117, 199, 201, 208, 463
Candlewick, gold decorated 463
Candlewick, hand-painted 118 *illustrated* 200

candy boxes 143 *illustrated* 143-144
Cane (aka Huckabee) 145 *illustrated* 145-146, 210
Cape Cod 227-253 *illustrated* 227, 229-253, 399-404, 657, 731
Cape Cod blown stemware 236 *illustrated* 240
Caramel Slag 14, 254 *illustrated* 254, 405-410, 701-702
Carnival glass (new) 255-256 *illustrated* 255, 416-429
Carnival glass (old) 364-367 *illustrated* 411-415
Casa Tile tumblers 288, 713
Cascade cutting 93 *illustrated* 93
Cased bowls 288
Cased glass vases 257 *illustrated* 257
Casino 288 *illustrated* 288
Casual Crystal 258 *illustrated* 258
Catawba Grape etching *illustrated* 208
Cathay 20, 259-262 *illustrated* 260-261, 430-432
Caveman Carvings tumblers 288 *illustrated* 288
celery vases 289
Celestial cut *illustrated* 287
cemetary vases 289 *illustrated* 289
Champagne color 10, 289
champagnes 289 *illustrated* 289
change tray 289
Charcoal color 289
Charcoal Brown color 290
Chartruese *illustrated* 189
Chatelaine 290 *illustrated* 290
Chesterfield 290 (see Colonial Crystal)
Chick 19 *illustrated* 19
Chicken, No. 145 14 *illustrated* 14, 159
China Rose cutting 290 *illustrated* 290
Christmas ornaments 290-291 *illustrated* 291
Christmas plates 263 *illustrated* 433
Christmas Season tumblers 291-292 *illustrated* 291, 712
Chroma, No. 123 69, 264 *illustrated* 264, 404, 434, 438, 698
Chrysanthemum 292 *illustrated* 292
Circus or Zoo line
  (see Animal decorated tumblers)
clarets 293 *illustrated* 292
Clover Pink 293
Clydesdale 19 *illustrated* 160, 163
Coach Lamp Jars 265 *illustrated* 265
Coarse Rib, No. 407 293
cobalt blue *illustrated* 188
Cobblestones 293 *illustrated* 293
cocktails 293 *illustrated* 293
Coffin Nail cigarette set 293
Collector's Coin plate 293
Collectors Crystal 4, 53, 266-268 *illustrated* 266-268
Collectors Cupboard 269 *illustrated* 269
Collectors Fruit 51, 270 *illustrated* 270
cologne bottles *illustrated* 189
Colonial 294
Colonial Bells 294 (see bells)
Colonial Bottles 271 *illustrated* 271

Pages 1-226 are in volume 1; pages 227-494 are in Volume 2; pages 495-762 are in this book.

Colonial Cabin tumblers 294 *illustrated*
Colonial Crystal, No. 600 272 *illustrated* 272
Colonial Eagles 6
Colonial Lady 294 *illustrated* 294
Colonial Tile tumblers 294
Colonial and Grapes, No. 700 273 *illustrated* 273
Colt (balking, kicking or standing)
  illustrated 161, 163, 657
Columbia 294 *illustrated* 294
Concord, No. 995 274 *illustrated* 274, 404, 435
Cone and Tie 294 *illustrated* 295
Conrad Birds 275 *illustrated* 275
console sets 276 *illustrated* 276-280, 436-437
Continental, No. 176 281 *illustrated* 281
continuous tank glassware 295
Corinthian, No. 280 282 *illustrated* 282-283
Convivial, No. 1680 295 *illustrated* 295
cordials 296 *illustrated* 295
Corn bottle 296
Coronet, No. 123 296 (see Chroma)
Cow Brand tumbler 296 *illustrated* 296
Crabclaw 296 *illustrated* 297
Crackle 296
Crackled, No. 841 284 *illustrated* 284
Cranberry *illustrated*
cranberry rim decoration *illustrated* 402-403
cranberry stained and cut 297
Crinkled, No. 851 297 *illustrated* 297
Crocheted (see Laced Edge)
Crown Glass Manufacturing Co. 298
Crown jelly mould 298 *illustrated* 298
Crowned Concord (see Concord)
Crystal Coil 285 *illustrated* 285
Crystal Coins 298 *illustrated* 299
Crystal, Fired on Gold 298 *illustrated* 444
Crystal Intaglio 298 (see Intaglio)
Crystal Satin 1, 14
Crystal Shell 299 *illustrated* 299
  (see Corinthian, No. 280)
Crystal Vase Collection 300
Crystal with fired cranberry decoration 300
  illustrated 439
Crucifix, No. 119 300 *illustrated*
cup plates 301 *illustrated* 300
Curlique Crystal 90-91, 301
  (see Cambridge Caprice)
Curved Star 301 *illustrated* 301
Custard, Midwest *illustrated* 438
cut decoration 9 *illustrated* 9
cut glass, imitation (see imitation cut glass)
cut glassware 286-287, 298 *illustrated* 286-287
Cygnet *illustrated* 162

Dad's Cookie Jar 306 *illustrated* 306
Dalmally Thistle etching *illustrated* 208
Daisy 306 *illustrated* 306
Daisy basket 306 *illustrated* 306
Daisy and Button basket 307 *illustrated* 404
Dandelion cutting 307 *illustrated* 307

D'Angelo 307 (see Part Cut)
DAR Bottle Collection 67 *illustrated* 189
Dawn, No. 3300 307 *illustrated* 700
decorated cranberry 307-308 *illustrated* 402-403
decorated tumblers 308
Denim Blue 308 (see Leaf)
Denise cut *illustrated* 287
Dewey 308
Dewdrop Opalescent 302 *illustrated* 302, 440-441,
  704
Diamond Block 308
Diamond Lace 308 *illustrated* 308
Diamond Quilted 308
Diamond Ring 309 *illustrated* 309
Diamond and Sunburst 309 *illustrated* 309
Dimpled tumblers 309 *illustrated* 309
  (see Big Cooler)
Dixie Dandies tumblers 303 *illustrated* 303
Doe Head bookend 19 *illustrated* 19
doeskin finish 1, 28, 310
Doggies tumblers 310
Dog-Gone tumblers 304 *illustrated* 304
Dolly Madison decoration *illustrated* 660
Donkey (aka Wild Jack) 18
  illustrated 160, 162, 164
Doodler cutting 310 *illustrated* 310
Double Dutch 310 *illustrated* 310
Double Scroll 310 (see console sets)
Draped Lady 20
Dresden Blue 65, 310
dresser sets 305 *illustrated* 305
Driftwood 2
Duck ashtray, No. 537 28 *illustrated* 28, 63
Duck, No. 146 14 *illustrated* 159
Dunce Cap decanters 311
Dusk color *illustrated* 713
Dynasty Jade 311 *illustrated* 311
Dynasty tumblers 311 *illustrated* 311

Eagle (see No. 1776)
Early American Hobnail, Nos. 741-742 312
  illustrated 312-314
egg cups 320 *illustrated* 320
Eisenhower pitcher/tumblers 315 *illustrated* 315
El Tabique de Oro tumblers 320 *illustrated* 320
El Tauro (see Bull)
electric shades 321 *illustrated* 321
Elephant (aka Eminent Elephant) 18
  illustrated 19, 161-163
Elizabeth II cut *illustrated* 287
Elysian 316 *illustrated* 316
Eminent Eagle Eagle bookend 18, 20
  illustrated 19, 165
Empire, No. 779 317 *illustrated* 317, 729
End O'Day Ruby Slag (see Ruby Slag)
Esquire 321 (see Doodler)
Essex stemware 321 *illustrated* 322
etched decoration 6 *illustrated* 6
Etched and Gold Candlewick *illustrated* 208

Etched Lustre 321
Etiquette, No. 544 318-319 *illustrated* 318-319
Evergreen 57, 321 *illustrated* 404
Expression 322 *illustrated* 322

Face and Fanny tumblers 331
Fancy Colonial, No. 582 323-324
  illustrated 323-324, 442-443, 729
Fancy Flowers 331 *illustrated* 331
Fashion 331 *illustrated* 331
Federal Column Eagle bookends 20 *illustrated* 19
Federal Eagle (see No. 1776)
Federal Glass Co. 9, 88
Fern Green 14, 332 *illustrated* 445
Fiddle vase 332 *illustrated* 257
Fieldflower 306, 332 (see Daisy)
Fighting Cock tumbler 332 *illustrated* 332
File 325 *illustrated* 325
Filly 19 *illustrated* 19, 160-162, 164
Fired Gold on Crystal 332
Fired Gold on Green 332
Fish ashtray, No. 531 *illustrated* 63
Fish Bookend 162 *illustrated* 165
Fish Ornaments, No. 12 20, 332
  illustrated 167-168
Flag decorations 332-333
Flame, No. 680 326 *illustrated* 326-327
Flare, No. 670 326 *illustrated* 326-327
Flask Brown 10, 333 *illustrated* 148, 445
Flat Diamond 333 (see Diamond Quilted)
Flat Iron 333
Fleur De Lis tumblers 333-334 *illustrated* 333
Floral and Optic 333 *illustrated* 333
Flower Fair 334 *illustrated* 445
Flower Flasks 84 *illustrated* 84, 189
Flower Pot, No. 692 (see Allways tumblers)
Flute 334 *illustrated* 334
Flute and Cane 334 *illustrated* 334 (see Cane)
Flying Mare *illustrated* 161-162
Forget-Me-Not Blue 65 *illustrated* 674
Forest 2, 10
Forester vases 334
Four-Seventy-Four 335 *illustrated* 335
Free Hand 27, 328-330 *illustrated* 172, 328-329,
  446-462
Freefold 335 *illustrated* 335
Frieze tumblers 335
Frog (see Little Pals)
Frosted Block/Beaded Block 49-51, 335
  illustrated 49-51, 182-183
frosted sueded finish (see sueded finish)
Fu Wedding Vase 32 *illustrated* 32
Futura, No. 692 (see Allways tumblers)

Gaffer bowls/vases 336 *illustrated* 336
Gaffer Gaines vases 337 *illustrated* 337, 438
Galloping Dominoes tumbler 346
Garden Arbor etching 338 *illustrated* 338
gas globes and shades 339 *illustrated* 339

Gas Light Era tumblers 340 *illustrated* 340
Georgian, No. 451 341 *illustrated* 341
Giraffe figurine 19 *illustrated* 19, 162, 165
Giraffe tumbler 346 *illustrated* 346
Goboons vases 346 *illustrated* 463
gold band decoration *illustrated* 536
gold decorated glassware 346 *illustrated* 463
Golden Green color 342 *illustrated* 342
Golden Harvest decoration *illustrated* 578
Golden Shoji 343 *illustrated* 343, 713, 729
Golden Smoke 10
Golden Spiral tumblers 347 *illustrated* 347
Golden Tackhead 347 *illustrated* 347
Golden Tile tumblers (see Tile tumblers)
Goose Duo 18 *illustrated* 19
Gothic Arches 348 *illustrated* 348
Grape, No. 473 344 *illustrated* 344
Granada, No. 136 348 *illustrated* 348
Grecian Key decoration 349 *illustrated* 349
Grecian Key, No. 200 345 *illustrated* 345
Greek Key cutting 349 *illustrated* 349, 573
Guinevere cutting 350 *illustrated* 350
Gypsy Rings tumbler 350 *illustrated* 350

Happiness tumbler 351 *illustrated* 351
Harlequin tumbler 351 *illustrated* 351
Hattie 351 *illustrated* 351
Hawthorne decoration 351 *illustrated* 200, 577
Hazen 352 (see Square)
Heather 2, 10, 69, 352 *illustrated* 404
Heavy Diamond 352
Heavy Grape 352 (see Colonial and Grapes)
Heisey by Imperial animals (see Animal figurines)
Heisey Collectors of America 20
Heisey moulds 31, 352 *illustrated* 657, 731
Heisey Tangerine 58, 71
Heisey Victorian (see Americana Waffle)
Helios 7, 353 *illustrated* 417
Hen 19 *illustrated* 19, 161-162, 166
Hen-on-nest 353 (see also Chicken, No. 145)
Heritage tumblers 353
Heritage Blue 21 (see also Antique Blue)
Herringbone and Beaded Oval 353 *illustrated* 68
Hex box and cover 353
Hexagon and Cane 354 *illustrated* 353
Hobnail 354 *illustrated* 354
Hobnail, No. 615 354 *illustrated* 438
Hobnial, No. 741/742 *illustrated* 729
Hobnail, Early American (see Early American Hobnail)
Hobo tumblers 354-355 *illustrated* 355
Hobstar 36-37, 355 *illustrated* 37
Hobstar and Arches 355 *illustrated* 355
Hobstar and Tassels 355 *illustrated* 366
Hobstar Flower 356
Hoffman House 356 *illustrated* 435, 464, 729
Holiday-Hostess Hospitality Trays 357
  illustrated 357
Holyoke cutting *illustrated* 574

Home/Office Tubs Trio 358 *illustrated* 358
Homestead 358-359 *illustrated* 358
Honey 54
Horizon Blue Carnival glass 359 *illustrated* 652-653
Horse Head bookend *illustrated* 160
Horse Head and Horse Shoe ashtray, No. 540
    illustrated 63
horseradish jar 359 *illustrated* 359
horseshoe bottom jelly tumblers 359
    illustrated 359
Huckabee 359 (see Cane)
Hunter's Mug, No. 464 56 *illustrated* 184

Ice 360 *illustrated* 360, 465
ice creams 368 *illustrated* 368
Ida 368
illuminating goods 368
imitation cut glass 361 *illustrated* 361
Imperial Blue 65
Imperial Jade 369 (see Jade)
Imperial Jewels 369 (see Art Glass)
Imperial Jewels Candle Holders 369
Imperial logos *illustrated* 651, 677
Imperial paperweight 369, 651 (see Change tray)
Imperial Ruby 369 *illustrated* 466
Imperial signs *illustrated* 651
Imperial's basket 368 *illustrated* 368
Inca Tile tumblers (see Tile tumblers)
Incan tumblers 369 (see Aztec)
ink stands 369 *illustrated* 369
Interior Rib 369
Intaglio 362-363 *illustrated* 362-363
Intune, No. 688 (see Allways tumblers)
Ipswich, No. 1405 369 (see Heisey moulds)
iridescent ware 364-367 *illustrated* 411-415
Ivory Satin 1, 14, 369 *illustrated* 674

Jack Daniels bottle 80 *illustrated* 189
Jade 370 *illustrated* 370
Jade Slag 14, 374 *illustrated* 467-468, 701-702, 710
Jamestown Festival items 374
Jar Tower 371 *illustrated* 371
Jefferson, No. 1401 372 *illustrated* 372, 698
jelly tumblers 374 *illustrated* 374
Jewels, Imperial 374 (see Art Glass)
Jonquil 71, 373 *illustrated* 189, 373

Kallaglas, No. 990 46-47, 375 *illustrated* 375
Katy 376 (see Lace Edge)
Keg tumblers 376 *illustrated* 376, 404, 710
Kennedy Coin Plate 376 (see Crystal Coins)
Kilt Green color *illustrated* 713
Kimberley cut *illustrated* 287
Kingfisher *illustrated* 162

Lace Edge 54, 377-380 *illustrated* 377-380,
    469-472
La France stemware 390 *illustrated* 390
Lalique finish 1, 390

Lamode, No. 685 (see Allways tumblers)
lamps 381 *illustrated* 381, 473
Lantern tumbler 390 (see Marine Lights)
Larkspur Blue 65
Laureate cutting *illustrated* 575
Laurel Crown cutting 390 *illustrated* 390
Lead Lustre 27, 382-384 *illustrated* 382-383,
    446-450, 474-478, 719
Leaf 391 *illustrated* 438
Leaf candy box 391 *illustrated* 391
Lemon Frost 1, 14, 391 *illustrated* 438
Lichen Green 391 *illustrated* 717, 723
Lindburgh 391
Linear 385 *illustrated* 385
Lion bookend 20 *illustrated* 164
Little Pals 20 *illustrated* 19
Loganberry 386 *illustrated* 386
Longhorn tumbler 391 *illustrated* 392, 713
Lost Soul tumbler 391 *illustrated* 392
Love Bird etching 392 *illustrated* 392
Lucerne cutting 387 *illustrated* 387
Lunar Dot cutting 388 *illustrated* 388
lustre iridescent 389 *illustrated* 389
Lustre Rose 392 (see American Beauty Rose)

Madeira 57, 507 *illustrated* 698
Magic Swirl 507 *illustrated* 507
Magnolia decoration *illustrated* 578
Mallards (aka Mallards Three) *illustrated* 160,
    162, 166
Mandarin Gold 507 *illustrated* 698
Manhattan cut glass 495 *illustrated* 495
Mardi Gras 507
Marine Lamp tumbler 507 *illustrated* 693, 710, 712
Marmota Sentinel 18 *illustrated* 19, 164
Martha Washington 507-508
match stands 508 *illustrated* 508
mayonnaise sets 496 *illustrated* 496
Maytime decoration (see black glass)
Meadow Green Carnival 14, 508 *illustrated* 418,
654-655
Menagerie set (see Animal decorated tumblers)
Metropolitan Museum of Art 508 *illustrated* 656,
    730
Mexicana tumblers 508
Midas *illustrated* 463, 689
Midnight decoration (see black glass)
Midwest Custard 509 *illustrated* 674
Milk Glass 7, 14, 28, 497-498 *illustrated* 497-501,
585, 658-661, 664, 698, 731-746
Milk Glass, decorated *illustrated* 660-661
Milk Glass and Golden Brass *illustrated* 659
Milk Glass and wrought iron *illustrated* 731
Milk Glass and Golden Brass *illustrated* 659
milk jars 509 *illustrated* 509
miniatures 509
Mint Green Satin 1, 14, 509 *illustrated* 662-663
Minuet Doll *illustrated* 166
Mirror Images 20

Moderna decoration (see black glass)
molasses cans 509 *illustrated* 510
Molly 509
Monticello, No. 698 502-505 *illustrated* 502-505, 664, 723
Moonlight Blue 65
Moonstone Blue 65, 509
Mosaic Tile tumbler 509
Mother Pig (see Sow)
Mother Rabbit *illustrated* 166
Mount Vernon assortment 506 *illustrated* 506
Mount Vernon (see Washington)
Mouse (see Little Pals)
Mulberry color 509 *illustrated* 713
Munsell 510
Murrhina 71, 510 *illustrated* 449, 665, 723
Mustard 510 *illustrated* 473

Nappy Promotion 511 *illustrated* 511
Narcissus decoration 522 *illustrated* 200, 577
Newbound 522
Niagra 512 *illustrated* 512-513
Noel cut glass assortment 514 *illustrated* 514
Normandie decoration 522
Nosy Jay Bird (see Scolding Bird)
Nuart 27, 522 *illustrated* 666, 719
Nuart decorated *illustrated* 667
Nuart shades 522 *illustrated* 666
NUCUT 515 *illustrated* 515-516
Nugreen 7, 522 *illustrated* 404, 443, 717
Nuruby 522
Nut Brown 14, 522 *illustrated* 190

No. 82/S 9 *illustrated* 9
No. 86 vase *illustrated* 718
No. 98 cakestand (see Baker's cakestands)
No. 100 boot *illustrated* 718
No. 132 vase mould *illustrated* 63
No. 176 tumbler 6 *illustrated* 6
No. 188 Hobnail ivy ball *illustrated* 718
No. 214 ashtrays 28 *illustrated* 28
No. 313 517 *illustrated* 517
No. 330 (Diamond Block) *illustrated* 729
No. 414 518 *illustrated* 518-519
No. 489 (see American Beauty Rose)
No. 514 Windmill 1
No. 550 goblet 22 *illustrated* 22
No. 627 decanter 6 *illustrated* 6
No. 666 24 (see Cane)
No. 671 (see Amelia)
No. 719 520 *illustrated* 520
No. 721 521 *illustrated* 521
No. 739 ashtray 28 *illustrated* 28
No. 821 Squirrel candy box 1 *illustrated* 1
No. 850 Giant Goblet 22 *illustrated* 22
No. 1608 ashtray 29 *illustrated* 29
No. 1632 ashtray 28 *illustrated* 28
No. 1748 assortment
  (see Animal decorated tumblers)

Oak Leaf cutting 530 *illustrated* 530
Octagon (see Bellaire No. 505)
Octagon, No. 725 530 *illustrated* 692
Ohio State University Centennial Bottle *illustrated* 189
Old English, No. 166 530 *illustrated* 531 668
Old Gold 530 *illustrated* 413
Old Sturbridge Village 523
Old Williamsburg, No. 341 524 *illustrated* 670-673, 730
Olde Jamestowne 525-526 *illustrated* 525-526, 669
Olde Jamestowne ashtrays *illustrated* 29-30, 173, 526
Olive 54
Olive, No. 134 530-532 *illustrated* 531, 668, 730
On-the-Rocks tumblers 527 *illustrated* 527
Opalescent glass 532
Opaque Blue 65 *illustrated* 188, 674
Opaque, colored 528 *illustrated* 528
Optic Flute 529 *illustrated* 529
Owl (see Little Pals)
Oxford, No. 5024 532 *illustrated* 532

Pacesetter tumblers, No. 855 533 *illustrated* 533
Packard 547
palladium band decoration *illustrated* 536
Pansy, No. 478 547 *illustrated* 547
Parisian Provincial, No. 563 548 *illustrated* 675
Parlour Puppies 18, 534 *illustrated* 18, 534, 661
Part-Cut, No. 678 548 *illustrated* 548
Pastime tumblers 535 *illustrated* 535
Patio tumblers 548
Patriot 6, 548
Peachblow 536 *illustrated* 676-677
Peacock iridescent 548
Pearl Amethyst (see Art Glass)
Pearl Green (see Art Glass)
Pearl Ruby (see Art Glass)
Pearl Silver (see Art Glass)
Pearl Venitian 549 *illustrated* 678
Pearl White (see Art Glass)
Pecan color *illustrated* 713
Persian tumblers, No. 8401 549 *illustrated* 713
Peruvian 549
Petunia (see Bel-aire etching)
Phoenix bowl 20 *illustrated* 19
pickle dishes 549 *illustrated* 549
Pie Crust Bowls 537 *illustrated* 537
Pie Crust, No. 588 538 *illustrated* 538-539
Pigeon 18
Piglet(s) 19 *illustrated* 19, 160-161
Pillar Flute, No. 682 540 *illustrated* 540, 729
Pinch, No. 675 630 *illustrated* 630
Pink Carnival 7, 14, 550 *illustrated* 418, 679
Pink Satin 1, 7, 14, 550 *illustrated* 679-681
Pioneer Glass Co. *illustrated* 727
Pizarro 550
Platinum Tile tumblers 550
Plum 550 *illustrated* 682-683, 718

pokal 550
Pony Stallion and Three Sons 18 (see also Colt)
Posie Bowl, No. 46C 550 *illustrated* 720
Pouter Pigeon 18
Proud Puffer 18
Provincial, No. 56 541 *illustrated* 541
Provincial, No. 1506 542 *illustrated* 542-543, 684-686
punch sets 544-545 *illustrated* 544-545
Pura 550 *illustrated* 666
Purple Slag 14, 546 *illustrated* 410, 546, 687-688, 698, 701-702, 710

Rabbit, No. 162 14 *illustrated* 159, 161, 166
Radcliffe cutting *illustrated* 574
Radiant Star 555 *illustrated* 555
Rainbow iridescent 555
Ranch Life tumbler 555 *illustrated* 404, 713
Rearing Horse bookend 19 *illustrated* 160
Red Glow 556 *illustrated* 729
Reeded, No. 701 551-552 *illustrated* 551-552, 689-691
Reflection 556 *illustrated* 556
Regal Ruby *illustrated* 192
Revere 553 *illustrated* 553
Ribbon Bow cutting 556 *illustrated* 557
Ringneck Pheasant 18 *illustrated* 160
Ritz Blue 65, 556 *illustrated* 194
Rockfern cutting *illustrated* 573
Roly Poly 556 *illustrated* 557
Roman Key 9, 554 *illustrated* 554
Rooster 19 *illustrated* 160-161, 166
rose bowls 559 *illustrated* 558
rose deep plate etching 559 *illustrated* 559
Rose Ice 560
Rose Marie/Rose Pink 4, 560 *illustrated* 152, 442, 667, 692
Rose of Sharon etching 116, 118 *illustrated* 201-202, 208
Royal Egret 18, 20
Ruamber color 560 *illustrated* 560, 724
Rubigold 560-561
Rubigold Sueded *illustrated* 147
Ruby *illustrated* 693, 709
Ruby Slag 561 *illustrated* 410, 694-697, 701-702
Rx Medicine tumbler 561

salts/peppers 588 *illustrated* 588
sandblast decoration 9, 588 *illustrated* 9, 589
SAR bottles *illustrated* 698
Satin Crystal 1, 562 *illustrated* 562, 681
Scolding Bird 18, 20 *illustrated* 19
Scottie 18 *illustrated* 19, 162, 165
Scottie Dog bookend 20
Scroll (see Atterbury Scroll)
Sculptured Rose 563 *illustrated* 563
Sculpturesque cased bowls, No. 55 588 *illustrated* 723
Sculpturesque ashtray, No. 58 29 *illustrated* 29

Sea Foam opalescent colors 50, 65
Sea Gull Flower holder, No. 1138 20
Sekai Ichi 590 *illustrated* 590
Semi-Colonial, No. 666 564 *illustrated* 564
servers, brass-handled 590 *illustrated* 720
Shaeffer 590
Shaker Sweets Jar, No. 617 *illustrated* 699
Show Horse 20 *illustrated* 160, 163
Signature tumblers 32 *illustrated* 32
Simplicity, No. 440 590 *illustrated* 590
Sittin' Duck (see Wood Duck)
Skanda, No. 530 565 *illustrated* 700
Skanda, No. 531 (Diamond Optic) 565 *illustrated* 700
Slag 590*illustrated* 701-702 (see Caramel Slag, Jade Slag, Purple Slag, and Ruby Slag)
Small Game Animals (see Animal decorated tumblers)
Smart Alec tumblers 566 *illustrated* 566
Smith-Scherr 2
Smithsonian Institution 567 *illustrated* 567
smoke shades 591 *illustrated* 591
Smoky Chartruese 2
Sortijas de Oro 591 *illustrated* 591
South Jersey assortment 591 *illustrated* 703
Southern Highlands 568 *illustrated* 568
Southern Highlands decoration 592
Sow 20 *illustrated* 160, 162, 166
Spangled Bittersweet 58, 71, 592
Spanish Windows tumbler 592 *illustrated* 592, 713
Sparrow *illustrated* 160, 166
Springerle sweetsdish 569 *illustrated* 569, 658
Spun (see Reeded)
Square, No. 760 570 *illustrated* 570
Stamm House Dewdrop Opalescent 592 *illustrated* 440-441, 704, 718, 730
Star and File *illustrated* 705
Star Holly 571-572 *illustrated* 571-572
Star Medallion (see Amelia)
stemware, cut 573 *illustrated* 573-575
stemware, decorated 576 *illustrated* 576-578
Stiegel bowls 579 *illustrated* 579
Stiegel Green 592 *illustrated*
Stirrup 592 *illustrated* 593
Storybook mugs *illustrated* 429
sueded finish 1
sugar dusters 593 *illustrated* 593
Sunburst Carnival 7, 14, 594 *illustrated* 698, 706-707
Sunburst engraving 594 *illustrated* 594
Sunset Ruby Carnival glass 580 *illustrated* 427, 580, 708
Sunshine Yellow 581 *illustrated* 581, 718
Sunup cutting *illustrated* 573
Svelte, No. 330 582 *illustrated* 582
Swan 18, 20 *illustrated* 19, 161, 166
Swan, No. 149 14
Swan, off-hand blown 19 *illustrated* 19
Swans (No. 1042, 1043 and 1044) 20

Swedish Pinched Crystal, No. 220 583 *illustrated* 583
Sweeney sweetsbowl 584 *illustrated* 584
Sweet Servers *illustrated* 709
swung vases 585 *illustrated* 585-586
Symmetry 587 *illustrated* 587

Tahitian tumblers 604 *illustrated* 604
Terra Cotta decoration 604 *illustrated* 438, 660
Terrace tumblers, No. 855 (see Pacesetter tumblers)
Terrace tumblers, No. 990 595 *illustrated* 595
Terrier, tail up 18 *illustrated* 19
Terrier, tongue out 18 *illustrated* 19
Thistle decoration *illustrated* 578
Tiara 596 *illustrated* 596-597
Tiara cutting 598 *illustrated* 573, 598
Tiger paperweight 20 *illustrated* 19, 160-162, 164
Tile tumblers 604 *illustrated* 713
Toltec tumbler 604 *illustrated* 713
Tom and Jerry set 605
Tomorrow, No. 760 599 *illustrated* 599
toothpick holders *illustrated* 710
Topaz color 605
Toril de Oro tumblers 605 *illustrated* 605
Trader Vic 605
Tradition, No. 165 600 *illustrated* 600, 711
Trellis tumbler *illustrated* 713
Tropical (see Bambu)
Tropical Fish Piece *illustrated* 161
Tropical tumblers, No. 787 605 *illustrated* 605
Tulip decoration 606
Tulip and Cane *illustrated* 705
Turn O' the Century 4, 53 *illustrated* 714
Turquoise 10, 606 *illustrated* 606, 674, 723
Twist, No. 110 601 *illustrated* 601-602
Twisted Optic 603 *illustrated* 603

Ultra Blue 14, 65, 607 *illustrated* 188, 607, 715

Valencia assortment 616
Valencia cutting *illustrated* 575
Valerie cutting *illustrated* 575
Vanessa cutting *illustrated* 575
Variant cutting *illustrated* 575
vases 608 *illustrated* 608-611, 716-719, 733
Vassar cutting *illustrated* 574
Velvet Pie Crust 616 *illustrated* 720
Venus Rising 20
Verde color 2, 10, 21, 616 *illustrated* 721-722
Vert color *illustrated* 713
Victorian candy jars 612 *illustrated* 612
Victorian, No. 123 613 *illustrated* 613

Viennese Blue 65 *illustrated* 188, 194, 730
Vigna Vetro 616 *illustrated* 719, 723
Vincent Price National Treasures 616 *illustrated* 189, 698
Vinelf 616 *illustrated* 714
Vintage Grape *illustrated* 722
Vintage Ruby 614 *illustrated* 614-615, 724
Vintage stemware 616 *illustrated* 617
Voodoo tumbler 617 *illustrated* 617, 712

Washington, No. 699 618-619 *illustrated* 618-621, 725-727, 730
Watch candy box 628
Waverly, No. 1519 622 *illustrated* 622
Wee Scottie tumbler 628 *illustrated* 628, 713
Weiss beers 628 *illustrated* 628
Wellsley cutting *illustrated* 574
Welsbach globes and shades 629 *illustrated* 629
West Point glassware 629
West Virginia Glass Specialty Co. 9
Western Apple decoration 623 *illustrated* 200, 577, 623
Western Rose decoration 623 *illustrated* 200, 577, 623
Western Wild Flower decoration 623
Whirlspool jars 629 *illustrated* 691
Whiskbroom 624 *illustrated* 624-625, 658
White Carnival glass 626 *illustrated* 428, 626, 728
White Flying Geese decoration 629
White Ice 627 *illustrated* 627, 660
Wild Animals (see Animal decorated tumblers)
Wild Jack (see Donkey)
Windmill pattern 629
Wood Duck 18 *illustrated* 19, 160
Wood Duckling *illustrated* 161, 166
Woodbury 629
Woodchuck (see Marmota Sentinel)
Woven tumblers 630 *illustrated* 630
Wright, Russel 630

Yellow Optics 631 *illustrated* 631-632
Yellow Poppy decoration *illustrated* 577
Yesterday tumblers 633 *illustrated* 633
You-Me-Us 634 *illustrated* 634

Zak 638
Zipper Loop lamps 638 *illustrated* 638
Zodiac ashtray, No. 520 *illustrated* 63
Zodiac, No. 1590 635-636 *illustrated* 635-636
Zodiac tumblers, No. 1234 637 *illustrated* 637
Zoo line 638

SPECIAL OFFER ON IMPERIAL GLASS ENCYCLOPEDIA, VOLUMES I AND II

Buy both books to complete the set and receive 20% off the retail price. If you already have these volumes, consider buying the three-volume set for a friend. The discount when buying all three volumes is 25% off retail.

IMPERIAL GLASS ENCYCLOPEDIA VOLUME I, A-CANE

*National Imperial Glass Collectors' Society,
Edited by James Measell*

Imperial Glass produced millions of items, many unattributed by collectors today. Imperial did it all — blowing, pressing, cutting, etching, and more.

The first volume of this series is packed with information on Imperial's history, as well as photos featuring **art glass, animal figurines, covered dishes,** and all topics and patterns whose names begin with A, B, and C (through "Cane," including Candlewick). About 1,000 pieces are shown in color (including ad/catalog reprints), plus hundreds of other items in black and white.

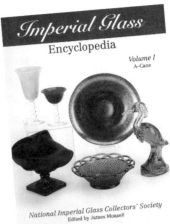

208 pages, 64 in color
8½ x 11 with 1995-96 price guide in book
$34.95 PB, Item #4076
$44.95 HB, Item #4077

IMPERIAL GLASS ENCYCLOPEDIA VOLUME II, CAPE COD - L

*National Imperial Glass Collectors' Society,
Edited by James Measell*

Major topics within this volume's alphabetical range include **Cape Cod** (No. 160), **Caramel Slag, Carnival Glass** (old and new), **Cathay, Free Hand, Ice, Lace Edge, and Lead Lustre.** Other subjects include patterns, colors, shapes, etchings, and limited editions.

Well illustrated throughout, the 80 color pages feature both original photos and outstanding reprints from Imperial catalogs. A comprehensive index lists all subjects covered in both Volume I and II. **Volume II has surprises for the most knowledgeable collectors.**

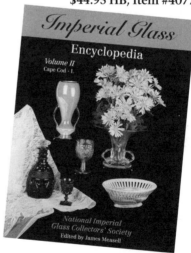

272 pages, 80 in color,
8½ x 11
with 1997-98 price guide in book
$34.95 PB, Item #4125
$44.95 HB, Item #4126

Ordering information: Send payment to **Antique Publications**, PO Box 553, Marietta, OH 45750, or use your credit card to order by phone (800-533-3433 or 740-373-6146). Shipping charges—U.S.A. $4.50 for the first book, $.50 for each add'l book; Canada: actual cost, plus 10% for handling (credit card only); Outside N. America: $9.00 for the first book, $1.00 for each add'l book. U.S. Funds only. Ohio residents add 6.5% sales tax.

Antique Publications
217 Union Street, PO Box 553, Marietta, Ohio 45750
(800) 533-3433, (740) 373-6146, info@antiquepublications.com
Check out our Website at **antiquepublications.com**

IMPERIAL GLASS ENCYCLOPEDIA
Volume III, "M-Z"
NationalImperial Glass Collector's Society, Inc. — Edited by James Measell
Value Guide 1999-2000

This value guide embraces more than 1,200 articles pictured in the color pages of this book, as well as 16 pages of Milk Glass. The price ranges given reflect items in "mint" condition. For some items, no price (NP) is indicated because the item is seldom seen and/or has not changed hands for some time.

Neither the author nor the publishers can be liable for any losses incurred when using this guide as the basis for any transaction.

Color Plates
1921 - NP
1922 - 150-175
1923 - 140-160
1924 - 75-85
1925 - 70-80
1926 - 25-35
1927 - NP
1928 - 20-25
1929 - 600-650
1930 - 250-275
1931 - 80-100
1932 - 30-35
1933 - NP
1934 - 250-275
1935 - 50-55
1936 - 250-300
1937 - 35-40
1938 - 60-70
1939 - 45-50
1940 - 30-35
1941 - 20-25
1942 - 70-80
1943 - 15-20
1944 - 40-45
1945 - 15-20
1946 - 15-20
1947 - 35-40
1948 - 30-35
1949 - 40-45
1950 - 25-30
1951 - 40-45
1952 - 25-30
1953 - 15-20
1954 - 30-35
1955 - 20-25
1956 - 150-175
1957 - 15-20
1958 - 70-80
1959 - 40-45
1960 - 25-30
1961 - 40-45
1962 - 25-30

1963 - 35-40
1964 - 40-45
1965 - 20-25
1966 - 35-40
1967 - 35-40
1968 - 30-35
1969 - 15-20
1970 - 20-25
1971 - 35-40
1972 - 25-30
1973 - 65-75
1974 - 20-25
1975 - 30-35
1976 - 30-35
1977 - 50-60
1978 - 20-25
1979 - 30-35
1980 - 20-25
1981 - 30-35
1982 - 35-40
1983 - 35-40
1984 - 240-260
1985 - 40-45
1986 - 40-45
1987 - NP
1988 - 50-60
1989 - 75-85
1990 - 40-45
1991 - 30-35
1992 - 20-25
1993 - 45-50
1994 - 40-50
1995 - 20-25
1996 - 25-30
1997 - 20-25
1998 - 25-30
1999 - 45-50
2000 - 60-65
2001 - 35-40
2002 - 55-60
2003 - 75-80
2004 - 30-35 pr
2005 - 50-60

2006 - 320-370
2007 - 50-60
2008 - 50-60
2009 - 50-60
2010 - 145-155
2011 - 40-45
2012 - 50-60
2013 - 50-55
2014 - 50-55
2015 - 50-55
2016 - NP
2017 - 100-115
2018 - 20-25
2019 - 50-60
2020 - 30-35
2021 - 25-30
2022 - 60-65
2023 - 25-30
2024 - 25-30
2025 - 40-45
2026 - 40-45
2027 - 40-45
2028 - 40-45
2029 - 40-45
2030 - 40-45
2031 - 18-20
2032 - 18-20
2033 - 30-35
2034 - 25-30
2035 - 30-35
2036 - 8-10
2037 - 80-100
2038 - 30-35
2039 - 15-20
2040 - 60-70
2041 - 55-65
2042 - 12-15
2043 - 20-25
2044 - 40-45
2045 - 85-95
2046 - 85-95
2047 - NP
2048 - 60-70

2049 - 25-30
2050 - 75-80
2051 - NP
2052 - 35-40
2053 - 60-70 pr
2054 - 18-20
2055 - 30-35
2056 - 20-25
2057 - 20-25
2058 - 20-25
2059 - 65-75
2060 - 65-70
2061 - NP
2062 - NP
2063 - NP
2064 - NP
2065 - NP
2066 - NP
2067 - NP
2068 - NP
2069 - NP
2070 - NP
2071 - NP
2072 - NP
2073 - 20-25
2074 - 30-35
2075 - 55-65
2076 - 25-30
2077 - 20-25
2078 - 16-20
2079 - 15-20
2080 - 20-25
2081 - 30-35
2082 - 30-35
2083 - 15-20
2084 - 45-50
2085 - 20-25
2086 - 35-40
2087 - 18-20
2088 - 25-30
2089 - 25-30
2090 - 25-30
2091 - 70-80

Value Guide

2092 - 85-95	2149 - 30-35	2206 - 15-18	2258 - 16-18
2093 - 45-50	2150 - 20-25	2207 - 16-18	2259 - 20-25
2094 - 15-20	2151 - 25-30	2208 - 12-14	2260 - NP
2095 - 85-95	2152 - 20-25	2209 - 18-20	2261 - 175-200
2096 - 40-50	2153 - 15-20	2210 - 18-20	2262 - 150-175
2097 - 65-70	2154 - 25-30	2211 - 9-11	2263 - NP
2098 - 50-60	2155 - 15-20	2212 - 9-11	2264 - 150-175
2099 - 20-25	2156 - 20-25	2213 - 9-11	2265 - 275-300
2100 - 100-110	2157 - 35-40	2214 - 14-16	2266 - NP
2101 - 45-50	2158 - 25-30	2215 - 15-18	2267 - NP
2102 - 40-45	2159 - 20-25	2216 - 15-18	2268 - 80-90
2103 - 30-35	2160 - 20-25	2216A - 16-18	2269 - 140-160
2104 - 35-40	2161 - 25-30	2216B - 18-20	2270 - 275-300
2105 - 40-45	2162 - 25-30	2216C - 16-18	2271 - 150-175
2106 - 16-18	2163 - 20-25	2216D - 18-20	2272 - 90-100
2107 - 16-18	2164 - 25-30	2216E - 20-22	2273 - 140-150
2108 - 25-30	2165 - 13-15	2217 - 45-55	2274 - 90-100
2109 - 32-35	2166 - 9-11	2218 - 35-45	2275 - 125-135
2110 - 35-40	2167 - 9-11	2219 - 75-80	2276 - NP
2111 - 20-25	2168 - 15-18	2220 - 80-85	2277 - NP
2112 - 45-50	2169 - 13-15	2221 - 50-55	2278 - 150-175
2113 - 25-30	2170 - 9-11	2222 - 50-60	2279 - NP
2114 - 100-125	2171 - 13-15	2223 - 60-70	2280 - 140-160
2115 - 225-250	2172 - 11-13	2224 - 35-40	2281 - 40-45
2116 - 250-275	2173 - 9-10	2225 - 35-40	2282 - 45-50
2117 - NP	2174 - 16-18	2226 - 45-50	2283 - 40-45
2118 - 100-120	2175 - 13-15	2227 - 30-35	2284 - 25-30
2119 - 175-195	2176 - 13-15	2228 - 16-20	2285 - 30-35
2120 - 185-210	2177 - 12-15	2229 - 16-20	2286 - 20-25
2121 - 140-160	2178 - 13-15	2230 - 25-30	2287 - 55-65
2122 - 175-195	2179 - 10-12	2231 - 40-45	2288 - 15-20
2123 - 150-170	2180 - 12-15 pr	2232 - 30-35	2289 - 70-80
2124 - 125-140	2181 - 10-12	2233 - 45-55	2290 - 30-35
2125 - NP	2182 - 8-10	2234 - 30-35	2291 - 35-40
2126 - 130-145	2183 - 8-10	2235 - 30-35	2292 - 15-20
2127 - 125-140	2184 - 15-20	2236 - 18-20	2293 - 25-30
2128 - NP	2185 - 30-35	2237 - 12-14	2294 - 20-25
2129 - NP	2186 - 12-15	2238 - 9-10	2295 - 30-35
2130 - NP	2187 - 16-18	2239 - 8-10	2296 - 20-25
2131 - 275-325	2188 - 20-25	2240 - 12-14	2297 - 30-35
2132 - 275-325	2189 - 40-45	2241 - 18-20	2298 - 15-20
2133 - 275-325	2190 - 15-20	2242 - 20-25	2299 - 25-30
2134 - 375-425	2191 - 20-25	2243 - 18-20	2300 - 20-25
2135 - 300-345	2192 - 18-20	2244 - 9-10	2301 - 25-30
2136 - 285-325	2193 - 9-11	2245 - 10-12	2301A - 20-25
2137 - 175-225	2194 - 9-11	2246 - 16-18	2302 - 55-65
2138 - 260-295	2195 - 15-18	2247 - 20-25	2303 - 30-35
2139 - 260-295	2196 - 16-18	2248 - 18-20	2304 - 20-25
2140 - 25-35	2197 - 14-16	2249 - 12-14	2305 - 15-20
2141 - 15-20	2198 - 15-18	2250 - 9-10	2306 - 20-25
2142 - 35-40	2199 - 9-11	2251 - 8-10	2307 - 25-30
2143 - 45-55	2200 - 18-20	2252 - 12-14	2308 - 20-25
2144 - 45-55	2201 - 14-16	2253 - 18-20	2309 - 18-20
2145 - 35-45	2202 - 16-18	2254 - 20-25	2310 - 15-20
2146 - 15-20	2203 - 16-18	2255 - 18-20	2311 - 15-20
2147 - 25-30	2204 - 14-16	2256 - 9-10	2312 - 40-45
2148 - 35-40	2205 - 50-60	2257 - 12-14	2313 - 40-45

Value Guide

2314 - 35-40	2371 - 12-14	2428 - 45-50	2485 - 15-18
2315 - 45-50	2372 - 12-14	2429 - 55-60	2486 - 90-100
2316 - 25-30	2373 - 12-14	2430 - 45-50	2487 - 80-90
2317 - 20-25	2374 - 10-12	2431 - 50-60	2488 - 125-140
2318 - 12-15	2375 - 13-15	2432 - 35-40	2489 - 150-160
2319 - 40-45	2376 - 12-14	2433 - 55-65	2490 - 160-180
2320 - 15-20	2377 - 13-15	2434 - 15-20	2491 - 55-65
2321 - 25-30	2378 - 18-20	2435 - 70-80	2492 - 45-55
2322 - 30-35	2379 - 20-22	2436 - 40-45	2493 - 45-55
2323 - 25-30	2380 - 20-22	2437 - 45-50	2494 - 45-50
2324 - 15-20	2381 - 60-70	2438 - 18-20	2495 - 50-55
2325 - 18-20	2382 - 50-55	2439 - 75-85	2496 - 25-30
2326 - 18-20	2383 - 60-70	2440 - 65-75	2497 - 50-60
2327 - 18-20	2384 - 80-90	2441 - 45-50	2498 - 25-30
2328 - 20-25	2385 - 45-50	2442 - 35-40	2499 - 50-55
2329 - 15-18	2386 - 55-60	2443 - 34-40	2500 - 35-40
2330 - 30-35	2387 - 45-50	2444 - 50-60	2501 - 45-55
2331 - 18-20	2388 - 70-80	2445 - 40-45	2502 - 35-40
2332 - 35-40	2389 - 70-80	2446 - 35-40	2503 - 40-45
2333 - 45-50	2390 - 110-120	2447 - 35-40	2504 - 80-90
2334 - 9-10	2391 - 35-40	2448 - 95-105	2505 - 90-100
2335 - 14-16	2392 - 85-95	2449 - 45-50	2506 - 75-85
2336 - 10-12	2393 - 170-185	2450 - 40-45	2507 - 90-100
2337 - 13-15	2394 - 160-175	2451 - 40-45	2508 - 80-90
2338 - 50-55	2395 - 75-85	2452 - 35-40	2509 - 45-50
2339 - 14-16	2396 - 55-60	2453 - 85-100	2510 - 65-75
2340 - 25-30	2397 - 50-55	2454 - 45-55	2511 - 50-60
2341 - 20-25	2398 - 20-25	2455 - 65-75	2512 - 20-25
2342 - 14-16	2399 - 30-35	2456 - 40-45	2513 - 55-65
2343 - 14-16	2400 - 75-80	2457 - 45-50	2514 - 40-45
2344 - 15-20	2401 - 150-160	2458 - 35-40	2515 - 40-45
2345 - 30-40	2402 - 100-125	2459 - 35-40	2516 - 40-45
2346 - 12-15	2403 - 80-90	2460 - 40-45	2517 - 25-30
2347 - 8-10	2404 - 25-30	2461 - 35-40	2518 - 35-40
2348 - 10-12	2405 - 55-65	2462 - 20-22	2519 - 50-55
2349 - 35-40	2406 - 55-65	2463 - 25-30	2520 - 50-55
2350 - 35-40	2407 - 75-85	2464 - 20-25	2521 - 50-60
2351 - 16-18	2408 - 55-60	2465 - 20-25	2522 - 25-30
2352 - 13-15	2409 - 1600-1780	2466 - 20-22	2523 - 25-30
2353 - 16-18	2410 - 250-275	2467 - 50-60	2524 - 25-30
2354 - 18-20	2411 - 25-30	2468 - 65-75	2525 - 45-55
2355 - 18-20	2412 - 110-120	2469 - 18-20	2526 - 25-30
2356 - 16-20	2413 - 165-185	2470 - 30-35	2527 - 15-20
2357 - 16-20	2414 - 225-250	2471 - 40-45	2528 - 50-55
2358 - 18-20	2415 - 600-650	2472 - 40-45	2529 - 25-30
2359 - 20-22	2416 - 70-80	2473 - 50-55	2530 - 110-120
2360 - 14-16	2417 - 200-225	2474 - 40-45	2531 - 135-150
2361 - 10-12	2418 - 165-185	2475 - 18-20	2532 - 80-90
2362 - 14-16	2419 - 225-250	2476 - 40-45	2533 - 75-85
2363 - 14-16	2420 - 50-55	2477 - 18-20	2534 - 65-75
2364 - 13-15	2421 - 30-35	2478 - 40-45	2535 - 50-60
2365 - 14-16	2422 - 25-30	2479 - 30-35	2536 - 50-60
2366 - 14-16	2423 - 45-50	2480 - 10-12	2537 - 55-65
2367 - 16-18	2424 - 50-55	2481 - NP	2538 - 55-65
2368 - 18-20	2425 - 60-75	2482 - 18-20	2539 - 20-25
2369 - 12-14	2426 - 50-55	2483 - 8-10	2540 - 40-45
2370 - 8-10	2427 - 55-60	2484 - 10-12	2541 - 40-45

Value Guide

2542 - 25-30 each
2543 - 25-30 each
2544 - 25-30
2545 - 15-20
2546 - 25-30
2547 - 25-30
2548 - 25-30
2549 - 25-30
2550 - 25-30
2551 - 20-25
2552 - 35-40
2553 - 35-40
2554 - 150-175
2555 - 45-50
2556 - 10-15
2557 - 10-15
2558 - 10-15
2559 - 10-15
2560 - 10-15
2561 - 10-15
2562 - 10-15
2563 - 10-15
2564 - 10-15
2565 - 10-15
2566 - 10-15
2567 - 10-15
2568 - 10-15
2569 - 15-20
2570 - 25-30
2571 - 40-45
2572 - 20-25
2573 - 15-20
2574 - 40-45
2575 - 35-40
2576 - 40-45
2577 - 8-10
2578 - 8-10
2579 - 7-9
2580 - 8-10
2581 - 8-10
2582 - 8-10
2583 - 9-11
2584 - 7-9
2585 - 8-10
2586 - 11-13
2587 - 8-10
2588 - 9-11
2589 - 7-9
2590 - 9-11
2591 - 9-11
2592 - 9-11
2593 - 7-9
2594 - 9-11
2595 - 7-9
2596 - 8-10
2597 - 8-10
2598 - 8-10

2599 - 8-10
2600 - 8-10
2601 - 9-11
2602 - 8-12
2603 - 6-8
2604 - 8-10
2605 - 8-10
2606 - 100-110
2607 - 155-170
2608 - 85-100
2609 - 250-280
2610 - 80-90
2611 - 225-245
2612 - 50-60
2613 - NP
2614 - 60-65
2615 - 90-95
2616 - NP
2617 - 40-45
2618 - 50-55
2619 - 220-240
2620 - 65-75
2621 - NP
2622 - 225-250
2623 - NP
2624 - NP
2625 - NP
2626 - 50-60
2627 - NP
2628 - NP
2629 - 55-60
2630 - 125-145
2631 - 90-110
2632 - 70-75
2633 - 50-60
2634 - 45-55
2635 - 35-40
2636 - NP
2637 - 55-60
2638 - 25-30
2639 - 30-40
2640 - 45-50
2641 - 35-40
2642 - 45-50
2643 - 30-35
2644 - 30-35
2645 - 40-45
2646 - 30-35
2647 - 25-30
2648 - 25-30
2649 - 25-30
2650 - 25-30
2651 - 25-30
2652 - 25-30
2653 - 20-25
2654 - 20-25
2655 - 20-25

2656 - 20-25
2657 - 20-25
2658 - 20-25
2659 - 20-25
2660 - 20-25
2661 - 20-25
2662 - 20-25
2663 - 20-25
2664 - 20-25
2665 - 65-75
2666 - 20-25
2667 - 70-80
2668 - 60-70
2669 - 35-40
2670 - 20-25
2671 - 20-25
2672 - 45-55
2673 - 90-100
2674 - 70-80
2675 - 75-85
2676 - 16-18
2677 - 16-18
2678 - 40-50
2679 - 45-50
2680 - 35-40
2681 - 35-40
2682 - 40-45
2683 - 40-45
2684 - 50-60
2685 - 14-16
2686 - 25-30
2687 - 25-30
2688 - 15-18
2689 - 15-18
2690 - 15-18
2691 - 12-15
2692 - 12-15
2693 - 12-15
2694 - 12-15
2695 - 12-15
2696 - 10-12
2697 - 12-14
2698 - 35-40
2699 - 35-40
2700 - 30-35
2701 - 25-30
2702 - 45-50
2703 - 40-45
2704 - 35-40
2705 - 30-35
2706 - 30-35
2707 - 30-35
2708 - 25-30
2709 - 100-110
2710 - 20-25
2711 - 45-50
2712 - 45-50

2713 - 25-30
2714 - 40-45
2715 - 40-45
2716 - 30-35
2717 - 30-35
2718 - 45-50
2719 - 30-35
2720 - 25-30
2721 - 30-35
2722 - 25-30
2723 - 50-60
2724 - 30-35
2725 - 100-110
2726 - 20-25
2727 - 40-45
2728 - 35-40
2729 - 40-45
2730 - 30-35
2731 - 60-70
2732 - 40-45
2733 - 35-40
2734 - 40-45
2735 - 45-50
2736 - 40-45
2737 - 45-50 pr
2738 - 20-25
2739 - 40-45 pr
2740 - 35-40
2741 - 40-45
2742 - 40-45
2743 - 45-50
2744 - 40-45
2745 - 40-45
2746 - 50-60
2747 - 40-45
2748 - 45-50
2749 - 50-60
2750 - 30-35
2751 - 30-35
2752 - 45-50
2753 - 16-18
2754 - 16-18
2755 - 65-75
2756 - 30-35
2757 - 30-35
2758 - 30-35
2759 - 15-20
2760 - 20-25
2761 - 15-20
2762 - 15-20
2763 - 15-20
2764 - 15-20
2765 - 15-20
2766 - 20-25
2767 - 15-20
2768 - 30-35
2769 - 20-25

2770 - 20-25	2827 - NP	2883 - 15-18	2939 - 16-18
2771 - 20-25	2828 - NP	2884 - 30-35	2940 - 14-16
2772 - 25-30	2829 - NP	2885 - 60-65	2941 - 12-14
2773 - 15-20	2830 - NP	2886 - 50-55	2942 - 6-8
2774 - 15-20	2831 - NP	2887 - 20-25	2943 - 6-8
2775 - 30-35	2832 - NP	2888 - 40-45	2944 - 6-8
2776 - 30-35	2833 - 30-35	2889 - 35-40	2945 - 6-8
2777 - 25-30	2834 - NP	2890 - 35-40	2946 - 6-8
2778 - 30-35	2835 - 16-18	2891 - 40-45	2947 - 250-300
2779 - 15-18	2836 - 22-25	2892 - 20-25	2948 - 130-145
2780 - 18-20	2837 - 15-18	2893 - 40-45	2949 - 150-200
2781 - NP	2838 - 18-20	2894 - 35-40	2950 - 250-300
2782 - 16-18	2839 - 30-35	2895 - 40-45	2951 - 45-50
2783 - 18-20	2840 - 10-12	2896 - 14-16	2952 - NP
2784 - 18-20	2841 - 25-30	2897 - 30-35	2953 - 75-100
2785 - 20-22	2842 - NP	2898 - 15-18	2954 - NP
2786 - 18-20	2843 - 16-18	2899 - 15-20	2955 - 50-60
2787 - 18-20	2844 - 16-18	2900 - 30-35	2956 - 50-55
2788 - 18-20	2845 - 12-14	2901 - 20-25	2957 - 40-50
2789 - 20-22	2846 - 12-14	2902 - 45-50	2958 - NP
2790 - 18-20	2847 - 18-20	2903 - 40-45	2959 - NP
2791 - 18-20	2848 - 16-18	2904 - 25-30	2960 - NP
2792 - 22-25	2849 - 16-18	2905 - 80-85	2961 - 18-20
2793 - 15-18	2850 - 14-16	2906 - 45-50	2962 - NP
2794 - 12-15	2851 - 35-40 pr	2907 - 35-40	2963 - 14-16
2795 - 12-15	2852 - 45-50	2908 - 40-45	2964 - 16-18
2796 - 12-15	2853 - 30-35 pr	2909 - 15-18	2965 - 50-60
2797 - 18-20	2854 - 40-45	2910 - 50-60	2966 - 225-275
2798 - 16-18	2855 - 30-35 pr	2911 - 40-45	2967 - 40-50
2799 - 25-28	2856 - 40-45	2912 - 45-50	2968 - NP
2800 - 35-38	2857 - 25-30	2913 - 18-20	2969 - 260-295
2801 - 30-32	2858 - 15-20	2914 - 12-14	2970 - 18-20
2803 - 18-20	2859 - 10-12	2915 - 14-16	2971 - 18-20
2804 - 20-22	2860 - 40-45	2916 - 14-16	2972 - 20-25
2805 - 18-20	2861 - 50-55	2917 - 12-14	2973 - 18-20
2806 - 18-20	2862 - 15-18	2918 - 6-8	2974 - 18-20
2807 - 20-22	2863 - 20-25	2919 - 6-8	2975 - 18-20
2808 - 18-20	2864 - 12-14	2920 - 15-18	2976 - 16-18
2809 - 20-22	2865 - 10-12	2921 - 35-40	2977 - 16-18
2810 - 18-20	2866 - 8-10	2922 - 8-10	2978 - 18-20
2811 - 18-20	2867 - 14-16	2923 - 16-18	2979 - 16-18
2812 - 20-22	2868 - 18-20	2924 - 18-20	2980 - 16-18
2813 - 18-20	2869 - 18-20	2925 - 12-14	2981 - 16-18
2814 - NP	2870 - 20-25	2926 - 25-30	2982 - 8-10
2815 - NP	2871 - 10-12	2927 - 25-30	2983 - 10-12
2816 - NP	2872 - 8-10	2928 - 50-55	2984 - 10-12
2817 - NP	2873 - 6-8	2929 - 40-45	2985 - 8-10
2818 - NP	2874 - 25-30	2930 - 40-45	2986 - 10-12
2819 - NP	2875 - 20-25	2931 - 40-45	2987 - 10-12
2820 - 16-18	2876 - 18-20	2932 - 10-12	2988 - 8-10
2821 - 16-18	2877 - 10-12	2933 - 10-12	2989 - 10-12
2822 - 18-20	2878 - 8-10	2934 - 10-12	2990 - 10-12
2823 - NP	2879 - 4-6	2935 - 10-12	2991 - 8-10
2824 - NP	2880 - 8-10	2936 - 10-12	2992 - 10-12
2825 - 22-25	2881 - 8-10	2937 - 10-12	2993 - 10-12
2826 - 20-22	2882 - 8-10	2938 - 16-18	2994 - 30-35

2995 - 30-35
2996 - 125-135
2997 - 35-40
2998 - 30-35
2999 - 20-25
3000 - 20-25
3001 - 15-20
3002 - 20-25
3003 - 20-25
3004 - 125-150
3005 - 12-14
3006 - 75-85
3007 - 18-20
3008 - 10-12
3009 - 8-10
3010 - 15-18
3011 - 40-45
3012 - 14-16
3013 - 10-12
3014 - 10-12
3015 - 8-10
3016 - 10-12
3017 - 20-25
3018 - 40-45
3019 - 10-12
3020 - 6-8
3021 - 6-8
3022 - 16-18
3023 - 80-90
3024 - 45-50
3025 - 90-100
3026 - 100-125
3027 - 170-190
3028 - 55-65 pr
3029 - 80-90
3030 - 175-200
3031 - 22-25
3032 - 45-55
3033 - 45-55
3034 - 40-50
3035 - 80-85
3036 - 80-85
3037 - NP
3038 - NP
3039 - 40-45
3040 - 50-55
3041 - 15-18
3042 - 40-45
3043 - 18-20
3044 - 30-35
3045 - 18-20
3046 - 18-20
3047 - 20-25
3048 - 18-20
3049 - 35-40
3050 - 18-20

3051 - 18-20
3052 - 25-30
3053 - 25-30
3054 - NP
3055 - NP
3056 - NP
3057 - 30-35
3058 - 35-40
3059 - 40-45
3060 - 20-25
3061 - 35-40
3062 - 30-35
3063 - 25-30
3064 - 20-25
3065 - 20-25
3066 - 25-30
3067 - 25-30
3068 - 35-40
3069 - 10-12
3070 - 12-14
3071 - 12-14
3072 - 16-18
3073 - 75-80
3074 - 8-10
3075 - 18-20
3076 - 15-18
3077 - 12-14
3078 - 8-10
3079 - 8-10
3080 - 15-18
3081 - 16-18
3082 - 10-12
3083 - 10-12
3084 - 14-16
3085 - 10-12
3086 - 25-30
3087 - 16-18
3088 - 16-18
3089 - 16-19
3090 - 65-75
3091 - 65-75
3092 - 18-20
3093 - 20-22
3094 - 30-35
3095 - 23-25
3096 - 40-45
3097 - 40-45
3098 - 20-25
3099 - 70-80
3100 - 35-40
3101 - 60-70
3102 - 45-50
3103 - 15-20
3104 - 30-35
3105 - 25-30
3106 - 60-70

3107 - 30-35
3108 - 35-40
3109 - 45-50
3110 - 30-35
3111 - 20-25
3112 - 30-35
3113 - 20-25
3114 - 20-25
3115 - 20-25
3116 - 30-35
3117 - 30-35
3118 - 30-35
3119 - 15-20
3120 - 20-25
3121 - 25-30
3122 - 20-22
3123 - 18-20
3124 - 25-30
3125 - 30-35
3126 - 30-35
3127 - 20-25
3128 - 12-15
3129 - 20-25
3130 - 45-50
3131 - 30-35
3132 - 30-35
3133 - 50-55
3134 - 30-35
3135 - 40-45
3136 - 12-14
3137 - 12-14
3138 - 20-25
3139 - 20-25
3140 - 100-125
3141 - 225-250
3142 - 100-125
3143 - 65-75
3144 - NP
3145 - 65-75
3146 - 35-40
3147 - 30-35
3148 - 50-60
3149 - 25-30
3150 - 15-20
3151 - 15-20
3152 - NP
3153 - 18-20
3154 - NP
3155 - 50-55
3156 - 125-135
3157 - 75-80 pr
3158 - 45-55

Milk Glass Items
P. 731
A - 40-45
B - 45-50
C - 50-60
D - 65-75
E - 165-175

P. 732
A - 40-45
B - 60-70
C - 140-150
D - 35-40
E - 35-40
F - 18-20
G - 18-20
H - 70-80
I - 25-30
J - 25-30
K - 25-30
L - 30-35
M - 25-30
N - 25-30
O - 10-12
P - 12-15
Q - 20-25
R - 12-15
S - 10-12

P. 733
A - 25-30
B - 20-25
C - 25-30
D - 12-15
E - 30-35
F - 45-50
G - 20-25
H - 15-18
I - 12-15
J - 15-20
K - 30-35
L - 30-35
M - 12-15
N - 12-15
O - 18-20
P - 15-18
Q - 10-12
R - 20-25

P. 734
A - 85-95
B - 85-95
C - 85-95
D - 185-195 set
E - 150-165 set
F - 125-140 set
G - 100-125 set

Value Guide

P. 735
A - 25-30
B - 10-12
C - 18-20
D - 20-25
E - 25-30
F - 15-18
G - 10-15
H - 10-15
I - 15-18
J - 12-15
K - 10-15
L - 55-65

P. 736
A - 30-35
B - 20-25
C - 18-20
D - 18-20
E - 30-40
F - 30-40
G - 30-35
H - 25-30

P. 737
A - 12-15
B - 12-15
C - 15-20
D - 8-10
E - 12-15
F - 20-25
G - 10-12
H - 18-20
I - 30-35
J - 20-25

P. 738
A - 20-25
B - 20-25
C - 20-25
D - 25-30
E - 12-15
F - 18-20
G - 30-35
H - 45-50
I - 50-55
J - 35-40
K - 35-40
L - 75-80

P. 739
A - 20-25
B - 15-20
C - 10-15
D - 15-20
E - 18-20
F - 15-20
G - 15-18
H - 40-45
I - 15-18
J - 40-45
K - 12-18
L - 40-45

P. 740
A - 20-25
B - 18-20
C - 10-15
D - 35-40
E - 15-18
F - 18-20
G - 65-75
H - 35-40
I - 20-25
J - 45-50
K - 40-45

P. 741
A- 20-25
B- 18-20
C- 18-20
D- 30-35
E- 25-30
F- 20-25
G- 20-25
H- 65-75
I- 40-45
J- 25-30

P. 742
A- 25-30
B- 25-30
C- 20-25
D- 35-40
E- 20-25
F- 15-20
G- 15-20
H- 65-70
I- 25-30
J- 20-25
K- 30-35

L- 30-35
M- 25-30
N- 35-40
O- 30-35

P. 743
A- 15-20
B- 20-25
C- 25-30
D- 25-30
E- 35-40
F- 20-25
G- 140-150
H- 35-40
I- 70-80
J- 110-125
K- 125-150
L- 125-150
M- 80-95
N- 80-90
O- 40-45
P- 20-25

P. 744
A- 10-12
B- 10-12
C- 12015
D- 12-15
E- 10-12
F- 12-15
G- 5-7
H- 7-9
I- 8-10
J- 10-12
K- 15-18
L- 10-12
M- 18-20
N- 18-20
O- 15-18
P- 15-20
Q- 15-20
R- 15-20
S- 18-22
T- 18-20

P. 745
A- 35-40
B- 8-10
C- 18-20
D- 15-18
E- 15-18

F- 15-20
G- 18-20
H- 20-25
I- 18-20
J- 20-25
K- 10-15
L- 25-30
M- 25-30
N- 20-25

P. 746
A- 50-55
B- 12-15
C- 50-55
D- 20-25
E- 25-30
F- 30-35
G- 20-25
H- 30-35